# Benjamin Verdery

*A Montage of a Classical Guitarist*

## Edited by Thomas Donahue

**Hamilton Books**
an imprint of
**Rowman & Littlefield**
*Lanham • Boulder • New York • London*

Copyright © 2018 by The Rowman & Littlefield Publishing Group, Inc.
4501 Forbes Boulevard
Suite 200
Lanham, Maryland 20706
Hamilton Acquisitions Department (301) 459-3366

Unit A, Whitacre Mews, 26-34 Stannary Street,
London SE11 4AB, United Kingdom

Library of Congress Control Number: 2018938126
ISBN 978-0-7618-7037-1 (paper : alk. paper)
ISBN 978-0-7618-7038-8 (electronic)

Printed in the United States of America

# Contents

# Appendices

# Foreword

## by

## Leo Brouwer

### Friend from Old Times, Good Ones

Once in the 1970s a young fellow with all the energy of a rock player
came to my masterclasses in France. . . . His instrument was similar to a
guitar (!) almost . . . but he played a couple things with such a talent and
quality that I recommended to him not to abandon his *métier* but to enrich it with some classical touch. So we start working immediately
around it.

Now, forty years later, Ben Verdery has become a man of culture, not
in academic terms but in reality. To everyone who works with him, I
recommend continuing. . . . His character is positive, not "easy." He's a
brave one.

Thank you, Ben. Stay as you are.

# Preface

The impetus for this book was Benjamin Verdery's achievement of attaining thirty years on the faculty at the Yale School of Music teaching classical guitar. While there are a number of ways such an accomplishment may be acknowledged, it was decided to let his friends and colleagues reminisce from their individual perspectives. The result is a collection of writings that (1) demonstrates how Ben has impacted and influenced these people in particular and the classical guitar world in general; (2) illuminates many aspects of his musical career as a teacher, performer, composer, and arranger; and (3) highlights his personality. In addition to those personal reflections, Ben took on the monumental task of reviewing his career and expressing his thoughts, ideas, and experiences in his own essay, touching on the topics of performing, composing, arranging, teaching, and recording. As noted by Ben himself, an additional benefit of this collection is that it offers a look at the classical guitar world during a particular period of time.

All essays are original, heretofore unpublished, and used by permission of their respective authors.

# About Benjamin Verdery

Described by The New York Times as "an iconoclastic player" and by *Soundboard* magazine as "an American original, an American master," Benjamin Verdery has been hailed for his innovative and eclectic musical career.

Benjamin Verdery's tours regularly take him throughout the United States, Canada, Europe, and Asia, performing at venues and festivals including Royal Theatre Carré (Amsterdam), Maverick Concerts (Woodstock, New York), the International Guitar Festival (Havana), Wigmore Hall (London), Concurso y Festival Internacional de Guitarra de Taxco (Mexico), and the Chamber Music Society of Lincoln Center and the Metropolitan Opera (New York). He has recorded and/or performed with such diverse artists as Andy Summers, Frederic Hand, William Coulter, Leo Kottke, Anthony Newman, Jessye Norman, Paco Peña, Hermann Prey, John Williams, hip-hop artist Billy Dean Thomas, beatbox/vocal percussionist Mark Martin, and Nano Stern.

Ben's discography includes over fifteen recordings, including: *happy here* with William Coulter; *Branches,* featuring works of Bach, Strauss, Jimi Hendrix, Mozart and the traditional *Amazing Grace*; *Start Now* (winner of Classical Recording Foundation Award in 2005); *Some Towns & Cities* (winner of *Guitar Player* Magazine's Best Classical Guitar Recording in 1991); and collaborations with John Williams (*John Williams Plays Vivaldi Concertos*) and Andy Summers (*First You Build a Cloud*). Future recordings include *Searching for A Chorale*, music by and inspired by J. S. Bach, and a recording featuring his classical guitar arrangements of Randy Newman, Neil Young, Prince, Jimi Hendrix, John Lennon, Eddie Vedder, The National, Cream, and Elvis Presley.

Many of the leading composers of our time have created music for Ben, including Daniel Asia, Martin Bresnick, Bryce Dessner, Javier Farías, Aaron Kernis, Ezra Laderman, Hannah Lash, David Leisner, John Anthony Lennon, Ingram Marshall, Anthony Newman, Roberto Sierra, Van Stiefel, Christopher Theofanidis, and Jack Vees. Of particular note was the commission by the Yale

University Music Library of a work by Ingram Marshall for classical and electric guitars entitled *Dark Florescence*; Ben Verdery and Andy Summers premiered this work at Carnegie Hall with the American Composers Orchestra. A prolific, published composer in his own right, many of Ben's compositions have been performed, recorded, and published over the years. He has been commissioned to compose works for the Assad Duo, guitarist David Russell, John Williams and John Etheridge, the Changsha International Guitar Festival, the Chilean Guitar Ensemble, the Pensacola Guitar Orchestra (Florida), Kyo-Shin-An Arts (New York), Wake Forest University, Thomas Offermann and the guitar ensemble of the Hochschule for Music and Theatre (Rostock, Germany), and the score for the documentary film *The Goyesque*. Ben's *Scenes from Ellis Island* for guitar orchestra has been extensively broadcast and performed at festivals and universities in the United States, Canada, New Zealand, and Europe, and the Los Angeles Guitar Quartet included it on their CD, *Air and Ground* (Sony Classical). Doberman-Yppan (Canada) is currently publishing his solo and duo works for guitar, and Alfred Music distributes the solo pieces from *Some Towns & Cities* as well as instructional books and video.

Benjamin Verdery uses D'Addario strings and guitars by Garrett Lee and Otto Vowinkel.

Recently, Ben brought us up to date.

The past two years (2016–2017) have been musically exhilarating! There was the release of *The Ben Verdery Guitar Project: On Vineyard Sound*, new guitar music from my extraordinary colleagues at Yale University, released by Elm City Records which I founded with my former student and dear friend, Sol Silber. There was a documentary shot in Korea for Arirang Television's ArTravel series, as well as three videos, including two protest videos: *Chant for Peace* and J. S. Bach's *Chaconne*, subtitled *An Interpretation Celebrating the Earth, Sky, and Sea*. In addition, I was honored to perform an evening of my compositions including a new duo entitled *From Aristotle* with beatbox champion Mark Martin for the Guitar Foundation of America. I also presented concerts and masterclasses in Holland, Germany, and England as well as hosting my annual Maui Guitar Masterclass.

I began 2017 with a premiere of *Searching for a Chorale* by one of my dearest mentors, Seymour Bernstein. That summer I recorded, released the video, and published that piece. I had collaborations with Michiyaya Dance Company, curating and performing at the 92nd Street Y's 2017 Guitar Marathon, and embarking on a new solo work entitled *the rain falls equally on all things* (published by Doberman-Yppan) for the 2017 Changsha International Guitar Competition in China. I was so taken with the warmth and reception of the Chinese festival audience in Changsha.

I am into my thirty-second year as the guitar professor at the Yale School of Music, and my tenth year as Artistic Director of 92Y's Art of the Guitar series.

I enter 2018 arranging Leonard Bernstein's Clarinet Sonata for classical guitar and string quartet, which is going splendidly!

A year ago, along with the 92Y, I commissioned Bryce Dessner to write a piece for guitar and string quartet to be premiered on May 10, 2018 at the 92Y with the fabulous St. Lawrence Quartet. In 2018 I will release two CDs on the Elm City Records label. One will consist of my music, the other of American chamber music with guitar featuring Bryce's piece and my arrangement of the Leonard Bernstein Clarinet Sonata.

I have just accepted the position of Artistic Director of the Connecticut Guitar Festival. I look forward to curating this event annually. In October 2018 I am off to Chile to teach masterclasses, and play and hear a premiere of a new work I will compose for The Chilean Guitar Ensemble conducted by Javier Farías and featuring Nano Stern. Finally, the Maui filmmakers Polyphonic Industries, LLC, filmed the 2017 Maui masterclass. The footage they shot was beyond what we could have hoped for in its scope and beauty. The filmmakers and our Maui "team" are confident that when it is all compiled, we will have something unique to share.

# 1

# Sérgio Assad

## Charisma

As soon as I was invited by the editor to write something about my dear friend Ben Verdery, I started thinking about one specific word that could in principle define his whole artistic and human potential. I puzzled over many words but the one that came out strongest was the word "charisma." Ben possesses a large number of positive features, and it becomes quite hard to point out just one of them. So the word "charisma" fits his personality like a glove, bringing out most of his high qualities.

Our friendship started a long way back, but before I got to know him personally I had heard of his talent as a very interesting and energetic guitarist. In 1980 my brother Odair and I were just starting our international career and went to Rome to play our first concert in Italy, invited by the Centro Romano della Chitarra. This important center was a private classical guitar school that promoted concerts for young players starting out on their first international appearances. Ben had been in Rome the previous year playing for that same society and caused a great lasting impression among all the guitar aficionados. I still remember very well the story told by Sergio Notaro, the director of that musical institution, referring to Ben as someone courageous, with great personality, and without any shadow of shyness on stage. At that time, Ben was already using the guitar cushion that over time replaced the footstool. Similar devices are very common nowadays, but they were a complete novelty back then. Apparently, as soon as he stepped on stage with the cushion attached to his left leg he provoked laughs from the audience when he announced firmly that the cushion was not a

1

growth on his leg. The joke may seem ordinary today, but at that time all of us young guitarists were taught to be very serious about what we did and we could not allow ourselves to relax that much. It was a norm in those days to wear smoking jackets as outfits and never say a word onstage. In his own way Ben was already ahead, and since that time he became, under our new way of seeing the whole picture, part of a select group of young guitarists with plenty to contribute and to say in the international guitar community.

It is said by many that all guitarists traveling regularly end up knowing each other. I can agree with that, because it did not take us more than one single year to meet Ben in person. One year later (1981) we met Ben in New York, where he lived. The meeting took place in the apartment of the famous American luthier Thomas Humphrey, with whom we had become friends the previous year. Coincidentally, Tom and Ben lived in the same building on 72nd Street on the west side of Manhattan. My brother and I were visiting Tom one day when he decided abruptly to call Ben on the phone and tell him to put aside whatever he was doing and come down to Tom's apartment on the second floor. Tom exclaimed, "You must get down here immediately and listen to these Brazilian brothers." Tom left the door ajar for Ben, since Ben said he would come down straightaway. We were playing the *Micro Piezas* by Leo Brouwer as Ben pushed the door gently with his arms outstretched and with both hands touching the ground. He moved his head up slowly and said, "Hi guys! Nice to meet you! Keep on playing! I'm only doing my stretching." The scene was kind of comical and just reconfirmed the rumors of humor and relaxation that were part of his reputation.

After this first meeting we got to see Ben regularly because we were always in Tom's apartment when we came to New York. After a few years Ben got married and moved away. Although we could no longer see him frequently, Tom made sure that we would get Ben's news. Tom harbored a deep admiration for him and, in his view, Ben was the most creative person he had ever encountered in the classical guitar world. I agreed with Tom, as the vast majority of classical guitarists at that time were too serious and unable to publicly declare their personal taste if it did not fit in with the status quo of the time. Ben loved the blues, rock and roll, was a great fan of Jimi Hendrix, and knew a lot about the rock scene. He wanted to start writing his own music back then, and in his creative imagination he already had ideas of incorporating blues and rock-and-roll elements into it. It is hard to believe today that there was this kind of dividing line between the musical styles, but this is not an exaggeration at all. Ben eventually formed a musical group called Ufonia that played multiple genres. He also formed The Schmidt/Verdery Duo, a wonderful flute/guitar duo with his wife Rie, that always had an open mind and is still active today.

It is hard for me to separate the artist from the person when I think of him, and so I want to return to the word "charisma" that expresses these two sides very well.

Among the many elements showing Ben's charisma is his capacity to share his great conviction with other people. Since the 1980s he was no longer seeing any barrier with the confused labeling of music, and was giving real value to music with quality, independent of its label. This conviction became even more evident with the passage of time and with the compelling musical gestures and actions he took when he became a defender of new original music written by American composers.

Another of his charismatic traits is to always exude a lot of energy and contagious joy. Just by exuding happiness he already exerts a magnetic pull on others because everyone wants to be next to cheerful and positive people. Ben is at once a great storyteller and also a great listener. In a direct conversation with him one can experience a full sense of freedom of expression establishing an immediate connection and complicity.

As a professional musician, Ben has been widely successful in his career and leaves no doubt about his artistic value as a performer and as an educator. As a composer, he is nourished by the basic foundations of North American music and manages to create his own work full of personality, taste, and elegance.

In 2010 Ben wrote a piece for two guitars called *What He Said*. The work is dedicated to the memory of Thomas Humphrey, and for my brother and me it was a true emotional exercise to play it in public. Tom passed away prematurely in 2008 and I personally regret the fact that he did not hear this composition. He would certainly have loved it, since it has many blues connotations that he enjoyed so much. We had the opportunity to premiere this piece in 2011 at the Kaufmann Concert Hall at the celebrated 92nd Street Y in New York, and have played the piece frequently.

Since 2008 Ben has been Artistic Director of the Art of the Guitar series at the 92nd Street Y. My brother Odair and I had the great privilege of playing in that guitar series in 2015 when we were celebrating our fiftieth anniversary as a duo. Before the concert, following the tradition of the house, I had the honor of being personally interviewed by Ben. That was one of the most relaxed conversations I have had throughout my life, even though it was being recorded for future presentation, already a tension-building factor. For that particular occasion, Ben wrote a moving essay about our first meeting in New York that was printed in our program.

Ben continues to be extremely creative and surprising. His latest surprise is his new musical partnership with the young rapper Billy Dean Thomas. A couple of their very creative videos are publicly available on YouTube. In these videos Ben appears daring, innovative, and completely at ease in an unprecedented situation in the world of classical guitar. The energy of Ben appears to be endless and I can only compare it to another friend we have in common, the expert on ancient music Richard Savino. Both are similar when it comes to hyperactivity. I had a chance of checking that out at the end of 2015 when Richard organized a visit to Napa Valley with my colleagues from the San Francisco

Conservatory. Ben came all the way from New York just to hang with us. David Tanenbaum, Marc Teicholz, John Dearman, and Andy Summers took part in that group. John and Andy made a special trip from Los Angeles to join us and we really had one of the most joyful, radiant, and memorable moments of the year. No need to say that the combination Verdery + Savino was quite amusing and involving indeed.

I am proud to have Ben as a friend and can only wish that he keeps following his brilliant journey for many more years to come, always with his peculiar vigor and *joie de vivre*.

# 2

# Seymour Bernstein

## Tribute

I do not recall the date of my first meeting with Ben Verdery, but I do remember that I was seated at the piano demonstrating phrase-shaping and other musical issues related to the repertoire that he had performed for me. He of course instantly assimilated all of my suggestions with the greatest of ease. I feel deeply privileged to say that such sessions have continued to this day, not only with Ben personally, but also with his gifted pupils, either individually or in a masterclass format.

The first image that I associate with Ben is a person seething with emotion. In everything he does, he wears emotion "on his sleeve" so to speak. Since music is a language of feeling, one might say with full conviction that Ben-the-musician and Ben-the-person are one and the same.

Perhaps the life of the true artist defines the very meaning of the word *seriousness*. In contrast to this, many world-acclaimed musicians might easily have careers as comedians. Chopin, for example, used to mimic all of his distinguished colleagues. Ben's proclivity for humor, often bordering on the absurd, is legendary. Since I, too, love to mix seriousness with humor, Ben and I often laugh through a large percentage of the time we spend together. (What is that B-flat is doing in that phrase?) A penchant for humor, then, is one of Ben's many formidable qualities. It endears him to his colleagues as well as to his pupils and his audiences.

Nothing is more difficult or more responsible than being acknowledged as one of the foremost musicians of our time. Ben carries this distinction with grace, with poise, and always with the ability of living up to the very image which he, himself, has created through his profound gifts as a renowned guitarist, teacher, and composer.

I feel honored to be a friend and colleague of this great man. It is a privilege to know him, and to contribute this brief essay at this important juncture in his life.

# 3

# Jackson Braider

## What One Cradle-Mate Has to Say About Another

I am ten months and six days older than Ben Verdery. These days that does not count for much, but when we first met sixty years ago, it *should* have meant something. True, for fifty-five days each year we are nominally the same age; still, at the tender ages of two and three we nevertheless became glued at the hip. We did all of things well-adjusted boys did in the late 1950s and early 1960s: played "sojer" (child-speak for "soldier"), smoked cigarettes, and raced bottle caps in the self-washing gutters on the streets of Avignon.

Now, I have to admit that I was not there when he first met the guitar—my family had moved away, and we would not be reunited for some five years—so, I was not present when Ben's music switch flipped. Still, I conjured up in my mind's eye a picture of young Ben rocking out to The Beatles on his Wilson tennis racket. I *know* it was The Beatles who turned on the boy's groove, because the guitar he had when we got back together was a Gibson J-160E, the very same model that John Lennon had been playing from 1964 to 1965. It was on that guitar that Ben taught me my first chord, E major. And it was with Ben that I had a last childhood adventure: hitchhiking to Danbury, Connecticut, around Thanksgiving in 1968 to get the newly-released "White Album" at the record store on Main Street.

The thing that startles me upon reflection is how expansive Ben's musical world was during high school. I fell in with a bad crowd in Cooperstown, New York—folkies—and later with an even worse bunch—singer/songwriters—in

New York City. I never played lead guitar, never wailed via Fender Twin Reverb amp. I would always be a steel-string acoustic guitar kind of guy.

By contrast, Ben was all over the musical map in his listening appetites. Of course, it was the early days of guitar heroes: there was Jimi Hendrix and Eric Clapton and Robin Trower and Leslie West and John McLaughlin and Rick Derringer and Jeff Beck and Carlos Santana and Frank Zappa and B. B. King and Bert Jansch and John Renbourn. (I apologize to the hundreds of guitarists who influenced Ben not mentioned here because I cannot remember their names!) Further, Ben's brothers, Daniel, but particularly Donald, were also adding to Ben's all-you-can-eat musical buffet.

As a player back then, Ben was proving to be voracious in his pursuit of musical challenges, from power-trio-ing à la Hendrix with Jared Bernstein—yes, *that* Jared Bernstein—on bass and John Marshall on drums, to endless afternoons jamming with fellow students at the Wooster School.

Still not tough enough, though, and Ben started taking jazz guitar lessons with Russ Mumma at the Music Guild in Danbury in his freshman year at Wooster. It is curious to think that Russ was Ben's first official guitar teacher, and that Russ is still in business!

All that, of course, was before Ben's junior year, when a young organist named Mary Jane Newman joined the Wooster faculty and proceeded to remap our collective musical consciousness. Before MJ's arrival, the organ in the chapel was there simply to play hymns, providing simple organ-y sounds to accompany the swell of the student body's collective voice in the literature of hymnology. A gifted performer, her welcoming enthusiasm and engagement provided us a wonderful introduction to something that had not been on our radar: classical music.

Finally, Ben had encountered a real challenge to sink his teeth into: the classical guitar. In less than two years before conservatory, he not only had to learn to play four pieces at least well enough to pass his audition, he had to learn how to read music. His first classical teacher was Phillip de Fremery, and Phil—bless his heart!—guided him well. Ben began to learn how to read music; he passed his audition to SUNY Purchase; and he then worked his tail off. Six years later, he made his official New York debut on December 8, 1980. It was the night John Lennon was shot.

All in all, I think we can agree that, if you are holding this book, you already know Ben has pretty much mastered the instrument. After all, that is one reason why the editor put this book together. Ben has evolved into an imaginative composer of surprising and beautiful music; so, that's good too. But the thing that has struck me over the last fifteen years or so is how well he has been incorporating in his work—as both a player and a composer—so much from the all-you-can-eat musical buffet of his youth.

What to say? To mix metaphors in a particularly egregious way, all the guitar music in the world has become Ben's oyster: but it is hard to find such a good half-dozen of others with the likes of those bivalves. . . .

# 4

# William Coulter

## Performer, Teacher, Colleague, Friend

PERFORMER. I first met Ben in 1984. I had just started my undergraduate degree at the University of California at Santa Cruz and saw an advertisement in the campus paper for a classical guitar concert by some guy named Benjamin Verdery. I had not heard of Ben before but I was hungry for classical guitar, so I went to hear him perform. Needless to say I was deeply moved by his artistry and passion for the music. Very inspired I was, so much so that I went backstage to try and meet him. I said, "Hi, great concert," and he said, "Hi, thanks, do you have a car?" I replied, "Yes," and he said, "I need a cigarette and some M&Ms®," and I said, "Cool, let's go." So we spent a few hours in Santa Cruz talking about music and life and guitars and it felt like I had met a kindred spirit.

TEACHER. The next time Ben came to Santa Cruz I went to a masterclass he was giving at Cabrillo College. I heard several students play, and I played the Leo Brouwer studies for him. It was the best classical guitar teaching I had experienced: fun, serious, supportive, all about the music and the breath and the technique. After that class I met Ben for more lessons: once at his apartment in New York City, once at his family home on Cape Cod. I learned so much about music and guitar from him from these few lessons and classes, and in my own teaching now I still catch myself sharing the same ideas that I heard Ben share with me. Others have noted the same thing about my teaching, and I know that I am not alone. There are now teachers across the globe who are carrying on with the same antics and deep thoughts that were learned from Ben!

9

COLLEAGUE. In 1995 I was recording a CD called *Celtic Crossing* for Gourd Music in Santa Cruz. I worked up the courage to ask Ben if he would be willing to record a few tracks of music with me, myself playing steel string guitar and Ben of course playing his Smallman guitar. We recorded two tracks together— our arrangements of melodies by the Irish harpist Turlough O'Carolan—and I have to say they were some of the most fun recording sessions I have ever had. The combination of our two styles of playing blended together so beautifully that we were inspired to explore more music together as a duo. The duo Bill & Ben was born. In 2001 we recorded and released *Song for Our Ancestors* and ten years later in 2011 we released *happy here.* I am so crazy-proud of the work we did together on these projects: blending our styles, sounds, and musical person- alities into what I think of as one giant gorgeous guitar. We also had fantastic experiences playing concerts together, from the coast of California to Maui to Portugal. There was never a dull moment.

FRIEND. It is difficult for me to put into words how deeply I appreciate our friendship. Through many of life's ups and downs I have been thankful for the support and words of wisdom that I received from Ben. On matters personal and professional he has always helped me find my true path. Life as a professional musician is challenging in so many ways. What I have learned over the years of teaching, recording, and touring is that having a deep friendship with the people that I make music with is the true joy of living this kind of a life. I never could have predicted that our chance meeting in 1984 would lead to so much love and joy and music together. Ben has been many things to me: performer, teacher, and colleague, but the most important of all these is, and will always be, friend.

# 5

# James D'Addario

## And the Lyric is . . .

We became close friends with Ben and Rie shortly after our first meeting back in 1980. Anyone who knows Ben knows he can be a bit of a clown with an infectious, often self-deprecating sense of humor. While enjoying dinner at our home one evening, we began trading stories about our life experiences. Before too long the steel-string guitars came out and we began playing and singing songs by The Beatles.

Nowadays if you want to learn the words or chords to a song you just go on ultimateguitar.com or YouTube and you pretty much have access to anything you desire. Back then you had to figure out the lyrics and chords by putting the needle down on a record, picking it up again, writing down a few words, figuring out a few chords, and ultimately having a piece of paper in your hand with the code to the song you craved to learn and play. And sometimes it was really hard to make out what a particular lyric was.

That evening, in tribute to John Lennon, we just finished singing "I Saw Her Standing There" when Ben had a look of surprise on his face after we sang the bridge which included the word "mine" with an extended vowel ("miiiiiiiiiiiine"). After the song, nearly in tears, he confessed that he could never figure out what that line meant because he thought they were singing "Ha-wa-iiiiiiiiiiii." That, my friends, is the true essence of my friend Ben and why he makes us so happy with his humor and his music. We laughed so hard we cried! It was a moment we will never forget, and only one of so many shared throughout the years of our friendship.

11

# 6

# Janet D'Addario

## On a Scale of 1 to 5

For several years during the 1980s and early 1990s, Benjamin Verdery was Artistic Director of the D'Addario Foundation. Once we decided to produce a classic guitar series in three United States cities, we received literally hundreds of tapes by young, aspiring guitarists all hopeful to receive a spot on the series, a possible New York Times review, and in essence, a mini-tour. It was our responsibility to listen to each and every one of them and ultimately decide which person to invite to be on the series in a given season.

Anyone who knows Ben is aware he cannot say anything bad about anyone. Try as we would to "rate" the performances we were hearing on a scale of 1 to 5, he would evaluate most of the recordings at either 4 or 5. We would sit on the floor in our den with a cassette player, surrounded by tapes that we tried to sort into piles. Back then, the repertoire for classical guitar was more limited; often the tapes were the same pieces over and over again and it became difficult to remember who played what and how.

Just when we thought we had narrowed it down to three players (from which we would have to choose one) he would say, "No, wait! What about this one?! Did we listen to this one?" We had, of course; it was marked with a 4.2 at which point he would say, "Nah, he's at least a 4.5!" At the end of the day, after hours of nonstop listening and comparing he would lament that it was just "too difficult to pick one" from so many talented guitarists. And for the better part of the following week he would tell me how he had trouble sleeping because he had so much music going on in his head and could not keep straight whom he was listening to. Our marathon listening was a yearly event, a memory I will cherish forever.

# 7

# Don Dawson

## A Guitar for Keith Richards

When you receive a call from The Rolling Stones asking if you can help Keith Richards secure a true old-school classical guitar—not just your basic store-bought nylon string—what do you do? You call Ben Verdery!

Actually, after receiving a call from a good friend who works for The Rolling Stones, I ran to Jim D'Addario asking what might be the best course of action in getting a selection of guitars for Keith to check out. Truth be told, I was just giddy with the excitement at the prospect of getting some guitars and possibly sharing some space with Mr. Richards. I clearly had to share that notion with someone. Jim suggested we call Ben and see if he might be able secure a number of instruments from Beverly Maher's Guitar Salon in New York City. She has a very impressive line-up of instruments that ranged from the affordable to the very expensive.

Another call went out the The Rolling Stones organization, asking more refined questions about type, tone, price, and such. We called Ben, who immediately became giddy about the idea that we would get to act as intermediaries and sell an instrument to the one and only Keith Richards. The criteria for instruments were fairly straightforward: price was less important than tone and feel; possibly Spanish. Having Ben as a guiding light on this project mean that there was no need to worry that the five guitars we would have in-hand would be anything less than wonderful.

I drove into New York and met up with Ben who had already obtained the instruments. Our destination was an uptown recording studio where Keith was tracking. After meeting up with my old friend and some introductions, we were ushered into a second studio and Ben got the instruments prepped for Keith to check out. I can remember when that studio door closed and it was just Ben and me. We were wild-eyed and waiting teenagers that could not believe our good fortune. We were about to hold court with one of the true icons of rock and roll *and* we were going to get to see him play an instrument in an incredibly intimate setting. Mind-blowing to say the least!

We waited for a bit (although we were prepared to wait weeks, even months, if need be) and then the studio door opened. In strolls Keith Richards and his tech, gracious and welcoming, thanking us for taking the time to gather the instruments and bring them up to the studio. Ben gave quick overviews on the selection and as simple as that, Keith picks up a guitar and starts to play. The casual conversation comes much too easy; nothing like one would expect from a god of the guitar realm. Keith and Ben have a very easy rapport, much like old acquaintances that have not seen each other in many years. I can only speak for myself because inside my head, I am doing my best not to lose that professional veneer and just begin babbling in some incoherent warbling about how much *Exile on Main Street* meant to me as a kid, but somehow both Ben and I keep it a lid on it. Keith begins to regale us with a story about learning some of the earliest Scotty Moore licks as a kid. He proceeds to play these licks on a very expensive classical guitar, which isn't a simple parlor trick. Technically, they are much easier on a steel-string guitar, but Keith manages just fine, thank you. He painted a wonderful picture about how he was first introduced to the world of open tunings. All the while Ben and I were enraptured by his story, with him pausing every now and then to allow a question or two. The next thirty minutes slid by as if mere moments stitched together by a few musical notes. In reality, this is simply four guitar guys sitting in a studio, talking guitar, playing guitar, and it ends with someone buying a guitar. However, in the annals of our minds, this should be an epic nine-hour big-screen movie, starring Keith Richards and his guitar.

And then it was over. Time to pack up. He played all five guitars, told his tech which one he liked: a 1960s Velázquez, if my mind still serves me. Ben made arrangements for invoicing. We shook hands and went our separate ways. I am not one-hundred-percent positive, but I have a dim memory of Ben and myself jumping up and down like school kids once we got outside of the studio as we began our journey back to relative normalcy.

# 8

# Bryce Dessner

## A Source of Energy

I met Ben for the first time in January or February of 1994. We were introduced by my then high school English teacher Robert Patterson who had known Ben since their childhood in Connecticut. Bob was teaching English in Cincinnati, Ohio. He had also been our primary music teacher, jamming with us after school and teaching us the blues. In addition to being an accomplished fiction writer, he was a phenomenal blues piano player who had played in bands throughout the 1960s, including The Paul Butterfield Blues Band.

After I was admitted to Yale University as an undergraduate, Bob suggested I meet Ben to talk about music at Yale and how I might keep developing as a musician. I am not sure if Ben even remembers our first meeting; he was running between a million masterclasses and coachings. But I was certainly impressed by his open-mindedness and incredible talents as a guitarist. From that time forward I followed pretty much all the recordings he made.

I arrived at Yale the next spring like all undergraduates: full of ideas about all the things I could study. I quickly realized, however, that Ben and the graduate school of music would be a great resource for me. While Yale undergraduates famously often go on to be lawyers, doctors, and scientists, very, very few pursue music professionally after school, and I saw the graduate performance school as a great opportunity to stay connected to music.

Ben allowed me to join all the seminars and classes I wanted and occasionally to play in class with the graduates who were all at least seven or eight years older than I, and at far higher levels. Around that time I started a band with my

15

brother Aaron, and Ben was always incredibly open and curious about my life outside classical music.

To call Ben a mentor or a teacher is an understatement. More than anything, Ben taught me about music as a source of energy. Ben is eternally curious and always searching. He has tremendous patience with his own work and as a listener and teacher of others. In works he has coached a thousand times he is always finding new details and new ideas. His vision of the universe helped me to see possibilities I would not have found otherwise. Ben's commitment to his own compositions, which I have always followed very closely, had a huge impact on me as a young musician. I began writing while in school and have never stopped. Ben taught us that the beauty is in the process, in the making of the work. This is a self-sustaining idea that offers limitless happiness if practiced deliberately. Regardless of success, artistic or financial, I learned from Ben to pour my energy into the music itself.

Ben helped me see that music was bigger than separating my worlds into "classical" and "rock," that in fact I was the same person no matter which room I was in. Ultimately this was empowering to me as I found my own voice in writing. In Ben's universe, Jimi Hendrix and John Dowland, Prince and Bach were all of equal importance. His vision is non-hierarchical and non-elitist, which, as an important pedagogue, is tremendously influential.

Ben makes music from the heart. He cannot play a note without having a strong sense of emotion inside every phrase. This beauty of his musical persona is infectious and infuses the world around him with a sense of possibility. In this way, the best lessons Ben teaches are through his own playing and writing. Simply by being such a wonderful example to others, Ben is able to inspire and open so much to those around him.

# 9

# Thomas Donahue

## Confluence with Ben

During the summers of 1983 and 1984, I studied organ and harpsichord in masterclasses with Anthony Newman at the State University of New York at Purchase. It was memorable studying Bach's music with a world-renowned keyboardist on a campus with four organs and numerous harpsichords and pianos. That experience stayed with me for a long time, so much so that many years later I decided to edit a book in 2001 honoring Tony entitled *Anthony Newman: Music, Energy, Spirit, Healing.* One of the persons who contributed an essay for that book was Ben, since Tony was a lifelong friend and mentor of his.

Following that publishing project, I found myself on Ben's mailing list for his guitar masterclass held on the island of Maui, which he had started in 1998. Initially I completely ignored the notifications, since a guitar masterclass seemed illogical for my circumstances: I am a keyboardist whose focus instrument at that time was the harpsichord. Even though I could play the guitar to save my life, my technique was certainly not at the level expected at a masterclass. However, by 2004 the idea of travelling to Hawai'i was becoming more and more inviting, so my wife and I decided to make the trip. Since the masterclass made allowance for auditors who did not have to perform, I felt I could live up to the true meaning of that word and simply take on the role of listener.

It turned out that there were two aspects of Ben's masterclass that proved musically quite beneficial and satisfying to me. First, while some of the class time involved discussions of guitar-specific details—posture, sound production, fingering, nail care, and so on—just as much time was given to discussing matters of musical expression that were applicable to any musician regardless of instrument: tempo, dynamics, articulation, phrasing, and so on. This is well expressed by a phrase I had seen on a T-shirt: "The music is not in the guitar." Second, I discovered that guitarists and harpsichordists share some of the same literature. This included not only the keyboard pieces for which guitarists have their own transcriptions—Prelude, Fugue, and Allegro, BWV 998, by J. S. Bach; *Les Barricades Mystérieuses* by François Couperin; sonatas by Domenico Scarlatti—but also non-guitar non-harpsichord music such as Bach's Six Suites for unaccompanied cello and the Partitas and Sonatas for unaccompanied violin. Guitarists have their own transcriptions of those Bach pieces, and as I had played them myself as keyboard versions, it was interesting to hear them presented in a different context. The manner in which a given piece could be communicated in a musically convincing way on a different instrument was quite instructive and illuminating.

Ben's musical interests are demonstrated by his wide-ranging repertoire (see Discography and Programs). However, my personal opinion is that the music of J. S. Bach resonates greatly with Ben's psyche. Undoubtedly this view is completely biased, as Bach is my favorite composer, and his compositions are my desert-island music. Even with this acknowledged bias, when I observe Ben teaching Bach's music at a masterclass, I sense there is an increased level of enthusiasm, and when I hear him play Bach's music in recital, there is a heightened intensity to his playing.

It was interesting to observe Ben's teaching style irrespective of the specific piece being studied. At first, some of his techniques border on the zany; for example, improvising a second guitar part as the student is playing; adding percussion using a hand shaker; and introducing improvised lyrics to whatever piece is being performed. Of course, this is not zaniness for its own sake: it is a method of conveying a musical point in a creative manner. For example, adding lyrics means he is *singing* the notes, which emphasizes the melodic nature of the line. I also take this to be a reminder that we should be having *fun* when performing music. (As someone once said, that is why we say we "play" music.) In addition, I believe that Ben's approach helps to make a nervous masterclass performer more at ease. And of course, part of the basis for Ben's antics is that they are a reflection of his marvelous sense of humor.

So strong was my feeling for the successful nature of Ben's teaching style that I came to his defense against a person who had a misguided opinion to the contrary. Prior to one of the Maui masterclasses, Ben gave a solo recital. During the intermission, there were two masterclass students standing between myself and this lady. She was talking with them, and, upon finding out that Ben was going to teach the class, she made the comment that "often a performer is not necessarily a good teacher." As I had been to several of Ben's masterclasses by this time and knew of his capabilities, I was not about to let her have the last word, so I spoke up: "Never say the words 'Ben Verdery' and 'cannot teach' in the same sentence." I took her silence as an acceptance of the observation.

After attending several of the Maui masterclasses, I became more and more familiar with the classical guitar literature, and I found myself wanting to play some of the pieces. So, in an interesting twist, I would occasionally play guitar music on keyboard, including *Julia Florida* by Agustín Barrios Mangoré, *Homenaje* by Manuel de Falla, and *Worry Knot* and *Now You See It, Now You Don't, Now You Do* from Ben's *Eleven Etudes*.

Even though originally I was an auditor at Ben's masterclasses, eventually there arose situations when I would play. On one occasion, a participant was performing a transcription of a sonata by Domenico Scarlatti. During the lesson, Ben asked me to play portions of the original keyboard version for comparison. This way of thinking should be no surprise given the fact that Ben has mentors that are keyboardists: Seymour Bernstein and Anthony Newman. There were also several occasions in which John Olson and I played guitar/organ duets, a rarely heard and seldom written-for combination, but one that I find rather interesting and musically effective.

One aspect of Ben's masterclasses is the performance of ensemble pieces involving all the participants. This group is now referred to as the Maui Honu Guitar Orchestra. (The word *honu* is Hawaiian for "turtle," an animal that symbolizes longevity and good luck.) I had the privilege of playing with the orchestra on several occasions. Two instances are prominent in my memory. In 2015, one of the ensemble pieces was Ben's *Scenes from Ellis Island*, and he asked me to play the woodwind parts on the organ. Also, I added a running eight-note figuration and an underlying bass line in the pedals at the end of the piece. This performance became yet another version of the piece.

The second instance was in 2017, when one of the ensemble pieces was a version of Ben's etude *Start Now*. Toward the end of the piece, there was a measure that consisted of a single chord. In rehearsal, Ben's explained that his idea at that point was to have the performers slowly strum that chord at will, get up out of their chairs, and walk around the building, which happened to be a church. Ben wanted me to play something on the organ at that point. Jokingly, I said, "You better be careful, I may end up playing 'In-A-Gadda-Da-Vida'" (the song by Iron Butterfly from 1968, which I had played in my rock-band days). After more serious thought, I decided on the opening to the Sinfonia from Bach's cantata *Wir danken dir, Gott, wir danken dir*, BWV 29, which uses an organ, and which is taken from the Prelude to the Violin Partita in E major, BWV 1006. I felt this was appropriate because there is a guitar version of this piece, and the Sinfonia was in D major, the chord the guitarists were strumming. The final performance went well and the Bach was interpolated. After the piece was over, Ben called for a reprise, a vamping of the last three measures. He then looks at me and shouts, "In-A-Gadda-Da-Vida!" So I switched gears, exchanged Iron Butterfly for Bach, and it worked. Leave it to Ben.

So my confluence with Ben is based on our mutual teacher Anthony Newman, the Maui masterclass, the music of J. S. Bach, the links between the guitar and the harpsichord, the process of transcribing from one instrument to another, and our rock backgrounds. As a result of his masterclasses, I find my life is now infused with interesting connections. The sound of the guitar instantly transports me to Hawai'i. Often when I hear a piece of non-guitar music I ponder the feasibility of a transcription for solo guitar, guitar/keyboard duo, or guitar ensemble. I also listen to more guitar music, seeking pieces that would be interesting to transcribe for keyboard. And in a most curious association, whenever I trim my fingernails—short on both hands for keyboard playing—I am reminded about the ritual of guitarists' nail care.

But it goes much deeper than that. Irrespective of any specific instrument, Ben's teaching has underscored for me The Great Musical Confluence among composer, instrument maker, and performer, for the benefit of the listener.

# 10

# Eliot Fisk

## A Tribute to Ben

I first met Benjamin Verdery soon after I moved to New York City at around age 22. I remember our mutual friend and inspiration Phillip de Fremery telling me about Ben's new commission from Anthony Newman of a huge work including the imposing title of *Variations and Grand Contrapunctus.* On the basis of Phil's glowing recommendation, I called up Ben one day and banged my way down the crooked staircases of my garret apartment at 560 West End Avenue to get to Ben in his first apartment in New York.

I remember meeting Ben and his wife Rie: Rie's quiet yet strong support for Ben and Ben's burning intensity as we listened to his impressive recording of the Newman work played on a new guitar by Thomas Humphrey. Ben's passion for music was inescapable, and even then he exuded a deep sense of purpose and mission.

Our first meeting was a little tense perhaps: we were two young guys trying to make it in the City that really represented at that time in history just what Frank Sinatra's famous song "New York, New York," so often blaring from restaurants and other public places, belted out: that if you are successful in this city, success is guaranteed elsewhere.

Soon after our first meeting, Ben and Rie moved to the legendary building at 124 West 72nd Street where Thomas Humphrey, the famous luthier, also lived and worked. Tom, the amazing, wildly imaginative builder who had such a big influence on all of us young "guitar Turks" trying to make it in New York in those heady, early years, was also the most jealous of all guitar makers. He would watch carefully to see whether we were all still playing his instruments and woe to anyone who dared to show up with the work of another maker! Ben, ever seeking new vistas, left the fold rather early, and Tom, who had adored Ben above all of his adopted guitar progeny, could never quite get over it. Yet when Ben spoke at Tom's funeral service many years later, his speech, improvised in the moment, dwarfed all other tributes. Turning to Tom's two daughters and widow, Ben told them just how much Tom had meant to all of us and how proud they should be of him. It was the most powerful moment in the entire service, by far!

When Ben and I were starting out back in the late 1970s, New York City had just emerged from near bankruptcy. When I came back to my no-doorman, fifth-floor walk-up at night ($280 a month was just barely possible for me in those days!) I not infrequently had to climb over a junkie passed out in the tiny vestibule. Once, coming back from a red-eye flight from California just after dawn, I was propositioned by a sweet prostitute, who looked like a "nice girl" from next door. (Like Mozart, in a famous letter to his father centuries earlier and for similar reasons, I turned down that invitation.)

Soon after this, Ronald Reagan cut all the money for the mental institutions, and homeless people began to flood the neighborhood. I was fifteen blocks above Ben and Tom so things were a little tougher on my block. In these days of callous and seamless gentrification, no one can imagine what the West Side of Manhattan was like when Ben and I started chasing our dreams there.

In those early days, Ben and I also shared a recording engineer. The avuncular, witty, and brilliant David Hancock, with his ever-expanding belly and genial ways, full of wisecracks, was a virtuoso of the razor blade. (For those in the younger generation, a razor blade—yes literally!—was used to splice a "master" tape preparatory to pressing the result onto 33 r.p.m. discs. Program notes were limited in length to what could fit on the back of an album!) David recorded and edited one of Ben's great early landmark albums, which presented his transcriptions of J. S. Bach's Violin Sonata in A minor, BWV 1003, and Sixth Cello Suite, BWV 1012.

In March 1980 I played a recital at the 92nd Street Y with various Latin American works: as I remember, the *Six Variations on a Theme by Milán* by Joaquín Maria Nin-Culmell, *La Espiral Eterna* by Leo Brouwer, the premiere of *Notes on a Southern Sky* by Robert Beaser, and in the second half all the *Etudes* by Heitor Villa-Lobos. As not infrequently happens, I had to learn the new work under difficult circumstances: in the three weeks previous to the premiere, I had mostly been bouncing around in little planes en route to playing outreach concerts in Alaskan logging camps (various bunches of mobile homes parked on the banks of Alaskan rivers). Coming back across five time zones to play in New York was not easy, and so I not only asked Ben for advice about his great friend Leo Brouwer's *La Espiral Eterna* which I had never played before, but also if he would turn pages for the Beaser premiere. Ben was not only an encouraging presence and a perfect page turner (!) he later learned the work, playing it beautifully himself!

At the end of 1980 I traveled to Gargnano, Italy, and won first prize in the guitar competition organized there by Oscar Ghiglia and some of his Italian colleagues. That was the *only* guitar competition I would ever win. It was perhaps not unhelpful that two of my former guitar teachers—Oscar Ghiglia and Alirio Díaz—were on the jury! That prize brought with it some small concerts in Italy and also a stopover for a last-minute concert in Köln, after which, to my amazement, I was immediately offered a full professorship at the Hochschule für Musik in that city. At the time both Hans Werner Henze and Karlheinz Stockhausen were on the faculty, and I was later privileged to know them both.

Not long after returning to America, and after much back and forth, I finally decided to accept the Köln job. In so doing I traded a ratty, falling-down music building at Yale—where I had founded the guitar department in 1977 with a grand total of two incoming students and a minimal salary—for an imposing, if unbearably ugly, modern building in the center of Köln with a generous German government job attached. This meant, however, that I would need a successor at Yale. After asking Bob Guthrie to sub for me for a couple of years, I ultimately recommended Ben for the job. In the many lean years before the Yale School of Music became tuition-free and before the buildings were spruced up to an elegance unrecognizable to those of my generation, Ben's charisma kept the program growing and vibrant.

After some years at Yale, Ben approached me about creating an "Eliot Fisk Prize." His first proposal was to take money out of his own not-very-abundant salary and to use that money for the prize, a typically generous gesture that shows not only the depth of our friendship but also the nobility of Ben's character. I did prevail on Ben to keep his money and let me play an opening benefit concert to jump-start the little fund that still supports this small but symbolic prize, given each year to a graduating member of Ben's Yale class.

Another great Ben memory involves a trip I took to London to play a recital at Wigmore Hall in 1989. The days I spent in London around that recital found both John Williams and Paco Peña at home and Ben visiting. As Ben had famously performed with both of these masters, it was only natural that we would all hang out. On successive evenings we gathered at Paco's place and talked about everything under the sun, but almost nothing about the guitar. I remember a particularly pointed debate between John and Paco about who were worse, American or British politicians. John was adamant that the latter was worse; while Paco held out for the former. Looking at the respective leaders of the two nations today, such a debate seems like a fond memory.

Over the next decades, Ben and I stayed in touch by phone or when I was passing through New York. I used to talk to him about personal things a lot, too, especially in the often tortured years of my first marriage: "Ben, how do you do it, man? How do you combine all this travel and all this craziness that we go through to play, with the family thing?" And Ben would reply: "If it's not right with my family, I can't do anything. I've got to have that under control."

We would go back and forth on the eternal question of the cats and dogs nature of women and men, and how hard it was to figure that one out. It was always a great comfort to have a musical guitar brother facing these problems from a different part of the universe. I could open up to Ben utterly and he to me. As Segovia once wrote about himself and Agustin Barrios, "There was never any petulance between us."

Innumerable times my path has crossed with Ben's at guitar festivals on various continents in many of the world's time zones. There are countless memories associated with these events. I remember with particular clarity Ben playing Martin Bresnick's Janáček transcriptions (*On an Overgrown Path*) at a festival in California curated by another great guitar brother, "Wildman" Richard Savino. One movement in the Janáček is called *In Tears*, and I remember to this day the poetry of Ben's playing there. He had me in tears, too.

Despite all the years of friendship, Ben and I had never played together. Finally in September 2015, we came together in a duo recital to premiere *Cortada fue la Tierra*, a work written for us by the talented and delightful Javier Farías, at an event organized at Wake Forest University by our esteemed colleague Patricia Dixon. Javier also wrote a solo work for me entitled *Geografía de un Canto* which I premiered as well, while Ben premiered another one of his magical solo compositions, *Homage to Neruda*. I especially enjoyed this project, part of a grand *homenaje* to the Nobel laureate poet, Pablo Neruda. We played the premiere of the duo in the evening concert and recorded the piece the next day. Before or afterwards there was not a lot of rehearsal possible or needed. We knew intuitively and immediately how to catch each other at all the critical places.

Another amazing evening at a California State University Summer Arts event curated by our great mutual friend Scott Morris, a distinguished graduate of Ben's Yale program, brought together on one evening Ben, Roland Dyens, Andrew York, and myself, each of us doing a bit of what he loved best. It was great to be in the company of that band of brothers and to create a once-in-a-lifetime kind of *Gesamtkunstwerk* for the *holde Kunst*. Sadly, it was to be the last time I ever heard or was able to speak to our dear colleague, Roland Dyens, who recently left us for some heaven of his own invention.

I have always admired Ben's ability to integrate aspects of popular culture (about which I know and understand so little!) into the classical guitar tradition: his piece for basketball and guitar (with the witty title *Pick and Roll*), his Bach experiment with rapper Billy Dean Thomas, or his big guitar ensemble piece *Give* in homage to Ted Kennedy are great examples of this. I was also deeply impressed by his landmark set of character pieces for guitar called *Some Towns and Cities*, a work of tremendous variety and originality.

After all these years, Ben and I are still just two kids in love with music and in love with life. We are two *American* artists with strong personalities and a fearless experimental bent. We would rather fall into the bottom-most pit of hell than live life in the etiolated security of limbo. We both love virtuosity and playing fast, but at the end of the day we both only know how to play one way: from the heart. We are brothers struggling against the same odds, and comforting each other when things get tough. My affection for him is infinite.

Most of all, Ben is a true original, an authentic voice on our beloved instrument. He has invented: Himself. Who else could?

# 11

# Frederic Hand

## Energy, Love, and Wackiness

I first met Ben in 1974 when he studied with me at the State University of New York College at Purchase. In those days, it was common for instrumental faculty (mostly living in the New York City area) to teach in their homes rather than travel to the college in Westchester County. Ben would arrive at my apartment at 8:30 in the morning, which for me was the middle of the night. Having already been awake for several hours, he was raring to go. His ringing of the doorbell served as my alarm clock and I would stagger to the door to greet him. His energy level was through the roof and he leapt through the door like an excited puppy dog, albeit a doggy who played Bach. After several cups of coffee I was still barely able to keep up with him while we worked through his repertoire of Bach, Brouwer, Berkeley, and Ravel. From the start it was very clear that Ben was extraordinarily gifted, with a natural athleticism on the guitar that is rare. And coming from a rock background, Ben brought a very dynamic and individual approach to innately musical interpretations; quite unique in those days and still so today. He excelled throughout his college career, taking on the most difficult music with great enthusiasm and virtuosity. One day when I was visiting Purchase College the elevator door opened and there was Ben with a lovely young woman he introduced as Rie, a flutist. He told me that they had been playing duets. I thought: "Hmm . . . playing duets, uh huh?"

After Ben and Rie got married, they moved into an apartment in Manhattan on West 72nd Street. It was the same building in which the famous guitar maker Thomas Humphrey lived. I had known Tom since he started making guitars in a

26

small shop on Carmine Street in Greenwich Village. I recommended that Ben buy one of Tom's guitars, which he did (for $700). I lost touch with Ben for a little while, but in going to visit Tom, I ran into him and our friendship resumed. Then in the early 1980s I was introduced to a Californian guitar maker, John Gilbert, and started playing his guitars. Not long after, Ben was playing John's guitars, too. John was brilliant and innovative, and an extremely colorful character. Ben and I would spend many hours exchanging "John" stories and mimicking his very unique way of talking. Many years later, our roles reversed; Ben suggested that I meet a wonderful young guitar maker, Garrett Lee, whose guitar I happily have been playing ever since. Ben now also plays a "Gary" as he calls it. I am so thankful to Ben for introducing me to Gary, a wonderful luthier and an extraordinary person, whose generosity of spirit is inspiring. In a lovely symmetry to our luthier connections, Gary's mentor was John Gilbert. It is interesting to observe the common threads intertwining people's lives. For Ben and me, one of several threads has been our relationship with guitar makers.

A formidable issue in young musicians' lives is "How do I make a living?" and this may be even more problematic for classical guitarists. We do not have the same opportunities as orchestral musicians. In the 1970s and 1980s there was a wonderful organization devoted to bringing the performing arts to small and not-so-small communities throughout the country. It was called Affiliate Artists and it connected large corporate sponsors with communities and young performers. The guitar was a favorite instrument because of its portability and universal appeal. Typically an arts appointment consisted of four two-week trips to a community over the span of a year. During that time we played two informal performances a day (called "informances") capped off by a full solo recital at the end of the residency. It was an invaluable training ground in learning to be comfortable with performing in almost any situation and making one's art accessible to a wide range of audiences. After I had done several residencies, Ben joined Affiliate Artists and, according to him (my memory of those years is spotty), I was his mentor and adviser. By this time I am not sure Ben needed much mentoring or advice, as he was maturing into a major artist. But we had lots of opportunities to share very rich stories about our numerous residencies and the people and places we encountered. One of Ben's appointments was in Hawai'i and he subsequently developed a life-long connection there that is still going strong.

Ben and I share a love of music that falls way outside the classical guitar world. We have introduced each other to our favorite music via CDs, YouTube, and mp3s, and as a result have broadened each other's musical tastes and influences. Each of us has formed ensembles that allowed for the expression of a wide range of music. For me, this manifested in my Renaissance/Baroque/jazz fusion group Jazzantiqua. For Ben, his band Ufonia embraced a range of styles and influences, not easily categorized. Ben has also had many happy collaborations with Andy Summers and Bill Coulter, and also in a wonderful recording of his own music entitled *Some Towns and Cities*. For that recording, I was honored to be one of his sidemen along with John Williams, Leo Kottke, and Paco

Peña, among others. The music is a beautiful representation of some of the places where Ben spent time as an Affiliate Artist. It is also a great expression of Ben's very unique and eclectic compositional and guitaristic style.

Ben and I have performed together on many occasions and he was one of the first guitarists (other than myself) to perform and record my music. We premiered *Prayer* on a WQXR live radio broadcast and Ben performed *Trilogy* in his Wigmore Hall debut. Rie and Ben recorded *A Psalm of Thanksgiving* for their beautiful second compact disc *The Enchanted Dawn*. We shared the concert stage on Maui, marking a long and close musical and personal relationship. One of the best things about working with Ben is the "hang time." I am not referring to the basketball reference of vertical leaping ability (though we love to talk basketball as well) but rather the countless hours we have spent schmoozing in and around rehearsals and performances. One year the Met produced Hector Berlioz's *Benvenuto Cellini*. It had a killer virtuoso guitar duet in the first act and another in the last act with about two hours in between. After numerous stories and jokes, late in the run of the production, we would venture out to Columbus Avenue in our tuxedos and have a four-course meal.

For most people, becoming a world-class virtuoso and giving performances and masterclasses all over the globe, year after year, and running the Yale classical guitar program would be, hmm . . . what's the right word . . . maybe . . . enough? But Ben possesses an energy level well beyond the normal human. And so in addition to all of the above, he has become a major producer of guitar events in New York, both as Artistic Director for the D'Addario Concert Series at Merkin Hall (Jim and Janet D'Addario are another wonderful connection that Ben and I share, and what a contribution they have made to the music world) and the Art of the Guitar series for the 92nd Street Y, plus numerous guitar festivals at Yale University. Just in case that was not enough, let's not forget Ben's annual summer guitar festival on Maui. I had the great pleasure and privilege of participating in many of these events. They are all a beautiful reflection of Ben's love of music, the guitar, his colleagues, and his students. A feeling of joy permeates the atmosphere and makes each gathering a great pleasure. This is one of Ben's very special gifts. He puts people at ease and the atmosphere is imbued with Ben's energy and love, not to mention a wee bit of wackiness (all right, maybe not so "wee").

Over the years, I have seen Ben and Rie's beautiful children Mitsuko and John grow up and become sensitive artists as well as lovely people. I fondly remember playing miniature basketball in Johnny's bedroom with the great flutist Keith Underwood. Both of us were trying to deny Johnny from scoring a lay-up and yelling at him "not in my house" (even though it was his house, and of course, he scored the lay-up).

Ben and I have talked about every aspect of our lives: children, family, students, friends, our trials and travails, aspirations, discussions about Buddhist philosophy and practice, politics, and every manner of experience. Ben has also spent hours talking with my wife Lesley about Buddhism, and Rie and I have shared the concert stage several times.

In the summer of 2012 Ben invited Lesley and me to join him for his summer guitar love-fest on Maui, where I performed and taught with Ben, and Lesley was a judge in the all-important and infamous Mustache Competition. The Maui classes are held in an old church by the beach, with concerts in various historic churches throughout the island, each venue being more beautiful than the next. A typical day involved both morning and afternoon teaching sessions, and was capped off with a visit to an exquisite beach and a swim in the ocean. We frequently started the day with a morning swim. Ben has a very deep connection to the natural world, and what better place for him to share this love than in Hawai'i. He generously gave of his time and took Lesley and me to bird sanctuaries, beaches, mountain streams, secluded waterfalls, national parks, museums, and treated us to the astounding beauty of his second home. For us it was the trip of a lifetime which we will never forget.

Ben and I have known each other for over forty years, and during the past several years it has been our habit to talk on the phone after a long teaching day. When we speak, the time flashes by. We usually start each conversation with the words "So much to discuss," and then after talking for over an hour, we have covered only a small part of what we intended. The keystone of our relationship through all these years is that we make each other laugh. I do not mean the typical ha-ha variety, I mean painful laughter to the point where neither of us can speak or breathe, where we beg each other, "Stop, please stop, I'm not kidding, I'm dying here." What a beautiful thing this is and how rarely encountered. It is a type of connection that defies analysis, though both of our wives have called us idiots (though not unkindly). Actually, that's a fair summation of our banter.

Ben Verdery is a true master of the guitar and a great artist. He embodies a unique set of musical skills and his influences are incredibly diverse, ranging from Jimi Hendrix and Prince, to John Williams, Leo Brouwer, and Julian Bream, to J. S. Bach and W. A. Mozart. Speaking of Bach and Mozart, I have to mention Ben's incredible transcription and recording of Mozart's Adagio, K. 540, originally for piano, and his most recent recording of the Bach Chaconne. Both are towering accomplishments and great examples of the depth and maturity of Ben's artistry.

He has made a monumental contribution to the guitar world as a champion of new works, as a dynamic concert performer who is always stretching the boundaries of the repertoire, as a teacher influencing generations of guitarists, as a composer whose works for solo guitar and guitar ensemble are performed throughout the world, and as an imaginative and innovative producer of guitar concerts and festivals. The guitar world is so much richer for Ben's beautiful life's work. For that and for a lifetime of friendship, music, and laughter: thank you, Ben, with great love.

# 12

# Hannah Lash

## For Ben

I went to Ben's 2017 Faculty Artist Recital at the Yale School of Music, where he and I both teach. I had been looking forward to this recital for some time; Ben's concerts are always a treat to attend. He has a way of drawing the audience in, making us feel welcomed, included, and participatory.

As is typical of a Yale recital, this one started a few minutes late. Students were still filtering into the hall. Everyone was dripping and cold from the freezing rain that was falling outside. As the lights dimmed and the announcement came to turn off cell phones, I could hear the students still chatting amongst themselves.

Ben came out. No, he did not just come out onto stage, he ran: small shuffling steps, but definitely a run. He sat down and began to play the Aria from Villa-Lobos's *Bachianas Brasileiras No. 5*, arranged by the recently deceased Roland Dyens. Total silence from the audience; we were captured. As is typical of Ben's playing, the phrases were all so beautifully shaped; each line was brought into realization with such care and love.

After this first piece, he spoke: a joke about the terrible weather, something about his surprise that anyone would show up in such a storm. His banter was charming, funny, disarming. And I realized that instead of simply feeling like a member of the audience, I suddenly felt like an invited guest at a party. Ben was not just giving a recital. He was hosting us, making us comfortable, and putting us at ease.

30

As a performer myself, this is a revelation. That the performer should be the one to put the audience at ease seems counterintuitive as you imagine what it feels like from the stage: the faces of your colleagues and students—the most intimidating audience imaginable—looking back at you. But in that moment I realized that this very thing is part of what makes Ben's performances so magical: that sense of engaging his audience and making them feel so included, so invited, a part of an experience rather than a witness to it. We were not just watching him play his repertoire. He was playing it *to* us, communicating with us, both through his between-pieces banter and through his playing.

Ben is not only a guitarist of the highest quality but also a fine composer. He played a few of his own pieces, which were a great pleasure to hear. What I find beautiful about Ben as both a composer and a performer is his sense of deep engagement with his music. You can tell he hears his own music profoundly as he writes it, and I am sure he deepens his listening of it and shaping of what it becomes through performing it.

The whole recital was brilliant. And with my own faculty recital less than a week away, I learned an important lesson and was inspired not only by Ben's playing as always, but by this warmth and charm he embodies as a human presence on stage, communicating with other humans who have come to listen, and who can come away having been given a gift.

I have known Ben now for several years. It was not long after I joined the composition faculty at Yale that he asked me to write the piece for his auditioning students. Each year he asks a different composer to write a short piece—two or three minutes—for the auditioning group of guitarists to learn and play for him. The idea is to write a piece but not put any expression marks, articulations, or tempo indications in the score. The potential students are supposed to make these decisions and present their interpretations in their auditions. This can help one determine a great deal about how students think, how creative they can be, or maybe whether they tend to cross a line of good taste in trying to be too creative.

As a composer, it is an interesting challenge, too. I tend to think that articulations, dynamics, and tempo are just as essential to my music as the notes and rhythms I write on the staff. Relinquishing those aspects to the performer can be excruciating. But I was game; I agreed to write a short piece for the auditioning hopefuls.

As I puzzled my way through my assignment, a title came to me that struck me as funny and apt: *Play These Notes*. Beyond these notes, it was up to the students to decide what to do.

I sat with Ben through the auditions that year, listening to twelve or so interpretations of *Play These Notes*. Some were painful, others interesting, and still others utterly flat. It was a fascinating experience. My piece was difficult: not the kind of thing that fits in the hand easily, as I could see as I watched and listened through these many renditions.

Sometime after that audition day, either Ben or I or both of us had the idea that I should expand *Play These Notes* into a larger piece for Ben. I immediately loved this idea, because I felt very strongly that Ben's sensibilities toward my music would be very special, and that what he could bring to it as a performer would be inspiring to me.

And so I began the process of writing a larger piece. The guitar is not an easy instrument to write for. I do not have any real experience with this instrument except for listening to other people play. I never played around on a folk or rock guitar as a kid. It was an instrument I had avoided writing for, because I was not even sure where to begin. But now, as I sat down to write something in earnest, I poked around the guitar repertoire, picking bits of inspiration from pieces I could get my hands on: Alberto Ginastera, Isaac Albéniz, and Leo Brouwer, to name just a few.

But as is usually the case for me, when I sat down to compose my own piece, the ideas I was working with took over my imagination and I thought more about what those ideas demanded than what was idiomatic to the instrument. So when I took a draft to Ben, I knew my piece was impractical in a number of ways.

Ben's unfailing enthusiasm for new music is impressive. Although I presented him with a piece that needed an enormous amount of massaging and some revision to work, he approached it with the kind of zeal that I (often) only see performers bring to standard repertoire. The kind of care he put into this project was truly inspiring. As we shaped the piece together and I took his suggestions for making certain practical changes, I found that it became clearer to me as a composer what the piece was. I titled my piece *For Ben*. Anything else seemed beside the point.

That summer, Ben recorded the piece. I was in residence at the Copland House at the time and he sent me a link to a Dropbox folder with his recording so I could listen and make any last suggestions before the final mixdown. I remember clearly the afternoon I got this link: I had been hard at work composing my first chamber opera, which was a sober and tragic piece that took a lot out of me. I had finished composing for the day and turned to my email, feeling the heaviness of my mood. When I opened the Dropbox link, downloaded the folder, and put in my earbuds, I was brought to tears. For a composer, there can be no greater gift than to feel that a performer has put as much of him/herself into the piece in interpreting and playing it as the composer did in creating it. Usually this kind of devotion towards a piece—this combination of fearless ownership and surrendering to what the music demands—is reserved for standard repertoire. But this is what Ben brought to my music in his recording.

There are many wonderful relationships one finds along the path of being an artist in a field that requires collaboration in order to bring the art to life. But a few will always stand out as being particularly special and meaningful. For me, Ben is one of the most inspiring artists I know. He will always be one of my greatest role models, one of my most valued colleagues, and one of my dearest friends.

# 13

# Garrett Lee

## Ben's Luthier

It is December 2011 and I step into Benjamin Verdery's office at Yale University. I am there to pick up Ben's 1995 Greg Smallman guitar so I can repair the soundboard that suffered a head-on collision with his cell phone. I take a quick scan of the room. In addition to the recognizable silhouette of the guitar professor, I see a couch, an area rug, a slightly used desk, boxes of strings, and a sign saying "Please remove your shoes." Memorabilia, photos, and artwork cover the walls of the spacious studio, and album covers of cherished LPs adorn the bookshelves. I had not met Ben in person before, although after more than twenty-five years of seeing him in concerts, masterclasses, and videos, and listening to his recordings and those of guitarists performing his works, I feel as if I already know him, because in part, I do. He is a rare breed of artist who is courageous enough to show you the depths of who he is in all he creates.

I always wanted to meet Ben because I knew that he was one of the most influential, giving, and personable figures in the classical guitar world. Such is the aura that Ben exudes even from afar. Little did I know that Ben would contact me first. To my surprise, Ben generously sent me an email message with the subject "Bravo!" He recently played the guitar I built for his student Hermelindo Ruiz and somehow found the time to send words of encouragement. He wrote:

> Among many attributes, it is a musical instrument. I know how silly that reads, like duh!! But you know what I mean! That is a quality in my humble opinion many instruments lack. (Benjamin Verdery, personal communication, 29 September 2011)

That email message still resides in my inbox and it came at a time when any feedback—positive or negative—from an artist of such stature was hard to come by, but critical for my own development as a builder.

Now stepping into Ben's office as his new repair person, I know he is taking a chance on me because a Greg Smallman guitar costs a pretty penny, and for a musician to play a guitar for sixteen years means he loves it as dearly as his own child. We sit down and the questions come, but they are not interview questions to probe my qualifications. They are sincerely asked with an excited sense of curiosity in order to get to know me as a person. After examining the half-inch puncture in the guitar's soundboard, I assure an obviously distraught Ben that it is going to be fine and not to worry. I know that my first job is that of psychological counselor: to repair the psyche first, then the guitar. Of course, I am not one hundred percent confident of my prognosis because I know that the thickness of a Smallman soundboard is infamously small—on the order of 1.5 mm—not to mention that Greg Smallman's advice to Ben was "to pick up any shards of cedar, place them in a bottle and give them to your repairman." I can happily say that the repair went well, so there is more about our relationship to tell.

World-class players typically want to develop a personal relationship with a luthier before playing that builder's guitar. There is mutual trust and teamwork that must grow between musician and builder. A player might be searching for different tonal characteristics and new possibilities for musical expression. The luthier begins to observe the player in action with more discerning eyes and ears, trying to imagine the guitar that would best suit the player. This is a never-ending process but it has to start somewhere. When Ben came to my home in New Jersey to retrieve his repaired Smallman, I vividly recall experiencing for the first time how he sounded on one of my guitars. He started with his *Prelude and Wedding Dance*, my favorite Verdery composition. This was also the first of many times observing Ben evaluating one of my guitars. It is fascinating to watch his face and the rest of body while playing a new guitar because it is obvious that his primary objective, even on a test drive, is fully serving the music. Asking how the guitar satisfies that objective almost becomes an afterthought, but when the music ends, rest assured, Ben will give you the full report. I have learned that a good guitar in Ben's hands simply does not impede his musical expression. One can hear it in the music and see it in his body language.

Over the next two years, I kept in close contact with Ben, shared a presentation with him at the Yale Guitar Extravaganza, and loaned him a guitar for a performance and recording. It is hard to know exactly when a player decides to change guitars, but the decision usually forms gradually. At the conclusion of a concert at the 92nd Street Y in New York City where Ben is Artistic Director of the Art of the Guitar series, Ben asked the question. He was ready for a new sound; did I have any guitars available? No, I did not, so I offered him my personal guitar, a recently completed instrument with a cedar/spruce double top soundboard. Paired with Brazilian rosewood back and sides, I suspected it would be a perfect match for Ben because of its clear voice, large tonal palette, and even response. I also realized it would be much better in the hands of a virtuoso player than in my own. Much of my job as a luthier is that of matchmaker, and a week later I found myself in Ben's Manhattan apartment with guitar in hand, ready to make the introduction of two strangers with a common purpose. Ben will tell you that he knows within thirty seconds if a guitar will *not* suit him. Passing that hurdle, it may take another week of deep exploration to know if it is The One. Thirty seconds into playing, I could tell the blind date was turning into a relationship; thirty minutes later, Ben and the guitar were engaged; and a week later, the marriage license was signed.

I have never experienced a player who has a more profound influence on the sound of a guitar than Ben. When new guitars are played, the vibrations gradually change the physical characteristics of the instrument. The wood learns to move more efficiently and the sound becomes increasingly resonant, supple, and responsive to the cues of the player. Over months and years guitars that are well-played can develop a kind of glowing, sonic patina. The rate of this "breaking-in" process is highly dependent on (1) the player's right hand strength, (2) the cumulative playing time, and (3) how extensive the range of pitches that are played, so strong players who spend a lot of time practicing complex pieces can greatly hasten the process. The phenomenon is subtle but can be extremely apparent to players and makers who are privy to playing and hearing a guitar since its infancy. In Ben's case, the change was anything but subtle. In less than three months, I could easily detect a change in the ease in which the guitar spoke across all ranges of pitch. Commenting on his heavy-handed attack, he would shrug his shoulders and say, "That's just the way I've always played."

Skilled players who use a large arsenal of right-hand angles to achieve timbral contrasts will also break in the higher harmonics that accompany the fundamental note. Thus, the shape of the nail, use of flesh, and direction of the stroke dictate the quality of the note and how it breaks in over time. In retrospect, the way that Ben opened his new guitar in terms of speed and note quality should not have surprised me. His compositions take us through a myriad of pitch and dynamic ranges, and he is recognized as a master at rendering a wide range of tonal colors. Speaking about his aesthetic approach to playing, Ben has often told me, "I'm most interested in color." When I mentioned my observation about the speed in which he broke in his guitar, Ben agreed, saying, "I think I break in guitars fast because I use a lot of altered tunings." Most astounding to me was Ben's ability to physically imprint a signature sound on different guitars. During the time I spent two weeks with his Smallman repairing it, I marveled at the notes on the second string. They had an ease and vibrancy in the way they emanated from the guitar, accompanied with a supple feel in the right hand when the string was struck. To my amazement, Ben had trained the second string in the guitar I built to have those same qualities. Since I played Ben's new guitar for nearly two months prior to giving it to him, I had a baseline of sound and feel fixed in my musical memory. I may have doubted my conclusion had it not been for the fact that the two guitars were extremely different in terms of design and overall sound, yet the commonalities were now strikingly present in both. I have never known another player to have such a strong impact on a guitar.

One of the reasons why Ben makes an indelible impact on his guitars and audience is that he plays with absolute conviction. Even in large halls, he will dare to render a *pianissimo* that most performers would only think to play in smaller, more intimate settings. On the other extreme of the dynamic range, he will push the guitar to the limit with tidal waves of *crescendos*. The soundboards on Ben's guitars tell the tale of hard playing with a permanent record of scars from the nails of his right hand, the most visible appearing below the first string like the trailing arcs of fireworks. John Gilbert, my mentor and builder of one of Ben's early guitars, once told me, "Benny must eat steak and eggs on his guitars!" I personally love to see nail marks on my guitars because I know the player is playing without constraint and pushing the guitar to its limits.

There are auxiliary features on Ben's guitars that he considers indispensable and which provide insight into his playing.

*Armrest.* A rounded strip of wood that follows the corner of the left lower bout, an armrest serves two main purposes: first, to slightly raise the player's right forearm off the soundboard to prevent dampening the vibrations, and second, to provide comfort from the otherwise sharp corner where the soundboard meets the side. Ben has one of the most active right arms, continually moving forward and backward as he strives for tonal contrasts. It is no wonder that the comfort of the armrest facilitates his highly developed use of *tasto, ponticello,* and everything in-between.

*Wide neck.* Ben prefers a wide fingerboard with specific string spacing. In particular, he is most comfortable when the distance between the first string and the edge of the fingerboard is large, so that descending slurs have almost no chance of pulling the first string over the ends of the frets and off the fingerboard. He confessed that, "In the heat of the battle, I don't want to miss." Several months after receiving his guitar, I replaced the original 52-mm wide neck with a wider version measuring 53.4 mm at the nut. This allowed me to move the strings farther from the treble-side fingerboard edge while leaving plenty of room for his left-hand fingers to work. My necks are detachable, so several years later when I built Ben a second guitar, I simply moved his favorite neck to the new guitar.

*Adjustable action.* One feature that my guitars have in common with Greg Smallman's is a neck that allows the player to change the action with the turn of a key. The adjustment slightly alters the neck angle in relation to the body, which in turn changes the height of the strings above the frets. Ben frequently changes the action depending on repertoire and weather conditions. Given the strength of Ben's right hand, I am surprised how low he sets the action without experiencing fret buzz.

*Electronic pick-up.* The option to amplify is essential for many of Ben's performances and allows him to expand the boundaries of the classical guitar by including digital effects and increasing its volume in mixed ensembles. Installing a pick-up is always one of the first modifications I perform on Ben's guitars. Notable compositions in Ben's repertoire calling for electronics are *Soepa,* written for Ben by Ingram Marshall (1999, with digital delay), and two of Ben's own compositions: *En Ti Los Ríos Cantan* (2014, with the pre-recorded voice of Pablo Neruda) and *From Aristotle* (2015–2016, with mixed vocals).

It is a privilege to work closely with such an extraordinary person as Ben and an honor as a luthier to contemplate that a guitar I crafted may have an influence on the way he plays, chooses repertoire, and composes. There are many parallels between a concert guitarist and a luthier: the creative pulse, the offering of one's work to the public for scrutiny, and the ebb and flow from exhilaration to soul-searching. Our free-flowing relationship has helped me develop my craft, stretching and teaching me in ways that I would not have imagined. There are few players I trust to point me in a particular direction in terms of new guitar design, but when Ben exclaims, "You must!" it's a good sign. Ben's encouragement led to the development of what would become his second guitar from me, which utilized a wood core in its double top instead of Nomex®.

I have made many house calls to Ben's New York City apartment to make adjustments on his guitars. His coffee table is my workbench away from home. As I work, we cover a gamut of topics: the details of guitar set-up and sound, the frustrations of our fickle instruments, musical interpretation, cooking, politics, travel, teaching, Shakespeare, Picasso, podcasts, tea. Sometimes there are quiet moments where each of us is concentrating on his own work. These moments reveal Ben's deeply introspective and disciplined side that is often over-shadowed by his spontaneous, larger-than-life personality. Or *is* it overshadowed?

It is February 25, 2017, and Ben is on stage at the 92nd Street Y in New York City, one of the world's premier venues for classical guitar. He is playing his arrangement of Mozart's delicate Adagio, K. 540, in front of a mesmerized audience. A married couple seated directly in front of me frames my view of Ben, who is quietly probing the depths of Mozart's masterpiece. As the main theme returns, the wife offers her hand to her husband and he takes it. Ben, guitar, music, love.

# 14

# David Leisner

## Smart, Heart, and Art

Three words come to mind when I think about my good friend Ben: Smart, Heart, and Art.

With all his joking and light-hearted joviality, one might easily forget that Ben is an extremely intelligent man. His mind works quickly, makes gigantic leaps, and comprehends a great deal in a short amount of time. Do not let the hilarity fool you: this is a very smart man. He also possesses another, even more important kind of intelligence, which is emotional intelligence. Ben is as sensitive to the subtleties of human interaction as a seismometer is to distant seismic waves. His intuitive radar is always open to the subtlest hints of emotional vulnerability, genuineness, conflict, and turmoil. His intelligence, in other words, is a rare example of a well-balanced sensibility that is both delightful and awesome to experience.

It seems to me that the biggest part of Ben is his heart. What a warm, loving, supportive presence he is in any gathering, whether in a roomful of people or speaking with him intimately, one on one. Nowhere does this emerge more than with his students. Whether in the context of his yearly workshop on Maui, or in masterclasses, or with his protégés at Yale, Ben engenders a spirit of generosity, communal warmth, a very loose sense of fun, and always a true feeling of caring. When a student, colleague, or friend experiences a triumph, a loss, a great happiness, or a deep sadness, Ben's empathy is hugely, palpably present. Of course, this emotional vibrancy is also always part of his music-making, in both his guitar playing and his compositions. He seems incapable of rendering any

38

musical notes, whether performed or written, without his heart fully present. It is beautiful to behold.

Above all, Ben Verdery is an artist. His wild imagination seems to stretch infinitely in all situations, harnessed only by his creative impulses, which must by necessity rein it in, so as to create a finite composition or interpretation. Of course, those compositions and interpretations are always in flux, as they must be with someone of Ben's extraordinary imagination, but artistry is necessarily bounded by limitations. Most artists struggle with these contrary impulses to explore/expand and refine/limit. Ben's almost unrestrainable urge to invent new ideas and combinations, often merging the high and low, classical and popular idioms, is always pushing through to the next level, like a daffodil inevitably rising through the earth. He then must, by necessity, find ways of taming these irrepressible urges so as to find some order within the chaos. I have often witnessed this struggle in Ben, knowing that this process is essential to any artist, but also knowing that this conflict in this particular individual is especially challenging because his imagination is so wild and free. He cannot help but be who he is, and he cannot help but create anew. These are marks of a genuine artist.

Anyone who comes into contact with Ben notices his unbounded energy, his positive spirit, his sense of loyalty to his friends, and his love of ironic humor. But to me, first and foremost, Ben is about Smart, Heart, and Art.

# 15

# Ingram Marshall

## Up Close and Personal

Not having been a guitarist at all—I could barely strum a I-IV-V sequence—it never crossed my mind to compose for this most ubiquitous of instruments; that is, until I met Ben Verdery.

One wintery night sometime in the early 1990s my good friends Libby Van Cleve and Jack Vees invited me to their house, saying there was someone they wanted me to meet, someone who was crazy about my music. Ben often stayed with them in New Haven when he was teaching at Yale. The story went that Ben was all excited about a piece of music he had heard on the radio driving up, something called *Fog Tropes* by a composer, Ingram Marshall. Did they know of him, was he local, west coast, Scandinavian, or what? Always eager to increase my fan base, I showed up and a warm and jolly evening ensued with music, wine, and food.

When I heard Ben play—it was something by Bach, one of the Cello Suites as I recall—I was drawn into his sound like a magnet. I remember sitting on the couch next to him as he played and I was practically in his lap. His beautiful tone and expressive nuanced way with the music made me want to crawl inside the instrument. I felt this was the way to experience guitar music: establish a bond between the listener and performer in an intimate setting on a couch.

Having heard *Fog Tropes* he knew my proclivity for effects (or "processing" to be more academic) and wondered if I might think about writing something for him using digital delay. Until this meeting, I had never thought to write for the classical guitar but I was so drawn in by his musical intimacy that I decided to compose something that was inspired by, if not borrowed from, Bach (which in fact it was). The B-flat major Prelude from *The Well-Tempered Clavier, Book I,* became fodder for a very important compositional venture. The result was *Soepa* for classical guitar and electronics. Several other pieces followed over the years: *Dark Florescence, The Mentioning of Love, Florescence Soledad.* And I should probably give Ben a co-composer credit as his willingness and happiness in doing it gave the music a certain authenticity. Getting up close and personal with Ben gave me the comfortable currency with which to compose like a performer.

Most composers would be happy to find performers who LIKE THEIR MUSIC and put their best energies and heart into collaborative ventures, but with Ben I found someone with a sense of *Innigkeit*—Robert Schumann's term for a special internal or mysterious quality—who was not only on the same wavelength but a dweller in soulfulness. So it was not just technical matters that we tended to in our meetings (although those matters never escaped our attention) but the ineffable business of authenticity, soulfulness, *Innigkeit.*

When Ben asked me and other Yale composers for pieces for a compact disc recording, I worried about the stylistic differences which might undermine the unity and wholeness of the collection. It turned out beautifully: Ezra Laderman, Jack Vees, Aaron Jay Kernis, Ingram Marshall, Hannah Lash, Christopher Theofanidis, David Lang, and Martin Bresnick were all swimming about in the Vineyard Sound.

A final word on Ben's musical intuition about form. When he started to play *Soepa* around (in all sorts of venues), retained passages had disappeared—unbeknownst to me—and I realized quickly not to be upset by this unauthorized editing, but welcomed it; we called it the "Reader's Digest Version" over the long form. It stands up today as the echt version even though there might be an *Urtext* buried in there. Future *Musikwissenschaft* diggers, have at it.

# 16

# Martha Masters

## The World of Ben Verdery

I was first drawn into the world of Ben Verdery when I was thirteen years old. Ben and Rie came to Washington, D. C. to play a concert at Georgetown University, and my sister (a violinist) and I had the honor of playing in their class the next day. I was a relatively shy child and this was my first masterclass. I did not know what to expect. In retrospect, I can say with confidence that having your first masterclass experience be with Ben Verdery sets an incredibly high bar for everyone that follows!

Ben immediately spotted my anxious nature, which was addressed by having me dance in my chair while I played, aided by some lovely dancing and swaying behind me on his part. At one point, the inflatable hammer came out. By the end of our lesson, not only was I comfortable (which seemed quite impossible when we began) but my sister and I both had a better understanding of what the piece was about, and how to deliver a more effective performance. I left the class feeling inspired, accomplished, and a better musician than when I had started. It was everything a masterclass should be.

Through the ensuing years, I saw Ben at many festivals, most often at the National Guitar Workshop where I was a frequent student and he a frequent faculty member. I have many memories of his teaching and his performances through these years. Eventually the student-teacher relationship turned into a collegial relationship as I started to be invited to teach at summer festivals with Ben. This changed relatively little about our relationship aside from the label, as Ben is as warm and open with a colleague as he is with a student. And as a colleague I continue to learn from his perspective, which is inevitably eye-opening on any subject that comes up, be it about music or about bigger life issues. The label that has not changed: mentor. His life serves as a model for a creative and compassionate existence to which I will continue to aspire.

During a visit in Los Angeles we had a long drive in traffic (not so surprising) during which we talked in depth about our pasts, including some difficult times we have each had in our lives. That kind of deep conversation does not happen easily with many people, but with Ben I felt safe sharing my most private thoughts, as he was not there to offer advice or to pass judgment. He was there to express empathy, and his empathy was real. That day in the car I felt as if surely I must sincerely be Ben's very best friend.

In reality, I know that Ben makes everyone feel this way; he connects on a deeply personal level with everyone he is able to reach. That is who Ben is, and why we all love him. Following that deep conversation, we sat down to lunch with Andy Summers at a small sidewalk café in Santa Monica. We talked about playing tennis, children's schools, rock and roll, photography, and travel. It was an upbeat and diverse conversation covering the gamut of subjects. Ben can find fascination in any topic that comes up, being one of the easiest conversationalists one will ever meet.

Some personalities are larger-than-life, and to be in the room with several of them at once is an unforgettable experience. During one of the New York Guitar Marathons I was backstage with Ben, Eliot Fisk, and Oscar Ghiglia, among others. These three men go back decades and have more stories to share than can be imagined: stories about Segovia, about crazy concert snafus, about travel experiences, and stories told through music. In a room full of people with several larger-than-life personalities, one might imagine that the atmosphere could be a bit crazy; and it was! But what never happened was any form of competitiveness. It was beautiful to see all these old friends just sharing the joy of being together, appreciating this lifestyle we have the pleasure of leading, and the lifelong friendships that it bears.

On another trip to New York, Ben and I had a rare opportunity to have an extended dinner without any work pending afterward. We passed quite a bit of time at our table in a popular restaurant in Manhattan, occupying space that the owners likely would have wanted us to pass on to the next customers. But they could not possibly be upset with us, as Ben quickly made friends with our server and the rest of the staff at the restaurant. It struck me that Ben hasn't met someone who isn't a friend. I once saw a business card that said "Future Friend" in the title area. This seems like a card that was made for Ben.

I think the only time that I met Ben abroad (that I can remember!) was at the Iserlohn Festival a few summers ago. Our time at the festival did not overlap by much, but in a room full of guitarists who I knew well, it was Ben I was happy to talk with all night at the opening reception. We caught up about each of our musical projects, our children and families, and our hopes for the future. It had been a few years since we had talked much, but he remembered about my children, what they were into, and made me feel like I was an important person in his life (again: as if I must be his best friend!).

We had another great meal the night before a Guitar Foundation of America Regional Symposium in Washington, D. C. followed by a tasty box lunch the day of the event. Ben was just as cool and just as enthusiastic with a pre-prepared for-the-masses lunch as with the amazing vegan food we had the night before. (I am not sure the rest of us shared his enthusiasm for the lunch, but that is what sets Ben apart!)

The real gem of that weekend, however, was not his appreciation of a box lunch. It was his work with the students in the Symposium guitar orchestra. The orchestra played *Scenes from Ellis Island*, and Ben finished off with a fantastic electric guitar solo. Seeing him work with the orchestra of primarily middle-school and high-school students brought me back to our first meeting when I was that same age. Sometimes passing years dampen a person's energy and/or drive a bit of a wedge in their ability to relate to younger generations. It was beautiful to see how neither of those typical outcomes was happening there. Ben is living proof that age is just a number.

One of my favorite personality quirks about Ben is his hilarious, warm, in-fectious approach to written communication. An email or a text from Ben is guaranteed to bring a smile to your face, and often an LOL. I looked up a few examples. Where others would write "Dear Martha," Ben writes, "Marvelous M!!", "Wonderful M," and "M Girl." Where others would write "Sincerely," Ben writes, "Thanks so mucho!!! Huge hugs! So looking forward!", "Bpoo!", "Bennyhana," and "Bboy." A short and sweet reply to simple information I had shared was "Dearest Lady M, It is written that YOU RULE! Your humble serv-ant, Bennyv." The use of excessive exclamation marks—I had one message where I counted over fifty!!!—seems like something that Ben could copyright.

But in between the sweetness and silliness of his greetings lies an artist, deep to his core. I remember over the years many performances of Bach from Ben. Each performance was something entirely different from what I was hearing others do. It always sounded distinctly like Ben, and yet somehow exactly as I imagine it would please Bach. In my second masterclass with Ben (a year after the first), I played the Prelude to the First Cello Suite. I can still hear how he demonstrated his ideas for me, I can hear the basses on his Smallman, the depth of sound he produced, the movement of the lines he achieved. Ben's approach to Bach has been with me since my early years and remains one of my favorite things to hear Ben play.

But that is not all that I remember about concerts with Ben. I remember him collaborating in chamber music; I remember him playing his own music and the myriad of impressions that this creates; I remember him playing with pre-recorded tape; and the one the will never leave me: I remember him performing with beatboxer Mark Martin at the 2016 GFA Convention. I must confess to being skeptical prior to the performance of how this would work. I have im-mense respect for Ben, so of course I wanted to hear it; but if I am being honest, I was not convinced that it was going to work, no matter how many exclamation marks Ben added in his note to me, telling me it was going to be "AWESOME!!!!!!!!!" What happened on stage that night was true artistry, using the guitar as an instrument to deliver a message, not as the focal point. Ben is an artist who knows no bounds. Why *wouldn't* a classical guitarist perform with a beatboxer? A thought only Ben could have. And it would have been easy to do something flashy with that combination and have it be a cheap but effective performance. But that is not what they did. They created, in my opinion, one of the most memorable moments in GFA Convention performance history. This is a performance I would love to go back and hear again. I was moved by the musicianship of Mark Martin. (I confess I did not know how artistic a beatboxer could be.) I was moved by the way the two interacted. I was moved by the social context of the work.

And this performance is a perfect synopsis of who Ben is: an artist creating experiences we have never seen before; a deep human, always seeking truth in the journey, and there to support others in their pursuit of the same; a humble man, reluctantly accepting praise only while returning it to you twofold.

Ben has led an incredible career to this point and I cannot wait to see where the next thirty-plus years take him on this journey. I will travel far and wide to continue to be a part of his world of creation.

# 17

# Anthony Newman

## Ben and Tony

Ben and I met at the Wooster School in Danbury, Connecticut in 1973. I could hear he was already a great guitarist with one foot in pop music, like Jimi Hendrix, and the other in Bach. My wife Mary Jane was a teacher at the school and introduced us. I was already with Columbia Records, and immediately saw possibilities with Ben for some Bach projects. In 1973 the firm of Henderson and Wilson installed a grand-sounding organ at the Wooster School on which I recorded Bach's 24 Preludes and Fugues. During that time I often heard Ben play, admiring his talent and friendliness. In 1974 I introduced Ben to Zen practice, which he adopted immediately and easily, as if he had once been a student of Eastern practice. This led to his attending a New York Zen center on a regular basis.

In 1974 he entered the State University of New York College at Purchase, where I was already a faculty member. In 1977 I wrote for him my largest guitar work, *Variations and Grand Contrapunctus*, which we recorded for Cambridge Records, and which got a great New York Times review. In 1979 he married Rie Schmidt, and I played at the wedding!

In 1979 I wrote him my pop guitar work *Gigue* which was featured in *Guitar Player* magazine, even with a plastic CD inserted therein. The same year the great guitar builder Thomas Humphrey commissioned *Suite for Guitar*.

With both Mary Jane's and my coaching, Ben recorded Bach's Sixth Cello Suite in his own transcription for guitar solo. At the same time I persuaded Newport Classic Records to take him on. We also recorded Bach's great Concerto in D minor together for Musical Heritage Society.

Ben played a *Chaconne* of mine for his debut at Wigmore Hall in London, and I also wrote a two-guitar work *The Gigue Is Up* for Ben and John Williams, which was premiered at the Queen Elizabeth Hall Festival. In 1994 I wrote *Ride the Wind Horse* which he made famous.

Ben often invited me to lecture at Yale University where he is professor of guitar, and in 2003 he played on my chamber series at St. Matthews Church in Bedford, New York. Ben is a wonderful guy and I am privileged to know and work with him. He is a delight to be with and a true guitar genius!

# 18

# John Olson

## Ben on Maui

Several years ago, I found myself waiting out a pretty severe tropical storm with a group of friends in a small rented condo on the west coast of Maui. The rain was torrential, the wind heavy and treacherous. The roads were not safe to drive, so activities for the afternoon had been cancelled. We sat inside, eating pizza from the one nearby restaurant that had stayed open, enjoying the situation and each other's company, entertained by the non-stop banter between two of my musical heroes, Ben Verdery and Fred Hand. We had all been drawn together on this island by our love of the guitar, and it was not the first trip here for most of us. Those visiting for the third or fourth or eighth time had initially come to study and to be immersed in the guitar, but had returned year after year, I am certain, for reasons that go well beyond music.

Ben Verdery has been holding a masterclass on Maui for close to twenty years now. I have participated in it for over ten and helped organize it for the past five. It started, as I understand, as an informal event, held upcountry for the small group of musicians who made the long trip across the Pacific Ocean to get there. Over the years it grew in size and organization, with Ben's wife Rie expertly handling the logistics for the first dozen or so years. By the time I first attended the class in 2004, it had moved down to the coast and settled into a satisfying rhythm of masterclass sessions, concerts, outings around the island, and other events taking place over the course of ten days. My wife Gioia and I had a great time that first year, so we signed up to return the next year, and then the next, and soon it became a much-anticipated part of our year. The class is

48

like no other festival I have experienced, and has truly been life-changing for me. From the number of other participants who come many years in a row, I think it is safe to say my experience is not unique. So what is it that makes this class so extraordinary?

Certainly central to anyone's experience of the class is the infectious personality and inspirational artistry of Ben Verdery. He is a remarkable teacher, with boundless energy and an amazingly creative approach to any repertoire he is asked to teach. Everyone, whether one of his Yale students, a talented high-school student, or an adult amateur, seems to come away from a lesson with Ben inspired and entertained, with new insights into the piece they just played for him. And his energy level is, remarkably, the same for the last student on the final day as it was for the initial student on the first.

In my own experience as a student in the class, I have benefited enormously from Ben's specific insights—articulation ideas in the de Falla *Homenaje*, for example, or phrasing in a Bach fugue—but even more from the overarching creativity he encourages in approaching music. And I do not just mean creative ways of interpreting particular pieces. Ben also has a way of encouraging students, including through his own example, to find and follow their own individual musical paths. Much of what I have found most satisfying personally as a musician in recent years I can trace clearly to the class and Ben's influence: ensemble playing, duets with organ, commissioning new music for guitar and voice. These endeavors have broadened me immeasurably as a musician, and my embrace of them are largely due to the influence of Ben's teaching on Maui. I bring up my own experience here as an example, but I have seen other guitarists benefit from the class in this way as well, and find their own unique trajectories under Ben's influence.

But a lot of festivals have amazing teachers. So what is it about this class?

The event is more than just the lessons with Ben. In recent years, Ben has invited some amazing guests to be part of the week and to share some of the teaching: artists like John Dearman, Fred Hand, David Leisner, Martha Masters, and Andrew York. And there are some incredible performances to experience, including Ben's opening concert that also features his guest artists, and usually also includes some brilliant musicians from Hawai'i, such as Jeff Peterson and Ian O'Sullivan. The students also perform in two concerts that close the class which include several pieces played by the full ensemble of participants, rehearsed over the previous few days. For those whose heads are not buried in their music, the ensemble rehearsals with Ben at the podium are as funny as any time spent in a comedy club, as a procession of characters take over and channel their way through Ben. Somehow the music gets learned and the ensemble brought together in time for the concerts.

But most festivals feature concerts by great performers and many offer performance and ensemble opportunities for participants. Perhaps it is the setting. Hawai'i is, of course, an extraordinary place. The physical beauty of the islands is breathtaking, the *aloha* spirit is wonderful, and the feel of the air when the trade winds blow in the afternoon is unforgettable. And the class affords plenty of opportunity to experience the island, with informal trips to beaches, waterfalls, streams, and the Haleakalā volcano. This kind of natural beauty is hard to find at other music festivals, so no question it is part of what makes this class so special. But I know there is more to it than even that.

Maybe it is the relaxed vibe of the class, which provides the chance to ask a master teacher about fingering choices or interpretation or performance anxiety, or to get career advice, all while lying on the beach at sunset. Or maybe it is the accumulated class lore, which includes the story of the pair of students who decided to go luau-hopping after the closing concert and walked or hitchhiked the twenty miles back to their condo, an endeavor which did not go as planned, but which did provide a great yarn and the need for a signed liability waiver for all participants in subsequent years.

Or maybe it is the Mustache Competition that closes the week. What other music festival has a Mustache Competition? I am no historian, but I am reasonably certain that Segovia's masterclasses did not feature such an event. In brief: the male participants shave their mustaches at the start of the class, and at the closing party, the female participants judge the contestants, asking them probing questions and closely examining their upper-lip growth. The judges typically approach their role with suitable gravitas, with the contestants exhibiting great creativity in their answers and sometimes in their methods of augmenting paltry facial hair. And it actually is an equal-opportunity competition; female students have been known to enter on more than one occasion. One may ask: Why is this contest part of the class? Does it reflect Ben's distaste for music competitions and his desire at his own class to instead offer an absurd contest as a comment? I am not sure, but I do know that the competition is a lot of fun and serves as a great way for everyone to end their time together on the island. (Full disclosure: I won in 2006.)

Everything I have mentioned contributes to the class's unique flavor, but even together they do not fully capture the experience of the class or explain why it has such an effect on so many who attend. Even the guest teachers, themselves veterans of countless masterclasses and festivals, seem to come away from Ben's Maui class with the feeling that they have been part of something extraordinary, something they know will stay with them for a long time.

For me, what ultimately makes Ben's class so special is that for ten days each summer a beautiful little community springs up on this island in the Pacific Ocean. That community is never the same from one year to the next, although there is a lot of continuity. And the community does not really end at the close of the class. I have made enduring friendships, carried on musical collaborations, and started professional relationships that have continued once we are back on the mainland. And beautiful things happen, like the time two members of this little community got married on the beach at sunrise during the class.

This community is so special to those of us who have experienced it because the individual at the center of it is himself so exceptional. Ben is a remarkable person; I could not begin to put into words how creative, compassionate, and funny he is. He is not just a great musician, composer, performer, and teacher; he is an extraordinary person of tremendous intelligence and depth. The class, with its many facets and with this human community at its core, is itself a beautiful reflection of who Ben is. A dear friend of ours, who joined me and Gioia for a week during the class last year, put it simply: "Ben is life." That pretty much sums it up. Who wouldn't want to experience that?

So I remember that night in the storm well. A group of friends, brought together by music, in our temporary little haven, experiencing the one thing so easy to find in Ben Verdery's presence: joy.

# 19

# Ian O'Sullivan

*Kumu* Verdery

Over the last thirteen years I have gotten to know Ben as an artist, as a teacher, and as a friend. His artistry is, of course, what draws many to him. His eclectic performances, original compositions, and electrifying personality are all attributes I could write about, but I will let someone else speak of those.

In Hawaiian culture, *Mo'o kū'auhau* (genealogy) is very important. To know where you came from and those who came before you gives the Hawaiian people a sense of place: to know who you are and why you are here. For instance, my name is Ian Hiroshi Nīa'uhoe Kekaulike O'Sullivan. I can tell you about my names: who they came from originally, what island my Hawaiian names are from, and the significance of each. The names we carry tell a history of who we are and where we come from.

In Hawai'i, the passing of information, skills, and tradition from *Kumu* (teacher) to *Haumāna* (student) is similar to western classical musicians who are often aware of their own musical lineage, very much like the pianists who can trace their pedagogical lineage back to Beethoven. Not only has Ben created his own musical *'ohana* (family) here in the islands, but he has been *hānai* (adopted) by many here in the islands as one of us.

There are now at least three generations of students that have come from Ben's years of teaching here in Hawai'i. It all started with Ben playing a concert at the Seabury School on the island of Maui back in 1985 sponsored by an organization called Affiliate Artists. At that time, there was a young boy by the name of Jeff Peterson sitting in the audience. Fast forward to 1998, and that young Maui boy was now a guitar student at the University of Southern Califor-

52

nia. While home in Hawai'i for the summer, Jeff heard about Ben's Maui masterclass, and because he had no way of contacting Ben, he decided just to show up. As a result of that leap of faith, and of course his amazing talent, Jeff was a participant in the first year of Ben's masterclass!

In 2002 I started taking lessons with Jeff Peterson at the University of Hawai'i at Mānoa where he was a guitar lecturer. A couple years later I attended Ben's Maui masterclass for the first time. I have been at every class since 2004. Classical guitar study can be difficult in the islands due to a lack of an organized classical guitar community, but such a community is exactly what Ben provided for me through his class. In 2009 I was accepted into the Yale School of Music where I completed my Masters in Classical Guitar Performance. I assumed Jeff Peterson's former position as a lecturer of guitar at the University of Hawai'i in 2012. That is when I began teaching a talented young Hawai'i-raised guitarist by the name of Aaron Cardenas. At that time, I had no idea that Aaron would be accepted in 2016 to the Yale School of Music and become the third generation of classical guitarists from Hawai'i descended from the guitar teachings of Ben.

Music is and has always been fundamental to Hawaiian culture. Just the utterance of the place fills the mind with images of palm trees and the gentle sounds of the 'ukulele. Undoubtedly for a variety of reasons, the classical guitar has long-struggled to gain traction here in the islands. We have had many great pedagogues and champions of the classical guitar in Hawai'i, including Byron Yasui, Lisa Smith, George Gilmore, and Darin Au. As great as those teachers have been, without Ben's influence here in the islands, the current state of classical guitar in Hawai'i would not be where it is. The future would not look so bright!

I released my debut album *Born and Raised* in 2013. The significance of this album is that it is the first album ever to feature classical guitar compositions by Hawaiian composers, and is the first time that a classical guitar album was a finalist in the Nā Hōkū Hanohano Awards, the Hawaiian Grammys. Thanks to the influence of *Kumu* Verdery, it is surely not the last.

# 20

# Paco Peña

## A Message to Ben

Since you and I met in Castres, France, all those years ago at the banquet offered by the town's mayor, we have had many chats and serious discussions about guitar, but also about the meaning of life and the world's problems, and the obvious solution we see to them: if only everybody just played the guitar!

I have to confess that *that* momentous occasion in Castres is somewhat vague in my memory, and I suspect this may be an unconscious (read: deliberate) lapse due to embarrassment, as, by your own account, I was at the time stuffing my face with French ham and other—perhaps not so delicate—delicacies, while doing my best to appear in control of a full glass, held I don't know how!

But there is another later occasion that is very present in my mind, and that was the time when Jim and Janet D'Addario had generously invited me to stay with them during a tour of the United States. Among great hospitality and many good times, they said one day that a great pal of theirs named Ben Verdery was coming for dinner. "Who is this Ben?" I asked, and they said he was a crazy guitarist friend whom they loved very much. "Crazy? What do you mean?" "Oh!" said Janet, "I can't explain; you'll know when you meet him!" And I did see what she meant! Crazy? Profoundly LOCO!!!!

Of course, we "locos" want to spend time together and we clicked immediately. I wonder why your innate *locura* was apparently not so much in evidence when we met in Castres? Could it be a certain jealousy that I was the one busy with the French refreshments? Were you too young? Was I too drunk? We will

54

never know. Anyway, at Jim and Janet's place we had great conversations about the guitar and about guitarists and the insanity that comes with being one of them.

The latest proof of it was, I explained, the festival I had just started in Córdoba: a wonderful idea in my mind, which established in the minds of most other people that I was crazy! I proceeded to invite you to come and show the city and the visitors what a real loco looks like! You did come and, sure enough, just as happened to me at the D'Addario's, everybody understood. Thank goodness for your lovely wife Rie, who brought some serenity and beauty, and rebalanced the situation. Many other visits followed through the years, sharing the company and activities of friends such as John Williams, Eduardo Falú, Sabicas, Paco de Lucía, and many others who, apart from being great friends, were not bad guitarists either! I always enjoyed your visits enormously, and I hope the whole thing was exciting for you, too.

At that time you were mostly playing pieces from the usual guitar repertoire, and very good they were. But I venture to say that perhaps the great environment of the festival, particularly the very special artists/friends that we hung out with, and your natural curiosity and ambition, prompted you to start composing your own pieces, and not a day too soon. You now have an impressive catalog of your own compositions, plus a number of arrangements of music by Jimi Hendrix, Prince, Bach, Johann Strauss, and so on, which are brave and successful, and show a wide spectrum in your interests, knowledge, and sensitivity. I salute you for that and I look forward to more! Your music always held qualities for me that may appear somewhat contradictory but actually complement each other: on the one hand it is guitar music of an immediacy that makes it easy to engage with as a listener, or indeed as a performer; but at the same time it contains an innate complexity that makes it demanding and difficult to execute with due justice. In the end, when one gets to fully appreciate it, one experiences a body of music of serious character, depth, and weight, full of fantasy and imagination, and occasionally sprinkled with the sharp, crazy humor that is nothing if not the hallmark of your own, larger-than-life personality, which I do love.

Let there be more!! Big hugs.

# 21

# David Russell

## Unique Magnetism

First and foremost, Ben Verdery is a good friend. We have known each other for many years, and right from the beginning I felt that we had many things in common. Of course, as guitarists we already had a connection through our love and passion for our music and our instrument. The guitar was our original link but over the years there have been many other sides of Ben that I have found captivating.

Whenever I spend time with Ben, we discover new elements in our personalities and I feel that he brings out the best in everyone around him. Our meetings tend to be short and intense, and I always look forward to the next one. We have had many good times sharing a good bottle of wine and exploring our ideas on life, the world, music, and so on.

Some years ago Ben wrote a piece of music for me entitled *Now and Ever* which I have enjoyed playing and which I also recorded. This beautiful piece has a deep message against slavery and shows Ben's commitment through his art against injustice in our world.

Ben has a unique magnetism which translates into wonderful playing and extraordinarily imaginative compositions.

# 22

# Richard Savino

## Electric Ben

Ben Verdery. When I hear this name I am overcome by a sensation that is similar to a wave of electricity running through my body and mind, the kind of electricity that was depicted in the 1935 movie *The Bride of Frankenstein* with Boris
Karloff. And that is the consequence of merely hearing his name. When you
meet Ben for the first time there are two possible personas you might encounter.
One is the introspective and thoughtful musician who is absorbing the environment around him in a peaceful, meditative state.

Then there is the Ben I know, the electric Ben. In my mind, no matter how
"classical" and well-trained he is as guitarist, to me Ben will forever be an *electric* musician. This might have something to do with my own personal nature
and the alchemy that results when we interact (see the movie *When Worlds Col-
lide*). Every single time I see or talk with him there is never enough time! Our
agenda is barely touched, the bottles of wine have been consumed, and we finally have to say to each other, "Okay . . . I gotta go practice."

Ben is the son of a preacher and is now a Buddhist, and a true advocate of
liberal ideals and social justice, extraordinarily admirable traits in this time of
overwrought cynicism. While we agree ninety-five percent on most issues, we
are sometimes at odds. He is always searching for the peaceful, constructive
path, while I am the product of my Brooklyn/Long Island Italian cultural fabric,
and when an impasse is reached my default position is "whack 'em." But Ben is
not a passive witness nor is he a "wet noodle." He is committed to his causes
with zeal and passion, and when it is time to take it to the streets, Ben is pound-

57

ing the pavement. His idealism is admirable and infectious, something that is apparent in his relationships with friends, family, and music.

While I have only known Ben on an intimate, personal level for about ten years, I have known *about* him for what seems to be my entire musical life. But how could this be? We are essentially the same age, we both played guitar, and loved the same music! We are both of a social fabric that had just entered into the hallowed grounds of the educated middle class. I grew up on Long Island and Ben in Danbury, Connecticut. We both spent summer days on Candlewood Lake, went to the same concerts (classical, rock, and jazz . . . and the Central Park Schaefer Music Festival!). We also knew dozens of the same people. It was as if the universe conspired to keep us apart fearing the pyroclastic explosion of energy that would emerge from our encounter.

This ended in the mid-1990s. By this time I had read his interviews in numerous guitar publications, learned of his very personal relationships with Bach and contemporary composers, and had listened to his arrangements of Prince and Jimi Hendrix, as well as his own compositions. Clearly I was impressed, and I invited him to teach and perform at the California State University Summer Arts Guitar and Lute Institute. Once this happened our relationship evolved into a bromance of "epic" proportions, kind of like an old-school arranged marriage: each of us going through our own personal crisis and then making the inevitable late-night phone calls. All the joy and excitement of living every day. And then there is the music. And I mean all kinds of music.

One night Ben had me over for dinner at his apartment in New York. Now is important to know that Ben is a committed vegetarian, and I am a complete omnivore with a particular proclivity toward red meat. Ben made me pasta with one of the best sausage/pepper/tomato sauces EVER. This is love. After eating we sat in his living room and with energy of a cyclone he shouted: "DUDE!!! . . . We need to examine something . . . McCartney or Lennon post-Beatles??? And no we can't get into the Harrison thing here . . . that is for another night. We need to listen, and on vinyl only, none of this digital!" We then proceeded to each pick and listen to a sequence of songs by one of the two great icons of our lives and then discussed and dissected their work for hours. On another night we did the same with King Crimson and Yes, on another how Santana ripped off Brahms and changed the meter of the third movement of the Symphony No. 3 in *his* song "Love of My Life" on the *Supernatural* album of 1999. And while he knows I am not a fan of rap *per se*, he has introduced me to things that I would never have sought out on my own. I recently left him a message saying that I finally "get it" and now understand it as a contemporary pop version of seventeenth-century Italian recitative. I still do not like it that much (and frankly, seventeenth-century Spaniards were not that fond of Italian recitative either) but I get it.

And then we go deep: Bach, Dowland, Kapsberger, Monteverdi, Sor, Giuliani, Regondi, Mertz, Ingram Marshall, Jimi, Prince . . . it never ends.

The electricity and exuberance that permeates Ben's personal life and inter-
actions is also a vibrant part of his identity as a guitarist and professor. When he
steps onto the stage there is a laser-like focus to his psyche and the energy is
intense. His technique flows forth uninterrupted, pushing the guitar to its limits,
both sonically and virtuosically. Yet all the while he has the ability to withdraw
to a pensive and meditative state that reflects his internal Buddhist ideals. There
is poetry as well as prose here, musical sophistication coupled with rhetorical
insight that nourishes our lives. His repertoire is huge. I know of no other guitarist who performs the Bach Chaconne and "Purple Haze" on the same program.
And in performance he regularly taps into his rich multicultural musical kaleido-
scope. His collaborations with rap artists, rock/jazz guitarists like Andy Summers, flamenco masters such as Paco Peña, and many others all provide testimo-
ny to a musician open to a deep reservoir of musical influences and practices.

Ben is also a champion and advocate for new music. He has had works written for him by some of the most important composers of our day: Aaron Jay
Kernis, John Anthony Lennon, Ingram Marshall, Bryce Dessner, and Seymour
Bernstein, just to name a few. Complimenting this are his own compositions that
are very personal statements. They often reflect specific places that have impacted his life in some way, pieces such as *Scenes from Ellis Island* or *Capitola*.
But to this day Ben is very modest about his works. (I keep telling him to get
over it!)

The first masterclass I saw Ben teach went basically as I imagined: lots of
musical insight, fantastic energy, technical analysis, and respect for the student.
None of the maestro stuff we had to endure. Oh, and then there is the humor.
Laughing and smiling are some of the greatest therapy tools known to man.
They can also be used in harmful, mocking ways, but I never saw this from Ben.
He laughs with the student and at himself, something that immediately defuses
nervousness. But there are also props. PROPS??? Isn't this a classical guitar
*masterclass?* To some it might seem like a gimmick, but to me it was sheer bril-
liance. Imagine the scenario: Ben is teaching a class and a student is not quite
getting it and Ben needs to repeat himself a number of times. He finally gets up
from his chair, retreats to a backroom, re-emerges with a HUGE inflatable base-
ball bat and proceeds to threaten the student with bodily harm until they "get it."

Did I say humor? The room erupts into a cacophonous chorus of laughter.
The students' nervousness, which was the primary obstacle here, instantly evap-
orates and they enter into a comfort zone which allows them to execute and
demonstrate exactly what it was that Ben was getting at. Unconventional? Without question. Effective? Beyond my wildest imagination.

I have also had the privilege of teaching some of his more gifted students in
masterclasses, and what is immediately obvious is that Ben always does his pedagogical due diligence in a most thorough manner. The students are prepared;
they have the best editions, be it an *Urtext* or a facsimile of the earliest publication; they are technically in command and not reaching far beyond their tools at
hand; and they have been imbued with sense of musical commitment and identity.

Without doubt, getting to know Ben has been one of the joys of my adult life. We disagree on a number of things, yet respect each other's philosophy. Our tastes are quite parallel in so many ways. Just this morning, as I write this from a secluded beach spot in Mexico where I am recovering from a minor surgical procedure, I received a text from Ben showing the cover of Bruce Springsteen's book *Born to Run*, while in front of me is a copy of Keith Richards's *Life*. Now *that* is synergy. As I like to say: we are definitely brothers from different mothers.

# 23

# John Schaefer

## The Mayor of Guitartown

In the early 1980s when I first began working at WNYC, we aired a series of programs called, simply, *Segovia*. It was a multi-part, once-a-week documentary about the great classical guitarist, who was still alive and playing at the time. I do not remember who produced it, although I know it was not an in-house show. But I thought the show was at once fascinating and appalling. One long stretch of *Segovia* involved the master explaining to the host how he maintained the fingernails on his right hand. His fingernails! On the radio! As a would-be guitar nerd myself, I thought this was a terrific use of the medium of radio. It was weird and unexpected, and by golly you could actually hear the man filing his nails on the air.

On the other hand, I had come to classical guitar-playing through rock, and to me, the way classical musicians and classical music fans (the host of the show included) talked about the music they loved seemed so pedantic and unappealing. So, even as I was listening intently to Segovia buffing his little moneymakers, I was thinking, "What would my friends from school (all of whom were rock fans) think if they were listening to this?" I did not like the imagined answer, and wondered, why don't classical musicians rave and slobber about the players and the riffs they love the way rock fans did?

The calendar says Ben Verdery is at an age where it would be unseemly to describe him as raving and slobbering. So I will simply say that talking to Ben Verdery is like the highly-charged, super-animated discussions you might have had arguing The Beatles vs. The Rolling Stones with your sibling or friend when you were fourteen: you know, the type of conversation that, if put in print, would be in eighteen-point type with a hilarious abundance of exclamation points.

Speaking of which, here is an actual recent email from Ben, sent before the 2017 Guitar Marathon concert at the 92 Street Y in New York, which Ben curated and I hosted. I have copied and pasted his message so as to maintain the quiet dignity of his majestic type size.

Aloha J S!!!!

We are all so over the moon you are doing this and joining us! And yes you are still my hero and I repeat, you should get an honorary doctorate from ALL schools of music!

I'm attaching my statement about the marathon which as you will read explains my excitement and reason for wanting to do this Marathon.
Given we are both coconuts busy we can chat over the phone, email or what ever is best for thee. I don't suppose you make it up the upper west side but should you we could get together.
Enjoy the snow flakes or maybe that's just an alternative weather report!!!!!!!!
Hugs,
B

This email was followed by a shorter, but almost inevitable follow-up:

Yikes, So sorry!
Forgot to attach!!!!
(Benjamin Verdery, personal communications, 8 February 2017)

Yes, this is how Ben Verdery writes. And even better, this is how he talks. He could be talking about Jimi Hendrix or he could be talking about Bach; it doesn't matter. He seems to understand that enthusiasm is contagious. I have no doubt that this is what makes him a great guitar teacher. I *know* this is what makes him a great interview, whether on stage or on the air.

In a perfect world this would not matter. The quality of the music and the quality and care with which it is presented would be enough. But in case you haven't noticed, we do not live in a perfect world. Great classical guitar works are unheard by legions of listeners—guitarists or not—who might enjoy them if just given the chance to hear them. This is why big personalities like Ben's are so important. They allow the signal—this often fragile, sometimes deliberately elliptical signal—to cut through all the noise of modern life. I have had the experience several times of presenting a series of guitar-themed concerts to a general audience, most of whom are probably there to hear the well-known rock or blues or jazz guitarist elsewhere on the program. But bring Ben onstage, give him a working microphone and a leading question, and that audience will be laughing along and waiting to hear what all the fuss is about. And that is really all any of us can hope to do: make people actually pay attention. Because then the music, and the quality and care with which it is presented, *is* enough.

One reason I say I have had this experience "several times" is that since first meeting Ben in the WNYC studios just over a quarter-century ago, I have found him to be an indispensable part of the guitar world. I co-founded the New York Guitar Festival back in the late 1990s with David Spelman (who continues to run it to this day) and whenever we put an event together that involved more than one guitarist, it was odds-on that at least one of them had a connection to Ben. So we learned very early on to invite Ben to our events, not only because of how good he was at communicating *from* the stage, but because of how good he was at communicating *across* it, to other guitarists.

Realistically, there was no compelling need for Ben to be at Joe's Pub on the evening of September 25, 2002. We were presenting Andy Summers, the guitarist of The Police, in duets with Victor Biglione, the Argentine-born Brazilian music specialist. The presence of Summers alone guaranteed a full house, but the performance of "One Note Samba" that ended the concert, with Ben sitting in on a trio version that seemed to be arranging itself on the fly, was easily the highlight of the evening. Ben and Andy would later record a whole album of guitar duets called *First You Build a Cloud*.

The point is this: there are many wonderful guitarists who choose their repertoire with care and with flair and perform with excitement and commitment. They are the good citizens of Guitartown. And Ben seems to know them all. At this point, it seems like he has taught half of them. They are not all classical players; some, like Bryce Dessner, have risen to the top of the rock heap. (Bryce is with the band The National, although he also doubles as an in-demand classical composer.) Others play contemporary music of every stripe on guitars of every kind. Guitartown has many neighborhoods, and in the old days if you lived in the rock neighborhood, that is where you stayed; ditto for classical, blues, jazz, and the rest. But if there is a mayor in Guitartown, then it is Ben Verdery. He travels freely through these neighborhoods, and while I do not want to stretch this metaphor too far (mainly because I am not sure what "kissing babies" in Guitartown might be a metaphor for), it is fair to say that a good mayor puts his town on the map and makes the other mayors want to visit, to see what is going on. Another 2002 performance comes to mind here: in January of that year at the 92 Street Y, we presented Ben's *Scenes from Ellis Island* for the first time. (The second time would be thirteen years later, at Brookfield Place.) This is a guitar fancier's dream: a work for an entire ensemble of guitarists with optional parts for other instruments. A class of high school guitar students from Staten Island handled the bulk of the heavy lifting, but along for the ride was reed/wind player Ian McDonald, co-founder of the band King Crimson, who showed up just because he wanted to be a part of the Ben Verdery experience.

But back to that 2017 Guitar Marathon, the one that had Ben so "e-excited." It turned out to be a masterclass in How To Be Benjamin Verdery. The event began with a simple enough question: What was the idea behind this daylong concert? The answer, too, was simple enough: it was a celebration of the art of the transcription and the arrangement, a day of guitarists playing music not written for guitars. But Ben delivered this answer with excited gestures while wandering all over the stage. (I had warned the stage crew to remove my host/interview microphone stand. "Some of these musicians tend to wander, and I'll need to wander after them," I explained. I did not specify which musicians I meant, but you can probably guess.) He went on about the guitarists' burning desire to play all the music. That was his exact phrase: "all the music."

Backstage, as the performances followed one another, Mayor Ben held forth. The Eden Stell Guitar Duo: "They're the funniest guys I know in the guitar world." Ana Vidović: "She's so good. And she's *so* nice;" a pause, possibly for effect, and then: "That's so important." That seemed to me to be a particularly telling moment.

I fear that all this "Ben is a nice guy" stuff is beginning to sound like the equivalent of your friend setting you up on a blind date with the cliché "he/she has a great personality." So let me hasten to add that Ben's own set that day did not suffer by comparison to the incredible talent around him. Faced with the unenviable task of following the Brasil Guitar Duo, Ben showed off his chops as a player and an arranger. His set included Mozart, Randy Newman, and Prince's "Kiss," which is a great song on record but which is not much to look at on the page. The melodic material is restricted in range, and simply repeats as the lyrics change. But the Verdery Version was full of all kinds of clanging metallic effects (on nylon strings!) and the arrangement maintained interest through a series of clever changes of textures.

His "Kiss" arrangement led directly into his well-known arrangement of Jimi Hendrix's "Purple Haze," which has evolved over the years since he first recorded it on his 1991 album *Ride the Wind Horse*. Here too, his ear for tone color was on display, in a performance full of *sul tasto* and *sul ponticello* effects. When the arrangement ended as it usually does with a quote from Hendrix's "The Wind Cries Mary," Ben let the final note ring out in the space while holding his classical guitar in the classic rock-god pose: guitar held out from the nether regions with the left arm fully extended, leaving the right arm free for windmilling. Only Ben didn't windmill. He reached up to the tuning pegs and detuned that final note, still ringing, until it completely faded away. It was brilliant, and silly, and kind of magical. It was textbook Ben Verdery.

# 24

# Andy Summers

## Incarnation

Clearly Benjamin Verdery is not of this mortal life, he is a god among us puking mewling humans who scrape around in the rocks and sand far below him.

The incarnation that he has chosen to share with us this time is the donning, if you will, and in a masterful way, of the guise of an American classical guitarist. It is brilliant, if not to say cosmic, and we below are the beneficiaries. In this role he has showered us not only with formidable guitar technique but also with many original and ingenious compositions for the guitar, all of which show a unique and adventurous approach to harmony and rhythm. The notorious music critic J. B. Havitoff has pointed out that Mr. Verdery has extended the somewhat claustrophobic boundaries of the classical guitar with his interpretations of Elvis Presley, Jimi Hendrix, and Strauss, the Viennese waltz king. He is currently and rather daringly merging his classical guitar playing with American rap music. This is a long way from Fernando Sor, and those with less illumination maybe see this as tantamount to pulling down the Vatican. What can one say but . . . Verdery—a word that speaks volumes.

The humble writer of this homage did in fact encounter our hero late one night in a small backstage dressing room in upper Manhattan—it was a dark and stormy night as I remember, a night where we had shared the same stage, amusing the populace with our various ironic pluckings and no doubt were both feeling the afterglow of six singing strings or rather twelve as there were two of us. As I was putting my right sock on the left foot (an ancient S___ good luck technique—but more of that later) the door thundered open and BV stood there smiling, or rather radiating. . . .

Of course it was instant recognition—not in a mortal way but rather in the mystical way that brothers know one another across vast eons of time and distance. For the truth is that BV and this humble author have been brothers in the ancient order of S___ since time first began.

This is a divine bond and therefore our re-encounter was to be celebrated, which we did with the blessing of the immortal grape.

This was our rejoining in a twin incarnation. It was joyous. Shortly thereafter we did indeed pluck together, make a gramophone record, and even appear onstage at the hallowed Carnegie Hall just down the street from whence we re-encountered. I became very intrigued by BV's modernistique guitar stylings, if not actually blown away. Although in our contemporary incarnations we were not exactly alike, me being on the electrical guitar and he on the instrument with strings of gut—made from the intestines of a wild animal—we did, though with the help of the grape, produce a musicke that at least the two of us enjoyed.

We last played our songs to a fine audience of Dutchmen in Amsterdam, a Dutch city where Dutch people live. It was generally agreed that our musicke had the feeling of clogs or that maybe you could ice skate to it on Amsterdam's wonderful frozen canals. We drank a lot of grog while we were there as it was—temperature-wise—below zero, but we would have drunk the grog in any case.

So here I raise my glass to BV and our wonderful brotherhood of the grape . . . and sometimes musicke. . . . The voyage continues . . . sail on, brother. . . .

# 25

# Thomas Sydorick

## The Touch of Talent

Ben was a student of mine at the Harvey School in the late 1960s where I taught English. It did not take long to see the bright creativity in young Ben. He was filled with an infectious enthusiasm about everything around him. In my class it was words and ideas; outside of class it was music. He embraced all music, but, as you would imagine at the age of fourteen and fifteen, he was mostly a rocker. And he was clearly good at it. He played often at school in his small trio that was always fresh and contemporary.

My wife and I were also fortunate to be frequently invited to Ben's home, which was at the Wooster School where his father was the Headmaster. There, in addition to hearing Ben play his thoughtful solos, we also saw and felt the home that spawned Ben. His mother and father were delightful people full of love and warmth. They had a large French kitchen that was always filled with interesting people eating interesting food. There was a constant flow of unusual guests, faculty, and students engaging in topics both current and classic. This kitchen was the percolator of Ben. This house and this kitchen salon embraced a spectrum of ideas, art, and opinion. My classroom was a small adjunct to this Master Class.

It soon became clear to me that Ben had the touch of talent. I gave him some poems of mine to consider setting to music. He can still remember those poems today and play the beautiful music he composed to house them.

But here is the best musical memory I have of young Ben in those days, and it is probably among his as well. I was part of a faculty/parent committee one year that was charged with putting together a fund-raiser for the school. I suggested that I could get John Mayall, a prime rocker at that time (and still touring today) at a good rate for one night as he traveled from a Philadelphia gig to a New York City gig. We arranged it, and I asked Ben and his trio if they would like to be the opening act for John Mayall. He, Jared Bernstein, and John Marshall were out of their minds with excitement and fear. Here was this junior high school trio playing their first big gig in front of one of the great rockers of their day. They played their hearts out that night and wowed a cheering audience with John Mayall clapping and smiling from the wings at these talented usurpers.

A few years later, I saw Ben play again with Anthony Newman at the State University of New York at Purchase as he began to reach into more classical guitar. Some years later I had moved to Los Angeles and I saw and heard Ben play in Pasadena. He had clearly morphed into a virtuoso classical guitarist. We had a catch-up lunch the next day. We have kept in touch, much to his credit, in the midst of a maelstrom of concerts, travel, and classes at Yale.

Last year I had the chance to visit him at Yale, and some fifty years after the Harvey School he was still the effervescent, enthusiastic student of life and music that I remember in my English classes and the French kitchen cradle I saw in his home. He continues to thrill me with his periodic emails that contain all that same effervescence. I hope many of you reading this have enjoyed similar emails. Ben brings joy and talent to all around him. It has been my good fortune to have seen it grow over some fifty years. I am a lucky guy. Thank you, Ben.

# 26

# Scott Tennant

## Banter with Benjamin

Dear Ben,

Following your Instagram posts, I have been, of late, flooded with memories of some of our more memorable and meaningful conversations. I just had to write you a letter. Remember these? Checking my answering machine:

> Hallo me Scotty Matey! It's your matey Benny! So good to see you in the Big App ol' chap! Give us a jingle back when you 've a teensy weensy little minute, eh, so we can have a jolly good chin wag? Thanks so very much chap! (Benjamin Verdery, personal communication, summer 1990)

> Hey Tennant! Verdery! I gotta talk to someone 'cause I think I'm going outta my mind here. These private lessons; whaddaya think? I dunno about you, but if I hear another Carcassi study or that there LAGRIMA I'm gonna LOSE IT! You? You tired of that ADELITA yet? God help us it's only the beginning of the semester. Geez! Excuse me, I gotta cry a little bit. I'll get back to ya . . . (Benjamin Verdery, personal communication, fall 1990)

> 'Allo Scottamin, it's your matey Benjamin! Sorry; mind if I call you Scottamin? Easier for me to remember. Or how about Scottamus? I like it! Scottamus Maximus; there ya go! That's it! HEY! Mozart on guitar: your thoughts please. OK. It's Benjamus signing out. (Benjamin Verdery, personal communication, end of spring semester 1991)

69

Scottmeister! It's the Benster. Hey. Just when everyone stops playing Adelita and Carcassi study 3, now it's this here Regondi etude thingy. Yeah, YOU know which one I mean. That first one. Someone help me! How many times in a week should I be expected to hear it? I think at least popping a capo on would help me out, but it's the same key EVERY SINGLE TIME. Your thoughts? It getting to you, too? I dunno . . . I gotta go. Gonna practice my harmonica. (Benjamin Verdery, personal communication, fall 1992)

These exchanges went on for years. We were each other's support system when a whole school year of hearing the same pieces over and over again got on our nerves. We were joking around, but it really did help! Because hearing the same piece every week played by several students does play games with one's mental health. But we are stronger because of it, right?

These all started after one of several visits to New York City early on in our career (The Los Angeles Guitar Quartet, that is). I was happy to sleep on Tom Humphrey's floor on West 72nd Street. The hard floor and the street noise did not bother me at all because I was in New York and could not wait to get out and about. You were living in the same building at the time, and if you were in town we would all hang out constantly. The hangs were my favorite thing about New York.

You already had a brilliant solo career going, and needless to say you inspired me to keep on track in my career quest. I had gotten hold of your recording of Bach's Sixth Cello Suite and played it over and over and over again. (I believe you sold it to me at cost. Thanks.) What a great performance. And I was a sucker for your stories of your visits to London, hanging out with Paco Peña and John Williams.

There are thirty-plus years of amazing stories and experiences with you. But I do have to get a little bit mushy here, mate. Your musicianship, dedication to new music, passion for helping students, and activities promoting world peace through the arts are only a part of being Ben. You make everyone a friend, and I am so very thankful to be in that circle.

Circa June 25, 2017: 2:04 p.m. I have decided to include a new guideline in next semester's private lesson syllabus:

Solo Repertoire: if you absolutely insist on playing a piece that everyone else on the planet is playing right now, PLEASE, for the love of all that is good, if you can't play it well, either practice harder or at least mix it up for my sake and put a capo on it. Add a little solo riff in there. Choreography is welcome. Or better still, play something else!

Your thoughts, Ben? Until next time, matey,

Scott

# 27

# Jack Vees

## Wizardry

It may be that Ingram Marshall's tale and mine smoothly dovetail and provide a seamless narrative of what the artistic life has been around Ben Verdery, interlacing like the cogs of gears in a well-oiled machine. It also might be that these tales spin and creak, break a few teeth, and end up smoking in a pile on the floor. But perhaps this gets ahead of our story.

I think that Ben and I had both been teaching at Yale for almost ten years before we actually sat down and had one of *those* conversations; that is, the one where you discover the other person has the same top-five album list you do, and few of those top five would be on any one-person-out-of-a-hundred's list (Procol Harum's *A Salty Dog* at number two. Really? *Yes!*) or that in fact it was Jeff Beck who was God.

In any case, as we quickly uncovered these details we realized there was a lot of lost time to make up for, and quickly got to making music with and for each other. It also became clear that Ben had matured into an artist of great depth; his interpretations of Bach alone are admired by musicians of all styles. I, on the other hand, had perhaps enjoyed a greatly extended childhood and was still playing with electric guitars and stomp boxes, and would sneak a listen to Pink Floyd's *The Piper at the Gates of Dawn* when no one else was in the car.

Another character who fits into this particular story line is Ingram Marshall, and you may already have read his contribution to this publication. These stories intertwine and overlap because of Ben's unflagging dedication to new music. It would be fair to say that both Ingram and I use technology elements in our

71

works in a way that tries to suit the performer, and not so much in a way that would peg either of us as an "electronic music composer." And in the case with Ben, I think Ingram and I each wanted to give him a vehicle that featured the performer, not the boxes. I wrote *Strummage* and Ingram wrote *Soepa*, and they both are on Ben's recording *Soepa* from 2001. Ingram uses digital delay and looping in an elegant way. My piece utilizes a pretty long delay (eighteen seconds) that almost pretends to be a repeated loop, except that it fades away after a couple of repeats, which, at eighteen seconds, piles up a bit of sonic landscape. Oh, it was also a little tricky in 1997 to find a digital delay unit with that much memory. However, we did, and Ben began to perform both pieces in his concerts.

Another aspect of Ben I want to bring up at this point is his fearlessness as a performer. Ingram and I both threw the technology wrench at him, and he ran with it. That does not mean it always runs smoothly. Perhaps the epitome of technical gremlins, at least for *Strummage*, came pretty early. Its European premiere was scheduled in Amsterdam at the Concertgebouw. At first it did not seem that I would be able to work my schedule out to be there, so Ben and I talked through what he would need to take. In many places they drive on the "wrong" side of the road, and everywhere they use a different voltage than we do. Yes, make sure to take a transformer for that.

As the date rolled closer, events in my own schedule shuffled around, and it turned out that I would be able to go over just in time for the performance. There would be very little time: just an hour or two before the concert to meet Ben, hear a sound check, then on with the show.

With the house tech personnel on break, Ben and I started to set up his gear. I do remember at one point saying, "Ben, could you hand me the transformer?" He tossed me a plastic cube that allowed one to plug in our American style plugs on one side, and the other had the European style to fit into the wall. It looked okay, but something just did not feel right. I ignored those instinctual alarm bells (note to reader: never ignore instinctual alarm bells!) and plugged it into the wall. There are instances in all of our lives in which the details of a moment etch themselves so deeply they extend the fabric of time and can be revisited, or they pay visits themselves time and time again with crystalline precision. The digital delay unit lit up brilliantly, emitted a cartoon puff of smoke, then went dark, a deep black hole of non-working digital equipment. I saw Ben looking at me, and in great Procol Harum tradition, he turned "A Whiter Shade of Pale." I must have too, as my field of vision started to close in on me. We together had blown up the only box in Holland with enough delay time to perform the piece. That "transformer" needs those quotation marks is because it wasn't really one. That is why it felt so light in my hand: no solid iron core of a good, old-fashioned transformer; 'twas only a plug adapter.

Though briefly adrift in some parallel universe timeline, we were quickly sucked back into ours, and the careening start of the concert coming up full speed on us. While Ben got the rest of the pieces together, I went downstairs to the now-available Dutch tech guys and explained our situation. Indeed, there was no delay unit with anything near the capacity we required, but there was an old analog cassette deck sitting in a dusty corner. The spark of a ridiculous idea formed in my brain, and the nice Dutch recording engineer helped us execute it.

Since it really was in concept a simple tape-delay piece, we could have Ben record the whole piece on cassette twice, one time about twelve measures (eighteen seconds) in, and the other delay on the other track of the cassette another twelve measures later. We would just have to get Ben into the studio and play it twice down flawlessly, with only about a five-minute leeway time before the concert, which he did. The thrilling premiere was almost an anticlimax, because the crazy jury-rigged cassette scheme worked, and so did Ben's live performance of his part along with his tape doppelgangers. He was a performance wizard.

Ben's wizardry extends beyond mere great playing. Wizards conjure up the new and unexpected in ways that defy our rational minds. Lately I believe this is referred to as "thinking outside the box."

One of the boxes that Ben took a wall out of is the typical audition practice. I remember many years ago that he was bemoaning the fact that he got to know very little of the total musical personality of those auditioning. It is true that prospective students' futures rely heavily on how they can recreate a few pieces from the "war horse" category, and that recreation is straight-jacketed by conventions that everyone knows. As Ben said, "I don't get to know how they would really interpret anything!"

His solution was simple, elegant, and shot-through with genius. He started a practice in which he would commission a composer each year to write a piece for the guitarists coming to audition at Yale. The guidelines for the composer? Write something short, maybe two or three pages. Use conventional notation (regular note heads, not avant-garde graphic shapes), and most importantly, *do not* put in any expression markings, dynamics, or anything that gives a clue that there is a particular "right" way to play the passage on the page. The students would all receive this music on the same day, about a month before the audition, with the instruction to take the score as a basic starting point, but to color it in however they saw fit.

The results were immediate and astounding. A good percentage of the students came up with ideas that only they would have thought of, and at the same time changed the atmosphere of the auditions themselves. A good number of these audition pieces were then fleshed-out by the composer, and some are finding their way into the repertoire. I may have lost count of all of the benefits, but it is at least a win-win-win-win situation, which is what you get when there is a Ben Verdery around.

# 28

# Andrew York

## Ben and Blues and Cervantes

I met Ben in 1985 when I was a student at the University of Southern California. He came to give a masterclass and concert. His Bach was most impressive, and for his masterclass I played for him in a duo, doing a couple of movements of Tchaikovsky's *Nutcracker Suite* which I had arranged for two guitars. Ben liked it and mentioned that he would be teaching the next year in Córdoba, Spain, and John Williams would be there also coaching duets, and we should come over. So the next summer I did. A friend flew to Spain to play the *Nutcracker* with me for the John Williams duet masterclass.

Cut to summer of 1986, arriving in Córdoba and staying in the ancient Judería in the heart of the old city, near the famous and beautiful Mezquita, the Great Mosque, with the church in the middle. I found Ben and he greeted me with a fistful of strings for my guitar. The next day began the class with John Williams, and when I announced we would be playing selections from the *Nutcracker*, Williams was skeptical, and rightly so; it seems at first blush that it would not work well on guitar. But after playing "March of the Tin Soldiers," "Dance of the Sugar Plum Fairy," and "Waltz of the Flowers," John said, "Fantastic!" and we began to work on the pieces with him.

Later I played for Ben my newest composition at the time, which was *Sunburst*. I had just composed it before traveling to Europe. After hearing it, Ben said, "You have to play that for John." Ben arranged for me to play in an afternoon concert the next day and asked John Williams to attend. I played two works: *Muir Woods* and *Sunburst*. Afterwards John invited me around the corner

74

for a coffee, in a tiny cafe by the Mezquita. He asked if I could give him the score to *Sunburst*. I had not notated it yet, but I told him I would send the score to him as soon as I committed it to paper. That is how John Williams came to play that piece for many years, and I have Ben to thank for it.

As wonderful as that experience was for me, it was topped by what happened that night. In the center of old Córdoba, not far from the Guadalquivir River, there is the Plaza del Potro, and in that plaza is a fountain with a small statue of a horse on top. That statue is five hundred years old and was mentioned by Cervantes in *Don Quixote*. Sitting on the steps of the fountain, some students of the festival were jamming, and then Ben showed up with his harmonica. Little did I know that Ben played a wicked blues harp. Ben and I have similar musical backgrounds, being steeped in rock and blues during our adolescence. So when Ben began to blow his harp like a madman, I backed him up with a twelve-bar blues, and under the Spanish stars, around the ancient fountain, in the land of flamenco and Moorish influence, two Americans were rocking out with a wild blues that echoed off the ancient stone and still reverberates in my memory.

# Afterword

by

# Benjamin Verdery

## What a Journey

### DEDICATION AND THANKS

I dedicate these writings to my wife Rie, my two children John and Mitsuko, my brother Don, my sister-in-law Laurelle Favreaux, my sister Joan, and her husband George Grey. Through the years they have given me great love and support. Don of course has been there for me since the day I picked up a guitar. Don and Laurelle have been my managers since, well, I think pre-Christian times! Without their support and hard work over the years I would be strumming away somewhere on the side of some road! John and Mitsuko are, yes, perfect children, and always were! And I am not biased! It has been a total joy to work with them these last few years.

Rie's contribution to my artistic life is a book in and of itself. Without Don and Laurelle, I might be playing on the side of some road but without Rie I would not be able to find the guitar or that road to play on! I will simply repeat what my father said to me early in our marriage: "God you are lucky. Look at Rie, she's not nearly as lucky as you!" It was said lovingly.

A huge *mahalo* goes to Tom Donahue who dreamt up this idea. Tom asked me on a beautiful Maui morning over breakfast if I would embark upon this project. I said yes but I had no idea what I was getting into and he *did* warn me!!! Again, *mahalo* Tom! Yes, it has been a journey!!

I have essentially had only two employers in my adult life: the Yale School of Music and the 92nd Street Y. I say much about my teaching at YSM in my essays but wanted to extend a specific "thank you" here to all of my various colleagues, staff, and of course students who have made my years there so enriching. My tenure as Artistic Director of the 92Y's Art of the Guitar series has been a complete joy and an education. I will always be grateful to Hanna Ari-Gaifman and everyone at the 92Y for giving me the artistic freedom to curate the various tribute concerts, as well as to organize and invite so many varied artists to our annual Guitar Day. Finally, I thank them for supporting my Guitar Talks series. The 92Y is undeniably one of the seminal cultural institutions of New York City. It has become my east-side home and I am truly honored to be a part of their community.

Finally, a huge *abrazo* and thanks to all who took the time to write what they did. I bow and love you all. Each one of you has given and taught me so much through the years. I cannot possibly thank you enough. I have read very few of your writings. It was too emotionally overwhelming for me to read the ones I did. I look forward to reading them when the book is published.

Eliot called and wanted to read to me over the phone what he wrote. I told him I was not reading any of them until the book was published. He proceeded to berate me, explaining he wanted to get some facts correct. Up until that point, I was paralyzed and just could not write a thing. I kept thinking, why would anyone want to read anything I have to say about music or my life? I still feel that way, but Eliot's essay made me look at the book in a less egomaniacal way and see it from a different perspective. I now see it as document about an American classical guitarist at certain time in history. Maybe years from now it will provide an insight into a corner of the American classical guitar scene.

Some of my articles are perhaps way too detailed and some maybe not detailed enough. They are largely written to and for younger players embarking on a career in music in the hope there might be some valuable tips. I can only hope that anyone who reads them will not totally fall asleep, will pick up a couple of useful hints, and will perhaps gain some perspective into the artistic life I have led.

## On Performing, with Special Reference to The Schmidt/Verdery Duo's New York City Debut

It is 7:00 p.m. on December 8, 1980. Rie and I are doing a sound check at New York City's Merkin Concert Hall. It is one of the most important nights of our lives. Years of practice have led us to this hall, to this moment. In one hour we will take the stage to perform our New York debut, a concert every classical musician aspires to. D'Addario Strings sponsored the concert. Jim and Janet D'Addario were new friends we had met through "my" guitar maker Thomas Humphrey. We were honored to have them sponsor such a monumental event in our lives. We knew the hall would be filled with our friends, colleagues, parents, and a New York Times reviewer. The best publicity agent I ever had was my mother Suzanne. Her equals were Rie's parents Ken and Fumi. They made sure everyone they knew in the tri-state area bought a ticket and was in that hall.

During the sound check our dear friend, radio documentarian Jay Allison, was doing a documentary about performers. Jay asked me as I am warming up how I feel. "Really nervous," I replied. Nothing is quite like waiting in the wings before a performance. All performers know the feeling and all have their own rituals before taking any stage. Even though you may have played the program many times, it can often feel like the first time. In this moment you connect with all of your heroes who have gone before you. Great performers of all disciplines have waited in the wings with some trepidation, humility, and wonder. You are not alone.

My heart pounded as my fingers ran up and down the fret board. Next to me stood Rie. I can still hear the sound of her flute keys moving as she breathed into the instrument *ppp*. We look at each other silently, with our eyes asking each other: Why are we doing this? Why do we perform? What makes some people so compelled to be in front of an audience and do what they do?

The guitar pushed me to perform. Performing seemed to go hand-in-hand with learning the instrument. As soon as I could get a song under my fingers I played it for someone. This led to the approval of that someone. The audience of one became an audience of five and their approval encouraged me to continue. Perhaps performing is somewhat in my DNA given that my father was a beloved minister, educator, and public speaker. He could read an audience instantly and always spoke from the heart. Watching the Reverend John Verdery—or Dad as we called him—preach and speak publicly as much as I did provided an early education in performing. I was lucky enough to have my parents attend many of my concerts. They were always encouraging. My father was aware that his positive comments would help me with my lack of confidence, which he himself suffered from in his youth. The confidence one needs to embark on a performance career is immense. It is built on a series of positive experiences.

Being in a band that was the opening act for The John Mayall's Blues Band—a musician I loved and had seen at the Fillmore East months before I learned Still Meadow, our band, would open for him—was something I could not have dreamed of doing at age thirteen. Still Meadow was a trio consisting of drummer John Marshall, a beloved teacher and performer, bassist Jared Bernstein, now a celebrated economist, and myself. Thanks to the curator of the concert—our favorite English teacher Tom Sydorick at the Harvey School—we were able to perform on the same bill as John Mayall. It was a memorable evening for all of us. That concert laid the first solid brick of confidence I needed to move forward. In addition, it gave me a real taste of playing original music in front of a substantial audience. In that concert, more than any previous performances, I "felt" the audience and fell in love with the feeling of communicating.

"Are you ready?" the Merkin Concert Hall stage manager asks. I look at Rie, who looked gorgeous in the dress her mother made. I was wearing an ornate velvet suit that her mother designed and made for me. Since that concert, my concert clothing has always been designed and handmade by Fumi, Rie's mom. My concert shoes are the same today as they were that night. "Yes," we reply meekly. The stage manager opened the door. Rie walked out first, then I did, one foot in front of the other. The concert began at that moment. I have always felt the concert begins as soon as the performer walks on stage, not when the first note is played.

As we walk on stage that sound begins: a group of people greeting you by clapping their hands. It is a ritual that demonstrates the audience's respect, excitement, and a degree of anticipation. Anticipation is part of performing. The fact is, you do not really know what will happen in any performance. I practice each phrase and piece as deeply as I can to try to eliminate any surprises. It is so that I can "take chances on firm ground" as the great pianist Artur Rubenstein said. It is so I can express the music as freely and beautifully as I know how. I aim to be as prepared as I can, because on stage there will be enough surprises. For example, I was performing at a retirement center and in the middle of Villa-Lobos's Second Prelude, a woman yells out, "What's that squeaking???" From that moment on, each squeak I made was magnified times ten in my head. Another example happened at the sound check in Amsterdam's legendary Concert-gebouw recital hall when I mistook an adaptor for a transformer. (This story is retold by Jack Vees in his essay earlier in this book.) There will be enough surprises.

Rie and I bow and take our positions. I double-check my tuning. Tuning for every guitarist is our nemesis. It is a much-told joke that our tuning often lasts longer than the piece. I look at Rie, she takes a breath and the first notes of the program are released out into the hall. Our program was very carefully thought out to represent us musically both as a duo and as soloists. We both played solos and played the whole recital from memory.

Each program I play is sometimes agonizingly thought out. It has shape and meaning. The music I greet the audience with, and the music I send them out onto the streets with, is critical. The most musically challenging works end the first half and begin the second. My concert programs are a direct reflection of who I am at that particular time, more so than even a recording. Solo programs in the last few years typically contain my music: something from the past and music that has been written expressly for me. It is as personal and as authentic as I can make it. If I am not one hundred percent committed to each piece or at least searching for the deepest meaning of the each piece, how can I expect my audience to be with me?

I find it takes me four to five days to get emotionally back inside a program I already know. The fact that I can play it through well is some consolation, but I need to be emotionally inside each piece. I need to be able to recreate the various emotions of each work. In that sense I have always felt akin to my acting sisters and brothers. Essentially you want to play each composer's piece as if you wrote it. As the saying goes, you want to become one with the music.

We have concluded our first piece. It went well. Rie exits the stage. I remain and tune for my solo. My thumb falls onto the sixth string of my guitar to play the first note of J. S. Bach's Sixth Cello Suite. A new journey begins. Anyone who has performed a work like a Bach suite from beginning to end will tell you it is just that. Each movement has its individual character, and all movements form a perfect whole. The Sarabande acts as centerpiece and is devastatingly beautiful. The second Gavotte puts me in a trance with its hypnotic hurdy-gurdy section. Onward to the Gigue with the brilliant falling figure directing you towards the suite's final beats. You played it and shared it with that audience at that moment. It cannot be replicated. Bach's notes and the emotion you poured into them have been dispersed into the ether . . . live music-making. It doesn't get much better.

When the last notes of Schubert's masterpiece *Die schöne Müllerin* evaporated into the hall at a 1997 concert, there was complete silence. The conclusion of such a masterpiece combined with the feeling one shares with the audience is sacred. When this has occurred in my solo recitals after the final bars of certain profound works, I often say a simple Buddhist prayer. Such is its special magic. The applause began. The legendary German baritone Hermann Prey, with whom I had the honor of accompanying Schubert's indescribably beautiful song cycle, took my hand and exclaimed, "What a journey, what a journey." I can still see the look in his eyes as he said it.

Performing a concert is a journey in which we share and communicate the composer's and our deepest emotions with a group of people. In so doing both parties can be transformed and transported in some manner, if only for an instant. When I am playing my best, I am transported. It is almost as if someone else is playing. I am for once not in my own way. The audience and I are in the divine moment. There is no future and no past. That only occurs when I am really listening. The experience is ineffable.

Anyone who has been fortunate enough to have played in halls like London's Wigmore Hall, Amsterdam's Concertgebouw, or New York's Carnegie Hall and 92nd Street Y will admit that there are ghosts in those halls that propel and inspire you. A space that has a history of great performances has an undeniable vibration you can feel that enhances the concert. That having been said, some of my most memorable recitals have taken place in a wide variety of unusual settings. One of the most moving concerts I ever gave was in a maximum-security prison outside of Washington, D. C. One of best reviews I ever received was after a concert in an outdoor train station depot. The concert was one of many informal recitals I was giving during an Affiliate Artists residency. At the end of the "informance" as they were called, a petite elderly Southern woman approached me in a beautiful dress and said, "You sure do make a lady out of that thang." Music can transform any space into a place of beauty.

A concert is the coming together of the performer, the composer's music, the instruments, the strings, the space and its acoustics, the audience and their ability to be good listeners, the clothes you wear, and more. All of these are taken into account when you think back on what made an especially good performance.

The last notes of our New York City concert debut had sounded. A feeling of great satisfaction—and yes, some relief—comes over us. We exit and are back in the wings offstage. The backstage area now feels completely different. The stage manager even looks different. We hear the beautiful rewarding sound of the audience's enthusiastic applause through the stage door, signaling us to re-enter and play an encore. This time our gait is different. We have been somewhere and experienced something profound. We say goodbye to our audience with François Couperin's *Le Rossignol en Amour.*

After meeting and greeting so many wonderful souls, Rie and I head back to our 72nd Street apartment. There is an after-concert party well underway. I remember distinctly seeing my Dad talking to Eliot Fisk and Joe and Marilyn Swartz. Other wild couplings of people were formed that only occur at unique events like these. The room was filled with joy. Not so long into the party someone entered saying that John Lennon had just been shot. We lived a block away from the icon. Jim D'Addario told us all that he thought he had heard something that sounded like gun shots after he had parked his car and was headed to our apartment building. We were all devastated. The party dwindled. The last guest left. We were blessed to have had such an evening and to be together at such a confusing, sad time. How ironic it was that the same night we made our New York debut, a "fan" shot the person who first inspired me to play music, and that it happened a block away. No sleep was had that night as our emotions ping-ponged from elation to sadness as the hundreds passed below our window singing Beatles songs. What did this all mean? I discovered rapidly that it meant there is little more powerful than music. John Lennon was one of the first to teach me that.

As long as humans exist on this planet, they will write and perform music. Live music is essential to our existence. It will never die. No amount of hate can quiet a beautiful song.

Thirty-seven years later I continue to perform. There is a mystery to live performing I will never quite understand. How I play live is a direct reflection of what I am feeling at that moment. It is live. It is to be treasured.

## ON COMPOSING

Composing remains one of the most profoundly personal and exhilarating endeavors I know. Once I have gotten into the flow of composing a work, time stops.

The genesis of my music can stem from an emotion, two or more notes, a rhythm from the windshield wipers, an idea, a concept, a line from a poem, a sudden burst of inspiration from hearing another piece of music, or a beautiful birdcall. They can emerge from all of the aforementioned and more.

Writing music has been a marriage of instinct, emotion, and learned craft. Any craft I have, if I have any, has mostly been gained through trial and error. It all leads—I hope—to a completed piece that, when it is performed, recorded, and listened to, embarks upon its own journey. I no longer own it. One could argue that maybe I never did.

## Tons of teachers

I have not formally studied composition. In fact, the music school I attended—the State University of New York at Purchase—did not offer composition at that time. Although I had four extremely positive years there, this omission on their part was practically criminal.

At age nine, I begged Santa for a guitar. Mrs. and Mr. Claus obliged. With the pick between my thumb and index finger, I began strumming the open strings of my new $20 acoustic guitar. Heaven! Over and over I strummed. The following day, the Wooster School organist Robert Reddington, who also played guitar, showed me a first-position D-major chord. I placed my three fingers down on the first, second, and third strings and strummed. The sound of the chord resonated through my body and shook my soul. Pure joy. After several celestial strums, I took a chance and lifted my second finger. Another beautiful sonic world unveiled itself. Now I had two chords of wonder: one with three fingers down and one with two.

"Day Tripper" by John Lennon was the first melody/riff I learned. The second song I remember learning was The Rolling Stone's "The Last Time." In that song I was playing the riff followed by arpeggiated chords (keep in mind I did not know what an arpeggio or archipelago was!) and singing the song. Years later, I played it for the song's composer, Keith Richards. I spared him my singing. Upon countless repetitions, variations of the riff and the chords would emerge, sometimes borne out of playing them incorrectly. They would eventually morph into something else. "Day Tripper" or "The Last Time" ceased to be important to learn. They became jumping-off points for what would become a song of my own. In effect, those songs—many of which contained brilliant motives as their core material—were teaching me and inspiring me to write my own. However basic and derivative they may have been, I owned them. I created them. Creating them was both mysterious and gratifying. My world would never be the same.

I have had the good fortune to improvise, co-compose, and record with some extraordinary musicians. They have all been teachers.

My first band was a trio. The Still Meadow Band, as we unfortunately called ourselves, played original music. Through the years our drummer, John Marshall, has introduced me to countless rhythms from around the globe that served as the foundation of several of my pieces. I deeply appreciated him teaching me the rhythm that ends *Scenes from Ellis Island,* which I have used in a couple of other works.

I made three new age recordings with vibraphonist, programmer, composer, and visual artist Craig Peyton under the name Latitude. Prior to those recordings, Craig and I were in two bands, both of which played original music. Among the many things I learned from Craig was how to create a great groove and be sensitive to the flow of a given passage. In addition, he taught me how to construct a solo and how a simple figure can transform a song.

One of my favorite musical experiences was performing and recording with my group Ufonia. At that time I wanted to lead a band in which I composed music. Flutist Keith Underwood and oboist Vicki Bodner were filled with masterful insights for every piece I wrote for them. Several times they would get me to rethink whatever the piece was, and in so doing, a better piece evolved. Bassist Harvie S. and percussionist John Marshall created their own parts to each piece. I would tell them what I was looking for, and they wrote their parts. Their contributions provided me with much inspiration for future compositions.

My solo repertoire had a tremendous impact on my compositions. *Capitola* from *Some Towns and Cities* is an example. It was modeled after François Couperin's jewel, *Les Barricades Mystérieuses*. *Capitola* is in rondo form, has three couplets, and many suspensions. The opening figure is a tip of the hat to the Allman Brothers song "Midnight Rider."

The piece *Tread Lightly for You Tread on My Dreams*, written for and dedicated to my late brother Daniel, was modeled after Leoš Janáček's stunning work *The Virgin Mary of Frydek*. It is thanks to Martin Bresnick's brilliant guitar arrangement of Janáček's *On an Overgrown Path* that I knew the work. That piece inspired and guided me through the writing of *Tread Lightly*.

Through the years I have been wildly fortunate to have several brilliant composers and performers give me honest and encouraging feedback on my pieces. Two in particular have been Jack Vees and Ingram Marshall. I can remember asking Ingram to listen to *Be Kind All the Time*, a piece directly inspired by his work *Soepa* and Jack Vees's work *Strummage*. I was unsure about the ending and asked Ingram about it. He listened and replied, "You know, I don't think your piece wants to end like that, I think it wants to fade away." He was absolutely right. I was forcing a type of virtuoso "wow" ending that was not working. I needed to listen and study more carefully where the work was headed as it concluded. Often as a piece progresses it can take on a life of its own. As a composer, I try to take heed and go with it. As the cliché goes, we need to get out of the way. Muscling fueled by will and ego will produce results that sound just like that. Ingram gave me a great lesson that day.

For thirty-two years and counting I have had the good fortune of teaching at the Yale School of Music. It has one of the most outstanding composition departments in the country, if not the world. I am honored that each member of the faculty has either written or arranged a work for me. In the case of David Lang, he allowed me to arrange a work of his and gave wonderfully insightful feedback about my playing of it. I have studied, recorded, and performed all of these works (they can be found on my recording *The Ben Verdery Project: On Vineyard Sound*). As a result, each piece and its composer have served as my teacher. Prior to the recording, I workshopped the music with each of these extraordinary composers. In so doing, I learned much. They did not know it but they were teaching me much in those sessions. For the above-mentioned recording, Aaron Kernis arranged a solo piano work of his for my wife, flutist Rie Schmidt, and me. Hearing how he departed from the original work and observing the choices he made to create a duo from a solo work was a composition seminar in and of itself. In the coachings, Aaron would question certain notes, chord voicing, and dynamics. I can still see him hurrying over to our out-of-tune piano, double-checking or rewriting a passage. Aaron's attention to detail was like few I have worked with. It was never forced or filled with self-importance. The composer wanted what was best for the piece. A great teaching.

In almost forty years of teaching the guitar, I have been fortunate to have taught many brilliant and wonderful young guitarists. I am honored to say several have performed my pieces. In some cases—like Ray Zhou whose interpretation of *For Those Who Came Before Us* is stellar—I would rewrite passages in their lessons. These changes made it to the final publication. Chris Garwood's contributions to the final score of *Now and Ever* were immense. To all of my students who have played my music over the years I extend huge thank you! You taught me much about my music.

## Process

From ages nine to eighteen, I made up songs to perform for myself and for the various bands I played in. I wrote solo guitar instrumental pieces and instrumental duets for acoustic guitar and electric guitar. I do not remember a time when I was not making up a tune or a song. Very little of it was recorded. Most all of it was stored in my head. At age eighteen when I began the classical guitar, I learned how to read music. Because of this, a major transition occurred. I was no longer satisfied keeping the music I had created just in my head; I wanted to notate it. I wanted to emulate the composers I was playing. In addition, I realized that if I did not notate it, few if any could or would play it. Notating my music provided me a welcome distance from the pieces at hand. At the outset, I liked that I did not have to keep playing the piece to remember it. I could step back and look at it and hear it in my head. I began to learn the joys of development. I had seen in my repertoire how other composers developed their musical ideas. Notating it made the development of these ideas easier. Articulation, dynamics, colors, and register acquired an importance that they previously had not. I noticed the role they played in the repertoire I was playing and how these critical ingredients improved my own music.

My journey from the aural process of composing to the written score is in no way uncommon. There are many virtues in composing at an instrument that are perhaps not so evident to a composer who does not actively play. I recall a meaningful conversation I had with Andrew York who told me that back in the day he kept a cassette file of a variety of musical fragments he had composed on the guitar. He pointed out that the particular articulation and inflection he gave to the phrase was critical to its character and ultimately to the composition into which it later developed.

Each composer has his or her own process. I have had more than one composer tell me they never write at the guitar or any instrument. They consider it a trap. They can hear it all in their head. I have also heard people say they never compose using Sibelius, Digital Performer, or whatever the program of the day there is. Would Couperin use Sibelius today if he could? Would Sibelius use Sibelius? Would Debussy compose using GarageBand? Does it matter? Those who record and preserve their music on cell phones: great! Jimi Hendrix and thousands of others did not notate their music. Jimi was so regarded—like The Beatles—that later people transcribed his music note for note. I generally have the guitar by my side when I compose. If the genesis of a piece arises out of my improvising, I will soon get to Sibelius and start to notate the phrase or harmonies I have discovered. But, timing is everything. I try not to kill the enthusiasm and flow of the moment by going too soon to the computer or the cell phone to record it. Sibelius is the notational program I was taught to use a few years ago, mostly by my students. It is not without its quirks but it has been a great help. Jack Vees very generously taught me the compositional benefits of Digital Performer. It has been a great tool in allowing me to shuffle and organize material.

Part of my process involves learning how to step away from a piece as it is being created. There comes a time in the day when a certain distance is needed between me and the piece. I remember a moment in writing David Russell's piece *Now and Ever* when, after a long session, I went home to my wife and proclaimed in the most modest fashion, "That's it. I'm a genius! I can't handle how beautiful what I wrote today is." She said nothing, as this was not the first time she had heard such a proclamation. The next day, as I delved back into the piece, I started to wince and talk to myself. (I am an overly verbal person and talk to myself a lot.) "This is horrible! What was I thinking?????" Yes, there were expletives, which I am sparing you. I had found that the numerous measures I had written, as my father-in-law used to say, were not making it for me. There were bunches of notes that meant little to those that preceded it. There can be many reasons for such an occurrence. That day it was a case of playing the passage on my instrument and getting carried away with the playing of what I was writing. I was isolating it, playing it, and not thinking how it was working to the form and shape it was taking. In short, I was falling back into a type of composing I had done from day one but to an excess. Taking a break with a walk or a tea maybe would have provided better results. It is all part of the process, which seems to be in a constant state of evolution.

More often than not, I become possessed and obsessed with whatever I am writing. During these times, my wife has been known to say things like, "You have that glazed look on your face you always get when you compose. Did you hear anything I just said?" There are prices to be paid for being possessed and obsessed by your music!

Like practicing my instrument, different areas of composing require different types of energies. Composing fresh material demands a different energy than adding dynamics that were not immediately apparent. Blocking out a piece prior to writing out pitches requires a different emotional energy than being stuck on a transition that is not flowing. Before composing several of my solo pieces, I have hunted around for the harmonies that will provide the work's foundation. In so doing, I will ponder and experiment with an alternate tuning (*scordatura*) on the guitar. When I discover a tuning that moves me, a sense of liberation and exhilaration overtakes me and the journey begins. The pieces *Prelude and Wedding Dance, Keanae, Mobile, Chicago, Newport, For Those Who Came Before Us, Happy Here, Now and Ever, From Aristotle,* and *the rain falls equally on all things* are a few of the pieces all written and inspired by the chosen *scordatura*.

I can remember a few pieces where I found myself sitting and staring at the page or computer, just thinking. Hours seem to have flown by. Just because barely a few notes got written did not mean I did not achieve something. It is all part of the process.

Writing pieces with sections open for the performer to improvise remain a joy. *Los Angeles, Firefly, Peace Love and Guitars, Dan and Peg, Seattle,* and *Scenes from Ellis Island* are works where improvisation is part of the structure. Because of this, no performance is ever the same. In some recordings I became quite attached to the instrumentalist's solo. Such was the case with *Seattle*. Keith Underwood's solo was so thrilling on the recording *Ufonia* that I asked him to help me notate it when I published the through-composed flute and guitar version. I make sure that the piece can survive even if performer is not an experienced improviser. When composing *Los Angeles* for *Some Towns and Cities*, I did not have an ending. I was stymied as how to end such an odd piece. Harvie S. had come so highly recommended that I hired him for the recording session. The minute I heard Harvie's sound and virtuosity, I was knocked out. After a few minutes I thought: wait a minute . . . we will end the piece with a bass solo. Harvie, never one to shy away from any musical challenge, was all in. It was one of the most exciting recording sessions I can remember, as well as one of my favorite endings to any of my pieces.

There is no one way to write music. How can there be? I write what I feel and am inspired at any particular moment in time by whatever means I have. Artists write music because they have to. We have no choice. We will create it however we can. Judging our process is time wasted. Improving our process is not. Opening ourselves up to a new ideas and ways to compose is not. One is never too old to learn and to improve.

## Ideas and Inspirations

As I stated earlier, ideas and inspirations for pieces come from literally everywhere. Improvising and what I call "noodling" on the guitar seems to be an eternal well.

It is not dissimilar from when I was nine years old and explored that first D-major chord. I will sit with the guitar and let my fingers roam. If I am lucky, I will stumble upon a group of notes or even two notes in a given register and in a rhythmic pattern that will resonate with me. It will give me pause. I will repeat it, embellish it, and soon I am beginning a new work.

My late dear friend Roland Dyens and I discussed how we got some of our best little motives and ideas improvising backstage before a concert. The idea for my short piece *Waves/Olas* came to me waiting to play at Eliot Fisk's wonderful Boston Guitar Fest.

Not all pieces emanate from improvising at the guitar. In the case of *Satyagraha*, I decided from the outset that I wanted to use a raga mode from which I would deviate only in the middle contrasting section. The boundary I set up for myself of employing strictly those eight notes for the outer sections allowed me a certain welcome freedom. I love modulation and I made sure the piece ended in the mode transposed.

Rhythm has always provided a great source of inspiration. I love the meters of 5/8 and 7/8! A rhythm will often dictate how a piece will unfold and affect the harmonies. This was the case in for the opening section of *Scenes from Ellis Island*, which I later used for *Peace, Love and Guitars*. Many of my etudes have their foundations in rhythm. In *Now You See It Now You Don't Now You Do*, I employ the same rhythm throughout. Like *Satyagraha*, it provided a boundary that was liberating. *Start Now* is combination of four different conga patterns strung together that I learned from John Marshall's book of world music rhythms. When I was asked by my dear friend Javier Farías to compose a work honoring the legendary Chilean poet Pablo Neruda, the rhythm of the piece was the first thing I decided upon. I knew I wanted most of the piece to be in the polyrhythm of three against two or vice versa.

Later, upon listening to a recording of Pablo Neruda reading his poem "Ah vastedad de pinos" ("Ah vastness of pines") from his *20 Poemas de Amor* (*Twenty Poems of Love*), I was convinced the piece would be based on a few of his spoken lines of that poem. His voice would be an integral part of the texture, similar to what I had heard many composers do previously. I envisioned a kind of duet for Pablo Neruda and guitar. Composer-bassist Jack Vees helped me greatly in extracting and manipulating certain lines from the poem using Digital Performer. One of the lines, "En ti los ríos cantan" ("In you the rivers sing"), became the title. I used the pitches of Neruda's voice in the phrases I chose from the poem. The semitone and particularly the notes B and C are used throughout. It remains one of my favorite pieces. *En Ti Los Ríos Cantan* and my guitar-orchestra work, *Penzacola Belongs To All* are examples of how valuable the program Digital Performer and Jack Vees's guidance were to the character of those works.

Subjects, people, and places often are the genesis of a work. When David Russell asked me to write a work for him, I had been reading about the horrors of slavery in America. His piece *Now and Ever* is my musical statement about slavery and all of the misery it has brought. At the outset I chose a *scordatura* that had a definite pathos to it and which guided the compositional language and tenor of the work. I was stunned when an audience member came up to me after a performance and said how the penultimate passage reminded him of the kora, an African instrument. Who is to say that subconsciously I might have been channeling that instrument? I certainly love and admire good kora playing. With such a heavy subject matter I knew that I wanted the work to end in a kind of musical prayer.

Fifteen different locations in America were the inspiration for my recording *Some Towns and Cities*. Each one is my little musical description or feeling about that place. The idea for the recording was taken from—or we might say, was an homage to—the piano pieces *Chants d'Espagne* by the legendary Spanish composer Isaac Albéniz.

Different pieces are inspired by a variety of emotions. Pieces like *Start Now, Milwaukee, Seattle, In the Garden: The Girl and the Butterfly*, and *Prelude and Wedding Dance* are joyous rhythmic pieces. *Tread Lightly for You Tread on My Dreams, Dennis, Mobile, Let Go, Song Before Spring, Dan and Peg*, and *The Wineless Cup* are more introspective, reflective, and quiet. That was their intent from the outset. *Firefly, Los Angeles, The Estuary, Be Kind All the Time, Start Now*, and *Tucson* are explorations of rhythm, sound, and color.

The New Jersey Chamber Music Society commissioned me to write a piece honoring Dr. Martin Luther King. I had just read Stephen B. Oates's wonderful book *Let the Trumpet Sound* which, along with much insight on Dr. King's life, gave me the title, *Soul Force*. Of course, the subject matter was a monumental inspiration. It is scored for cello, guitar, flute, and percussion.

I joined the thousands before me in making some statement about peace. Given the constant violence in our world I decided to re-record and re-orchestrate *Chant for Peace*. We made a video of the second version which includes the wonderful lyrics and performance of Billy Dean Thomas and the brilliant Chilean singer/songwriter Nano Stern. In addition, it features the then young dance company Michiyaya. I am one who thinks you cannot have enough pieces inspired by peace.

*Partial Recall, Tread Lightly for You Tread on My Dreams, Dennis, Prelude and Wedding Dance, Let Go, Mahalo, Firefly, Song Before Spring, Dan and Peg, In the Garden: The Girl and The Butterfly*, and *Satyagraha* are all pieces that are written for family members and extended family members. Writing music about someone and to someone is very emotionally satisfying and not always so evident.

Various instruments that I own or that have been loaned to me have been the inspiration for pieces. In 2001, I was staying at a friend's house in Honolulu, practicing away before a tour in Japan. A next-door neighbor approached me as I was headed to my rental car to go for a bite. He commented on the bass resonance of my Smallman guitar. I complemented him on his good taste and ears. He continued to say that he was an amateur *'ukulele* maker and asked if I would like to play his double neck *'ukulele*. I was all about it. Upon the first pluck, this instrument possessed me! I had been reading about how ancient Hawaiians had different names for different rains. Each evening, a gentle rain would fall and I loved it. In a day or less, I wrote *Ua Apuakea* on this enchanting instrument. With the help of the dear friend Hawaiian guitar virtuoso Jeff Peterson, I booked a local studio and recorded it. A four-string baja guitar generously loaned to me inspired *Fix the Funk*. Similarly, the great steel string guitar scholar John Stropes generously lent me his Dyer harp guitar, which inspired the work *San Francisco*. Keith Underwood gave me a cavaquinho from Brazil, which can be heard on a solo on *Firefly*. I love all the sisters, brothers, and most-distant cousins of the guitar. If you lend me one, I will in no time start composing something on it!

The multi-guitar piece *Scenes from Ellis Island* was commissioned by my dear friend Lou Mannarino for his Curtis High School Guitar Ensemble. Given that the students lived on Staten Island, I knew how often they would take the ferry to get to Manhattan. In so doing, they would have to see Ellis Island. I wanted them to know and feel something about that part of our country's history. I was deeply moved by the monument and recommend it highly to everyone who visits Manhattan. Before writing a note, I mapped the piece out to a degree. I decided the work would be comprised of seven short movements plus a grander eighth. Each movement was inspired by some of the extremely powerful photos that were on display at the museum. The last movement juxtaposes an East Indian rhythm referred by some as the "cow's tail"—because of its diminution from groups of six to groups of two—with European Baroque-like harmonies and melodies. It acted as a musical example of one our country's most beloved qualities. It remains to this day my most-performed ensemble work.

Given the fact that my dad was an Episcopal minister, most Sundays I was singing Anglican hymns, which I loved, and I was fortunate to be exposed to the glories of Bach's organ music. Every composer I know bows to Johann Sebastian Bach. He is a limitless source of inspiration and awe. One of the most revered cellists, the brilliant Pablo Casals, referred to Bach as the God of Music. In playing and listening to his fugues, I became enamored with imitation. I remain an eternal student and worshiper of his music.

Like a microphone, we take quantities of information daily. I try to remain open to it all and never know where it will appear in a piece at any given time.

## Writing for Specific Performers

I am often asked if I consider the guitarists for whom I am writing. Do I write to their guitaristic voice and musicianship? The answer is both yes and no. It has been a bit of a dream come true to have had some of today's most beloved guitarists ask me to write for them. Of course, from the outset I am thinking about the aspects of their playing that I love before I write a note. For example, because of my love for John William's and David Russell's tremolo technique, I was pretty sure I wanted a tremolo passage in their pieces. The Assad brothers' ensemble playing and rhythmic precision has always been riveting. I had never heard anything like it. From the outset I envisioned a piece with rapid call-and-response passages with rhythmic drive. I admit that there were passages that I thought to myself, yeah, he or she or they will really dig this. I love writing for dear friends for that reason. Seeing a group of musicians or a soloist you admire really sink their teeth into something you have written is wonderful. Hearing what passages a player likes in your piece can be a revelation. I wrote this silly piece for Ufonia dedicated and inspired by one my favorite movies, *Groundhog Day*. After the flutist Keith Underwood sight-read the melody, which granted is super corny, he said, "I love it, it's tasteless." It remains one of the greatest and funniest things anyone has said about my music. I am humbled to say that Keith has performed my flute-and-guitar and/or piano piece *Dennis* in several recitals.

One area that I have struggled with is consciously making a work playable. As a performer, it is wonderful when the piece both feels great under the fingers and sounds great! Working with the player to make a passage more playable is time well spent. John Williams has a sixth sense about what the guitar does best. He changed the order of notes in one of the arpeggios in *Peace, Love and Guitars*, a duo piece I wrote for him and John Etheridge. He felt the music flowed better with this change. It did. At a sound check before his concert with John Etheridge in New York City's Zankel Hall, John Williams approached me from the stage and asked, "Ben, you know the section where I use the other guitar because of the alternate tuning . . . what if I changed the fingering and play it on the same guitar? Would you mind? Here . . . listen." He played it really well and added, "I'll work on it at intermission." The performance of *Peace, Love and Guitars* that night knocked my socks off. John practiced the part at intermission and it sounded brilliant. Did I really like it better without the *scordatura*? I am not even sure. Did I think he had a point? Yes, and a valid one. I learned much.

David Russell: "Ben, I'm thinking of changing the ending of your second movement. I really think it should end with a chord and not a fade-out as you have written. Would you mind?" Ben: "Ah . . . well . . . sure, if you really feel this works better for you." What a dilemma! I write a piece for one of the world's greatest classical guitarists who is a dear friend and he wants to change the ending??!!!!!! An ending I love, no less! I wanted the piece to end with barely a whisper. Yikes! David's recording of the piece and the performances I heard were spellbinding. I have to thank him for asking me to write *Now and Ever* as it remains one of my favorite original compositions. Changing the ending and filling out certain chords in the way David did were not deal-breakers and it meant he was part of the creative experience. Lucky for the piece, both endings have merit.

I have found most performers enjoy having some creative input. What any composer wants to hear from the instrumentalist is that they like or even love the piece you wrote for them. The collaboration that occurs when I write for another player is exhilarating. At its best, both the player and the composer are bringing their life experience to the table to make a better composition. If they are both excited about the piece, their enthusiasm will provide a positive embarkation for the work's future.

As a player, I took the opposite approach with the work *Joaquin is Sleeping, Joaquin is Dreaming* by one of my dear friends and colleagues at Yale, composer Martin Bresnick. For years I struggled with a passage in the second movement. I knew from playing four of Martin's extraordinary guitar arrangements of

Janáček's *On an Overgrown Path* that he stands firmly behind the pitches he has put down on the page. He is going to give you quite a good argument as to why they are there. I did not alter the awkward passage because (1) I wanted to honor what Martin wrote, (2) I liked what he wrote, and (3) I was not up for seeing my buddy shake his head in displeasure! Finally, a few years later, a new fingering became evident and the passage flowed as Martin intended. The fingering arrived just in time for a performance honoring his seventieth birthday.

Often we instrumentalists are too quick to change this or that in order to make a passage more user-friendly. History has demonstrated that composers have furthered the technical and musical horizons of our instruments. In the world of violin, Brahms and Ligeti come to mind. As much as I want the performer to like the work, in the end it is more important that *I* like it and can stand behind it one hundred percent. Truth be told, when the composition is in full swing I tend to forget the person and their likes or dislikes and I get immersed in the work. Trying to tailor-make a work for a certain performer is totally understandable and in some cases completely valid. However, much as you write a piece "for" someone, you still have to remain true to your voice. In the end it is the performer who decides whether he or she really loves the piece you have written for them and wants to keep it in their repertoire.

## I Want to Write a Masterpiece. . . . It's Going to Be a Hit, I'm Sure!

I would love to write a masterpiece! Where do I sign??? I would be happy to have written a piece that became as popular as Roland Dyen's *Tango en Skai* or Andrew York's *Sunburst* or Carlo Domeniconi's *Koyumbaba*. Will I? Maybe? Is it going to make me a happier, more fulfilled person? Maybe, but I doubt it. I always give each new piece my all. Anything less is, well, less. Of course, I want each new piece I write to be better than the last, or to break new compositional ground. There are times when I have felt quite confident about a work's validity upon its completion. There have been other times when I have had great doubt.

After a performance, I complained to Ingram Marshall about my discontent of my piece. He responded in his wise and quiet manner by saying, "Look, you can't always hit a home run." Setting out to write a masterpiece or a "hit" is natural. Maybe it stems from our competitive nature, maybe from our insecurity, or maybe just from our enthusiasm for what we do. It is human and not necessarily negative and can give one great incentive. That aside, it can sometimes lead to a lesser work and great frustration. Benjamin Britten was already a world-renowned composer when he wrote *Nocturnal*. It was his only solo guitar piece, dedicated to and written for his friend, the much beloved master guitarist Julian Bream. He chose to base the work on a song by the Renaissance master John Dowland. Britten set quite a high bar for himself and delivered. Most every guitarist and several composers I know consider it to be a masterpiece. The reason we think this will differ from musician to musician. Did Britten set out to write a masterpiece? I doubt it. He just wrote the best piece he could at that time. He was not seeking a hit. He was, after all, a master composer. Let's not forget that. My point is that his intent was to serve his art as truly and as honestly as he could.

There is a well-known Zen saying: just sit. I try to just compose. The joy is in the doing of it. My dear friend Cotter Smith, the brilliant actor, told me once that auditions were the actors work. Getting the part and getting to act it was the icing on the cake. My work as a composer is to write the best and most honest music I can. Whatever critical acclaim I receive for the pieces is icing on the cake. The players and the public will decide my music's future, not me. Frankly, I feel quite fortunate to be able to do it at all!

## Cool and Beautiful

In whatever piece I write, there usually are a few places where I get animated while writing and feel this fabulous rush of joy. It may occur when I hit on a rhythm, a group of notes, or a progression that is, well, cool. "Cool" is an American expression I love. Many in the world have embraced it. It has a variety of meanings depending on how you say it. When I hit those cool moments while writing, my heart literally smiles. It's the best! I might be a bit more animated at the time and say to myself, "That is so freaking cool!!!" Rarely is a whole piece cool but I try to have cool moments. I am well aware that what I think is cool someone else might not, but one can hope. Beautiful is as imperative as cool. Again, these are subjective. I can get the same feeling when I arrive upon a melody that I consider beautiful. It is a more reflective feeling but equally as powerful. If I can get the two together, I jump for joy and praise all things great and small.

A piece I always thought was cool and beautiful was my short duo piece *Mobile, Alabama* originally written for Leo Kottke. *Mobile* actually begins cool and leads into beautiful. I have performed *Mobile* with a host of fabulous musicians, including a virtuoso kayagum player in Korea. Another example of where cool meets beautiful is the progression and melodies and rhythm that conclude *Scenes from Ellis Island*. When that unveiled itself to me, I must have played it a million times over. What joy it brought me, and continues to do so. Is cool and beautiful more important than form or overall architecture? Not really. It cannot be imposed. Finding a form that was not apparent at the outset is a huge thrill. I loved that the form of *Mobile* was A B C. The architecture of *Scenes from Ellis Island* was one that I had preconceived but had no idea would work to my satisfaction. It was both cool and beautiful to see that it actually worked.

## Beg, Borrow, and Steal: If It Ain't Broke, Change It!

Leonard Bernstein has been quoted as saying, "If you're a good composer, you steal good steals." When complaining about something I was writing years ago at Tom Humphrey's apartment, Odair Assad said to me, "Just take something you wrote and re-write it in a different way. Sometimes Sérgio does that." He said it ages ago and it has stuck.

Sometimes pieces will beg me to give them a new life. If I think a piece can be realized in a different manner, I will do it. Why not?

The first Bach piece Fred Hand had me learn was the Suite, BWV 995. I was delighted to know it was Bach's own arrangement for lute of his Cello Suite, BWV 1011. Observing how he and so many composers have "stolen" from themselves and sometimes, as "Lenny" said, "steal steals," is inspiring.

The first time I was guilty of theft was my solo piece *Capitola*. Originally, that melody appeared on my last recording with my Latitude duo-partner Craig Peyton. The tune was called *Sharing a Smile*. When John Williams heard our recording, he immediately suggested that I make a solo recording of it. I did, and it remained as one of the five solos of *Some Towns and Cities*. A few years later, John called and asked if I would make a duo arrangement of it for his upcoming recording with the great Australian composer Tim Kain. How could I say no? So this little melody I wrote who-knows-when has had three incarnations. The solo pieces *Milwaukee* and *Keanae* were also transformed into duos.

*Start Now* is a solo and part of my *Eleven Etudes*. When I was considering what could compliment the recording of *Black Bach* with hip-hop artist Billy Dean Thomas, I thought immediately of *Start Now*. I played it for Billy and I can hear her now, saying, "Oh, I'm all over that!" I altered it slightly and played it on my Otto Vowinkel baritone guitar. Billy brought a whole new life to it. When I heard that Matt Rohde, Scott Borg, and Adam Levin were forming the wonderfully important Kithara Project, I made it into a trio. I was befuddled trying to find an ensemble piece to conduct one year in my Maui masterclass and thought: *Start Now*!!!! I then made it into a quartet. Thinking about what duo to play with my mentor and former teacher Fred Hand, I thought again of *Start Now*. Will I write *Start Now: The Opera*? Stay tuned!

*Scenes from Ellis Island* was first an ensemble piece. Bill Kanengiser approached me and asked if I would make a quartet version for the Los Angeles Guitar Quartet. It was such an honor and thrill to be asked to write for one of my all-time favorite bands that I got right to it. The bulk of the piece consisted of the ending of the original with some added passages prior to that. *Ellis Island* had another incarnation as I made a version for my then-new band Ufonia. I decided to use the ending of *Ellis Island* as I had for the quartet version, but in addition, compose an extended opening section using the changing meters from 7/8 to 6/8. This would lead into an extended drum solo and then to the end of the work. It remains one of my favorite *Ellis Island* versions. We recorded it on our first CD. For Ufonia's second CD I did yet another abridged version. One of the highlights of that version is Keith Underwood's brilliant layering of many bamboo flutes in the opening of the piece.

When Thomas Offermann commissioned a multiple-guitar piece, my wife suggested—as Odair Assad did so many years ago—to steal from a past piece. I was a bit under the gun and took her advice. The work became *Give* for eight guitars. I borrowed the opening from Ufonia's first version of *Ellis Island* and wrote new material from there. Liking that as much as I did, I used the first two sections of *Give* in *Peace, Love and Guitars.*

Creating new versions of older pieces remains a delightful challenge and joy. In so doing, I am both arranging and composing. The composing has always maintained the original language of its source. I add completely new sections as well as altered beginnings and endings. You could say my motto has been "if you like something, milk it for all it's worth." A great patron and friend, John Kiehl, once said to me, "Ben, take a break from *Ellis Island,* will ya?" I did, but I am not promising I won't write the symphonic version some day!

## I Am a Guitar Composer

Throughout my life, I have written primarily guitar music. I have never written a string quartet or a major chamber music piece, and certainly not an orchestral work. Does that make me less of a composer, not a "proper" composer? Maybe to some. With life moving at a fast clip, with concerts and other people's music tugging at my heart and taking my time, I have turned continually to the instrument I know best to express myself compositionally. The very little music I have written for other instruments has broadened my compositional horizons and opened up my inner ear. I always encourage my students to write for other instruments simply because it will open their ears and musical minds. If they only write for solo guitar, they should not judge themselves but rejoice in the journey. Writing a gorgeous and truthful two-and-a-half-minute guitar piece could change someone's life. It is real. I look forward to writing a string quartet, vocal music, and even an orchestral piece. The good news is, if that happens, I will have good list of great composers to turn to for advice.

## ON ARRANGING: AN ARRANGEMENT CAN CHANGE YOUR LIFE

Arranging music is in the DNA of almost every guitarist I know. A song, a mass, an instrumental solo piece, a symphony, and sounds of nature and of humankind have inspired musicians to recreate on their beloved instrument what they heard. Mudarra, da Milano, Giuliani, Mertz, Tárrega, Llobet, Pujol, Segovia, Díaz, Williams, Bream, Brouwer, Hendrix, Fisk, Yamashita, Assad, Summers, Tanenbaum, Kanengiser, Smith, Hand, Leisner, Russell, and Dyens, to name a few, are guitarists who have enriched our repertoire with their arrangements. They had no choice but to do it.

I remember Roland Dyens telling me he did not go to my concert at a festival in Monterey, Mexico, because he was arranging something and could not tear himself away. It led to a fabulous discussion about how we loved to arrange. We discussed not having to create the material; it was there to begin with, and our challenge was to make it work on the guitar. Roland was one of the greatest arrangers of my or any generation, along with Sérgio Assad.

I had been playing Couperin's *Les Barricades Mystérieuses* on a tennis racket to Anthony Newman's recording of it for over a year. I highly recommend strumming on tennis rackets to good recordings for those of you who do not want to actually practice. (Wooden ones—although not used these days—sound better! Just sayin'.) In 1973, across from my kitchen table, my teacher Phillip de Fremery was playing away. After finishing a bit of the Aranjuez Concerto he began to play *Barricades*. My head literally exploded! What, you mean to tell me that a piece written for the harpsichord could be played on the guitar? I just about assaulted the poor guy begging him to teach me that piece! Phil played the great Alirio Díaz's arrangement. To this day, *Barricades* remains a trusted friend and a beloved piece to many guitarists.

Maintaining the character of the piece you are arranging for the guitar is our first priority. Much of *Barricades* is constructed around its magical suspensions. Whether one plays it in the key of C major or D major on the guitar, those suspensions cannot all be realized as they are on the keyboard, but we can play enough of them well, and with a little trickery and imagination we create the illusion of the others. Thus, the heart and the soul of Couperin's mini-masterpiece remain intact.

When we successfully arrange a piece, we catapult our instrument into a broader musical universe. Consequently, we invariably win over a greater public.

Today, it is common knowledge that Bach's Sonatas and Partitas for unaccompanied violin and the Suites for unaccompanied cello sound wonderful on the guitar. They are staples in our repertoire. But this was not always the case. Imagine being in Paris in 1930 attending Andrés Segovia's first performance of his arrangement of Bach's monumental Chaconne. Through the last sixty years, guitarists have demonstrated how idiomatic Bach's string and keyboard music sound on the guitar.

Bill Coulter: "Hey, I'm producing an all-Mozart record for Windham Hill"—a very prominent new age record label at the time—"and need you to be on it. Do you have any solo Mozart?" Ben: "No dude, I so don't! I like Bill Kanengiser's arrangement of *Rondo alla turca*, but other than that, I have never liked the sound of Mozart on the guitar. I'm afraid I'm not your man." Bill: "You know you will be paid . . ." Ben: "Wait . . . whoa . . . did you say Mozart?" I bang the phone to make sure it was working. "No, no, no, Mozart? I'm down. Let me look into it." I dial 1-800-Mozart and I get this recording that says: "For symphonies, press 1. For operas, press 2. For string quartets, press 3. . . ." And on and on until about number 401 it said: "For ideas on guitar arrangements, press 401!" Okay, so there was no 800 number, but I was fortunate to have something similar in Seymour Bernstein. I immediately call Seymour and explain my dilemma. He tells me to hold while he gets some music. He begins playing a minuet. Ugh . . . just what I didn't want. "No, that's way too minuetish" I say, a bit frustrated. Seymour: "Okay, goonbag"—one of the many names Seymour calls me; you have no idea the names I call him!!!!—"listen to this." He plays the first three measures of the Adagio, K. 540, and I am stunned. A beauty breakdown occurs. Of course Seymour's divine phrasing and playing of it sold me as well. I immediately got on the subway to West 76th Street to Seymour's to copy the score. The key of the Adagio is B minor. The first thought was that it might work in D minor. As I progressed measure by measure, to my utter delight and amazement, it all seemed to be playable. With some pieces, one is inclined to add notes, as many do with Bach's Cello Suites. In most keyboard music it is often the opposite; such was the case with K. 540. Registers had to be changed, chords revoiced, and left-hand accompaniments were slightly altered. To say it was a journey from when Bill called me to the publishing of the masterpiece is an understatement. When I started to lose my patience in the process, I remembered how diligently my wife worked on her brilliant arrangement of Ravel's *Daphnis et Chloé* for five flutes. That was a much more challenging endeavor than what I was facing. In total, I made about three different versions. Along the way, I received brilliant suggestions from both Seymour and John Williams.

Before publishing, a wave of insecurity flowed over me. I needed one more opinion from another great musician. Enter my former professor from SUNY Purchase, Robert Levin. Bob was always exceedingly generous as a professor. His Mozart course was one of the more inspirational classes I took at Purchase. He is recognized as one of the world's foremost Mozart scholars. He was *the* person to have the final word.

A word of advice to you youngsters: do not stay up all night with your oldest pal (Jackson Braider) drinking copious amounts of Côtes du Rhône wine or any alcohol the night before having a lesson with someone who is practically a reincarnation of that composer! By 3:00 p.m., I was somewhat functional and managed to play the piece well enough. After the final chord sounded, there was a very pregnant pause. Bob Levin was silent for what seemed an eternity. He then said solemnly, "We can only imagine what Mozart was feeling when he wrote this." That comment set the tone for what was one of the greatest lessons I have ever received. Oh, how I have wished I recorded it. In a couple of passages, Bob eliminated the left-hand accompaniment to allow greater expressivity and freedom in the upper line. Before doing this, he played for me numerous examples of similar passages in other Mozart works. Knowing the composer's work you are arranging gives one authority to make critical decisions. Bob reiterated a truth about arranging music I adhere to: when one makes an arrangement, essentially a new work is being created. We walk that fine line of being faithful to the original score but not being imprisoned by it. Because you can play all the voices of the given piece does not necessarily mean you should. I often imagine what the composer would have done if he or she were working on the arrangement with me. When the lesson was over we were both confident that a new piece had been created for the repertoire that sounded like a guitar piece. Upon each practice session and or performance of the Adagio, I am humbled and awed. What a gift to be able to play it on the guitar.

I was always humbled and awed by the music of Jimi Hendrix. Unlike the Mozart Adagio, I did not feel the same pull to consult anyone about my arrangements of Jimi's music, as it is in my blood. Jimi single-handedly changed the course of the electric guitar. Books have been written and documentaries have been made about Jimi, who tragically passed at the age of twenty-seven. His musical imagination and courage knew no bounds. Who else could or would have thought to close their set at the biggest musical event in history—Woodstock—with our national anthem in the manner that he did? I consider it to be one of the seminal interpretations/performances by anyone in twentieth-century music. To some degree, I owe the inspiration of my Jimi arrangements to Paco Peña. It was in Córdoba, circa 1983, in the Plaza del Potro at 3:00 or 4:00 in the morning, filled with wine and smoking cigarettes, that I conversed with a fabulous Chilean flamenco guitarist Ricardo Mendeville who put it to me, "Ben, why don't you play the music you grew up with?" It was the right question at the right time.

In Córdoba, as in all Andalucian towns and cities, people live their music. To witness this was a tremendous inspiration. At this time in my career, I noticed how many classical players were playing arrangements of gorgeous Latin American, Spanish, and other folk melodies from around the globe. I began to do the same, but then I reflected on Ricardo's comment on that blistering hot July evening. I thought: hang on . . . Hendrix melodies and guitars riffs are also gorgeous and I grew up with them! I should find a way to play them on the classical guitar. "Purple Haze" begins with a riveting tri-tone followed by the now iconic melody. As I played the opening chords followed by the melody, I could feel the guitar smile. With the rhythmic drive of the added eighth-note pedal tone on low E, I smiled with the guitar, feeling like I was actually playing with Jimi. In "Purple Haze" I briefly quote other Hendrix tunes: "Manic Depression," "Voodoo Child," "Machine Gun," "The Wind Cries Mary," and "Hey Joe." I was delighted to find that the solo fit wonderfully by adding Noel Redding's bass line. Immediately after finishing "Purple Haze" I launched into arranging "Little Wing," one of Jimi's most beloved ballads. A few years later, I combined "Burning of the Midnight Lamp" with "Freedom" into one arrangement. I now had a three-piece Hendrix tribute with which to end my concerts.

My basic approach to arranging songs is to try to learn all of the songs parts, including the drums. For example, "Little Wing" has a fabulous drum break that I felt had to be featured. I then put the various parts together, a bit like a collage. I try to maintain the harmonic language of the song in whatever notes I contribute. Often I will pick songs that have a great riff, a great solo, or a compelling chord structure. I was so thrilled with how the opening of Prince's "Let's Go Crazy" and "Purple Rain" worked. I was equally delighted to find that the powerful opening line of Neil Young's "Cinnamon Girl" sounded like he had written it on a classical guitar.

Completely altering a song's tempo and emotion can be dangerous but really excited. This is how I approached The National's "Ada." I played it at more than half-tempo, which seemed to work, and to my delight the songwriter approved. In the case of Randy Newman's "In Germany Before the War," I had almost nothing to add. It is more a transcription than an arrangement. It worked perfectly from beginning to end.

Hendrix, Prince, John Lennon, Neil Young, Joni Mitchell, Randy Newman, and The National are great musicians whose music I adore. It has been a joy and a challenge to make their music sing on the classical guitar.

Early in my career I received less-than-enthusiastic responses from certain of my peers for playing Hendrix and Prince on the concert stage. I am happy to say that playing these arrangements has introduced people to the instrument that might have passed them by. I will be arranging or composing something until I fade away.

## ON TEACHING

It is Sunday afternoon. I am on a green-tea break from practicing and the cell phone rings. OMG, it is Rami Vamos. I had to answer. I immediately burst into the silly melody I "set" to his name. (Before every lesson, like a ritual, I would sing this to him. It set the tone for a joyful lesson.) Rami asked if he could come over immediately as he was in the neighborhood and had a gift for me. I am never one to refuse gifts! He explained: "I came to a realization this summer that I really haven't thanked my teachers enough. So I decided to write and dedicate a piece to each one. I just went to visit my Dalcroze teacher and remembered you were in the same neighborhood. Do you have time for us to pop by and play you my piece written in gratitude for all you gave me at Yale? It's a short piece; it won't take long." What does one say to such a request? I was practicing but it had to be interrupted. Of course the answer was a resounding "YES!"

He arrived with his wife—Nurit Pacht, a wonderful violinist—and their two children Matan and Yonah. It happened to be a beautiful early fall day, allowing us to go to the playground at the back of our building. Rami and his wife played me what I think was the world premiere of this joyful and inventive little piece entitled *Ben*. I am tremendously moved that Rami took the time to do this.

Upon reflection, I asked myself: Did I ever say thank you to my teachers in such a profound manner? Did I even thank them at all??? I think I have, but I am sure I could have done better. When I think back on how much Phil de Fremery, Fred Hand, Anthony and Mary Jane Newman, Seymour Bernstein, and—in masterclasses—Leo Brouwer gave me, it is humbling.

The responsibility one has when one takes on the role of a teacher is big. Some would say huge.

In the many times I have been fortunate enough to see His Holiness the 14th Dalai Lama give Buddhist teachings, I noticed that he would bow to the seat before he would walk up the few steps to begin. Such is the reverence he has for both the teachings and the critical role he plays in delivering them.

An instrumental teacher is paid to teach his or her students how to better play their instrument. We are expected to teach technique, musical interpretation, and the instrument's repertoire. We help them to understand their bodies in relationship to the instrument and to play with as little tension as possible so as not to get injured. We teach them how to practice efficiently and effectively. We train them to become secure and convincing performers. We help them discover who they are artistically and how to create and follow their own path. We assure them that they can make the world a more wonderful and meaningful place through their art.

As thorough as that job description may be, it does not cover it all. What we music teachers do is even more involved and complex.

Over the past thirty years, guitar pedagogy has risen to an extremely high level globally. As I travel and give classes, I remain truly inspired by the extraordinary teaching my colleagues are doing. The proof is in the fabulous young players we hear everywhere. Thanks to so many dedicated guitar teachers and performers, the instrument has never been in better standing. I am honored to be a part of this wonderful musical community. I have had the great fortune to teach at the Yale School of Music for thirty-two years and counting. I teach primarily graduate students, with some exceptions. It has been a dream job for many reasons. I will share a bit of what teaching has taught me.

## The Audition Process

One of the greatest days in my teaching career came when Robert Blocker, dean of the Yale School of Music, announced that the School was going to go tuition-free. I should never stop thanking Robert for his brilliant fundraising and the generous Adams family for their contribution to the School. One of the things I loathed about my job was the recruiting process. Trying to convince students that they should spend their parents' hard-earned money, their own hard-earned money, or their future hard-earned money to study with me at Yale was a mild form of torture. Every early January I would get a pit in my stomach and think: no one wants to study with ME. Ugh! But to my surprise, every year, somehow, some way, I managed to fill my studio.

I am aware that many of my students have come to Yale for all that the extraordinary university has to offer. If you have ever spent any time at Yale, you would be in the minority if you did not come away inspired and impressed. It is a kind of mecca for seekers of knowledge. Its resources in all disciplines make me think it is a type of mini-Vatican.

I also know that unless I have hit record on the level of, say, the legendary Stevie Wonder's "Superstition" (and hey . . . who knows?) I will always be introduced in following manner: "This is Ben Verdery. Ben is the guitar professor at Yale." Their response is usually "Oh, wow!" The name of Yale is known globally and has become, like so many schools, a bit of a brand. This has not been a hardship and has helped me in quite a few situations. I have had students audition who had not heard my recordings, my music, or heard me perform, never mind taken a lesson. They are there because of the reputation of Yale. I appreciate those who actually take the time to take a lesson with me or who come to my Maui masterclass prior to auditioning.

The Yale School of Music went tuition-free the same year our son John began his freshman year at the Rhode Island School of Design. Part of the admission requirement at RISD was to submit an extensive portfolio plus three draw-ings on a specific type of paper and size, drawn with a specific pencil. One drawing was to be an interior, another was a free choice, and the final was a drawing that had to in some way relate to a bicycle. It could be literal or ab-stract, but had to involve a bicycle. RISD held an exhibition of all the drawings the day the parents dropped their children off. This exhibition was inspirational and revelatory. The drawings ranged from exquisitely detailed drawings of the bike spokes, the wheels, the bike as a whole, people riding it, to a charm bracelet with a tricycle attached, to a horseshoe crab on a beach with tire tracks in the sand beside it.

The bicycle-drawing requirement inspired me to rethink my audition pro-cess. Upon reflection, I decided to have a Yale faculty composer write a short piece that contained no dynamic markings, no tempo markings, and no articula-tion; just the pitches and rhythms. (In later years we have included the tempo.) The piece, usually no longer than four to six minutes, is sent out to the invited auditionees a month prior to the audition. It does not need to be memorized, although many have played from memory. At the audition, the applicants are required to play selected movements of three contrasting concert works in addi-tion to the set Yale audition piece. Of course one can tell much about the stu-dents' abilities and musicality from their chosen three works, but the set piece often has brought to the surface compelling aspects of the applicant's abilities. More than once it has been the deciding factor in accepting a student into the program.

Several times the audition piece has led to a more extended work from the composer. This was true of Ezra Laderman and Hannah Lash. I am deeply, deeply grateful for all the composers who so generously contributed a piece throughout the years; among them are Martin Bresnick, Katherine Cochran, Bryce Dessner, Paul Kerekes, Ezra Laderman, Hannah Lash, Ingram Marshall, Tanner Porter, Brendon Randall-Myers, Christopher Theofanidis, Van Stiefel, and Jack Vees. My recording *The Ben Verdery Guitar Project: On Vineyard Sound* was born out of the Yale guitar audition pieces. I am happy to say that the guitar repertoire has been enriched by these wonderful pieces.

While there is much one can learn about the student from the audition, the more I could learn about them the better. Similarly, the more the student can learn about Yale, the better. The same year I began the Yale guitar audition piece I decided to institute a meeting with all the applicants and two current stu-dents on the day of their audition, but prior to performing. This meeting consists of me explaining the program, its requirements, my teaching philosophy such as it is, the School of Music, and the University in general. During my talk I will often turn to the current students for information only they can give. We then answer any questions from the applicants. The meeting accomplishes much. I found that it calms the applicants down a bit and makes the audition a little less stressful for them. I also get a glimpse into the various applicants' personalities. The final part of the audition is a questionnaire of about twenty-two questions. They range from questions about guitar history, how the internet and YouTube have affected their learning, what they learned in their last masterclass, what they believe they need to improve the most in their playing, and why they want to attend Yale. I even ask if they can name some of my recordings, videos, some of the composers who have written for me, and some of my compositions. For the record, I have accepted students who were unable to answer any of the questions concerning my career. In the very beginning years of this new audition process, a student entered and played quite well. During the audition he exhibited some slight arrogant behavior. Despite this, I thought, the person really plays well and is from a highly regarded conservatory. I'll give it a go. Then I read the applicant's responses from the questionnaire. The answer that caught my attention was to the question "What key is Bach's solo Violin Sonata, BWV 1001, in, and what key would you play it in?" The answer given by this student was "G minor, A minor is for chumps." While I am a fun-loving guy and clearly am a chump as I prefer this piece in A minor on the guitar—even though I love hearing Eliot Fisk play it in G minor—I was fairly certain that I did not want to teach someone who assumes this kind of familiarity in such a situation. It was a deciding factor in me not accepting the student.

The student-teacher relationship does not end when the student graduates. It assumes a new life. Letters of recommendation are continually asked for. Phone calls and meetings occur concerning their future. I have remained not just friends but close friends with many of them. I am fortunate to have taught some unbelievably creative souls. I have performed and recorded with them. In the case of a recent graduate, Sol Silber, I formed an incredibly life-affirming and exciting music platform called Elm City Records.

## The Studio

The atmosphere in the teacher's studio is in many ways reflective of the teacher. Recently I taught the gifted students of Thomas Offermann at the Conservatory in Rostock, Germany. The pupils were so enthusiastic and receptive in each lesson. The experience was a total joy despite the long hours and my jet lag. This was due to Thomas's ability to create a wonderful atmosphere in his studio. I had the same experience a week later at the Oberlin Conservatory where my dear friend Stephen Aron has been the chair of the department for twenty-eight years.

Over the years I have tried to create an ambience of great dedication, respect, and humor. Taking ourselves too seriously can to lead to trouble, just as not taking ourselves seriously enough can. A balance of these is critical.

Bach's Sarabande from the Suite, BWV 995, is one of the more extraordinarily serious and profound pieces anyone can play. My father had to conduct a Good Friday service and asked me be part of it. I played that Sarabande for the service. To me it is the Good Friday Sarabande, but it also will always make me think of my lesson with Thomas Clippert, a much beloved teacher and player in the Chicago area. In one lesson, Tom was working on BWV 995. He entered the room as per usual. I sat in front of him in my then tiny studio in Stoeckel Hall, which I actually loved, and I asked, "So, which movement do you want to work on?" He looked me in the eye dead seriously and replied, "Bande, Sara-Bande." I died laughing, and to this day I cannot teach any Sarabande without thinking of Tom's James Bond reference. After the laughter subsided, Tom played it with the utmost sincerity and gravitas.

Humor can defuse almost any situation. I use it a lot to get the most serious of points across and to get the best performance I can out of a student. It does not always work but has been a noble companion in my teaching years. I have enjoyed having a studio of contrasting personalities and musical strengths. One or two students will be technically proficient in standard repertoire but lacking in imagination. In the same class is a student who is overflowing with creative ideas and musicality but whose playing is unrefined technically. And there has been everything in-between.

Respecting each other's gifts is imperative. The weekly seminar, among other things, is where the students learn to give constructive and compassionate criticism of their peers. It is also where they learn to be articulate when discussing music. This is something that is not a given.

It is easy to say that arrogance is not tolerated in my studio, but it is not realistic. For many students, if not all, their playing defines who they are. Their identity is completely wrapped up in the guitar and how they play it. A student's emotional state, like many professionals, is governed by his or her last performance or practice session. Because music is such an emotional art form, a seminar can be a highly emotionally charged environment. Some students just cannot help themselves from expressing their passionate views with a razor's edge. I have witnessed those same rigid personalities over time become more flexible and tolerant. I have also witnessed the more introverted students, in time, express themselves in a more dynamic manner.

One of the joys of teaching is witnessing the transformation of a student both artistically and emotionally. Occasionally I remind the students that they are training to be professionals and in most cases *are* professionals. I often recommend them for jobs during their tenure at Yale. How they conduct themselves in the studio is very possibly going to be how they are going to be out in the world. It is difficult to recommend someone who is difficult! That having been said, it happens. I have learned that there is way more to each student than meets the eye. In short, they are human. More often than not they are far more sensitive and complex than I might have thought.

## A Few Teaching Ideas and Practices Over the Years

Generally, I teach people between the ages of eighteen and thirty. Most of my students have been men. Thankfully the demographics are changing, not just in America but also around the globe. There are more women playing the guitar than ever before. In addition there are more women guitar makers than in the past. This is good!!!!

I am going to list some things I have observed and learned over my nearly forty years of teaching. I hope they will be of some value to anyone who is currently teaching or about to embark on a teaching career.

*We are Blessed.* How lucky are we to teach the divine music of J. S. Bach and/or a masterpiece by Benjamin Britten? How lucky are students to be learning this music? How painful is it to discuss the value of scale and arpeggio practice? The music teachers that I know, whether they are instrumental teachers or classroom teachers, feel most days that they are blessed to be teaching music. Now more than ever, I certainly feel that way.

*Gratitude.* Gratitude is a welcome sentiment in the studio: gratitude that students—in whatever period they are in their lives—are not bitter about what they have or have not achieved with their career in music; gratitude for the composer, the guitar maker, the string maker, the music stand maker, the metronome maker, the studio you are in, and more. I often say "thank you" after a student plays a piece, as I am genuinely happy and grateful to have heard their interpretation.

*Bringing Back the Joy.* A student's undergraduate performance degree program can be a life-altering positive experience, a life-altering negative experience, and everything in-between. I have often said that the way to squash the joy of music out of a student is to send them to conservatory. I say this partly in jest, but not entirely. So many students have come to me fresh from conservatories filled with a ferocious competitive and often negative attitude about their music-making. It is as if they regard their playing solely athletically. While there are many comparisons between the two, we are artists, not athletes. I hear phrases from students such as, "I want to nail it" and "I have to play it perfectly." I understand well what "to nail it" means and I have many times said I wanted to play perfectly, but I loathe both expressions. I do not believe they have much to do with art. Students can be so hard on themselves that the beauty of a simple Catalan folk melody eludes them. I often spend the first semester or more re-introducing them to the joy of making music on the guitar.

*Don't Fix It If It Ain't Broke.* As the Yale School of Music is a graduate school, the students have had four years of undergraduate guitar study prior to coming to me. If their technical approach to the instrument is working, I am certainly not going to change it. I will, however, be quick to point out their strengths and make sure they are as aware of them as well as their weaknesses. I set out to improve what I do not think is working for them, as well as promote what *is* working, both physically and musically.

*You Are Your Own Teacher.* The legendary American pedagogue Bruce Holzman taught me to ask my students (1) how many hours they actually practiced, and (2) how many hours of lessons they had in a week. They do the math and realize *they* are their main teacher. They learn how to be great practitioners and teachers to themselves. We only see them one or two hours a week compared to their solitary three to six hours of daily practice.

*Time Management.* Assuming students know how to manage their time might be too great of an assumption. I remind them that they alone choose how to spend the time they are given. They will choose to make or not to make time to practice well. Given the advanced level of my students, their commitment is never an issue. That having been said, we all can analyze and improve how we use the precious time we have.

*Recital Preparation.* In preparation for their recitals—besides playing regularly in seminar—I ask students to perform their program for me six weeks in advance. For those who are not regularly playing recitals, I encourage them to schedule mini-recitals in their hometowns or for their peers prior to the degree recital. We spend the six weeks prior to their recital refining the program. I also ask them to try and schedule a concert of the program *after* their degree recital. So much can be learned from playing a concert after one that is as emotionally and critically important as their degree recital. Those that are able to do the above inevitably glean more from the experience.

*Discovering and Nurturing a Hidden Potential.* What I hope I can spot early in the student-teacher relationship is a student's hidden potential, something that is not immediately apparent. Addressing that hidden potential with the student and nurturing it is the next step. During the course of the year, each student has to write an etude and make an arrangement. In the case of the etudes, the students do not play their own piece; each plays an etude that one of their colleagues wrote. This is not so with the arrangement assignment. The arrangements can be for solo guitar, duo, trio, quartet, as well as for guitar with other instruments. The arrangements must be performed and presented formally in our seminar. Because of these assignments, I have discovered that many of my students have quite a compositional gift. If this is the case, I urge them to compose a piece for their graduation recital. There have been students like Dominic Frasca whose etude appeared on his groundbreaking recording *Deviations*. Other students like John Kossler have gone on to make brilliant arrangements, several of which have been published. A student can have a hidden extra-performing ability that needs to be addressed and encouraged. Looking and discovering a hidden gift in a student has been a great joy.

*I Won't Teach That Piece!* If you are excited about the music, the students will be also. Generally I love or can learn to love teaching any piece. Naturally, like all teachers, I have repertoire I adore teaching. Once a student told me she wanted to study Barrios's *La Catedral*. It is one of the most-beloved and most-performed pieces in the classical guitar repertoire. At that time, my initial response to teaching it went something like this: "You know Katrin, I really think that is a piece you could study after Yale or on your own. I'm not sure I would have as much to offer on that piece compared to several others." There was an awkward silence. I thought to myself, "What are you saying? You've loved that piece since the first time you heard John Williams play it in a sixteenth-century cloister in Arles, France, in 1974. You've taught it many times before, why the new negative attitude?" I quickly retracted my sentiments and said, "No, no, I am wrong, let's work on it." I then proceed to have a ball teaching it. I even fell back in love with the piece and I am considering recording it! So often we seasoned teachers can grow tired of the standard repertoire. We forget that a work such as Tárrega's *Recuerdos de la Alhambra* was the reason many started playing the classical guitar. It is a shame—maybe criminal—to squash a student's enthusiasm for certain repertoire because we feel that it is hackneyed and out-of-fashion, and we are simply tired of hearing it. There are worse things in life! That having been said, I do not feel a teacher is obligated to teach any piece. The experience has to be engaging for both.

*Knowledge of the Repertoire.* "I just don't like the Chaconne," said my extremely gifted student Tyler recently in seminar. There was a hush in the room and then I fell off my chair! We discussed his views briefly and learned that he had grown tired of hearing the masterpiece, as it was performed constantly in his undergraduate years. It happens. I do not force repertoire on my students but urge them to research the varied and rich repertoire that exists. I try to be as informed as I can be about the guitar's repertoire and still discover pieces I had no idea existed. We are in such a fertile time in which a wealth of wonderful guitar music is being written that it is dizzying! One of the challenges and joys of teaching is introducing a student to repertoire that is a perfect fit for them at that time in their development.

*Chamber Music.* Few musical experiences transform young musicians as the playing of chamber music. I am happy to say we give guitar chamber music concerts twice a year at Yale that are very well attended. The repertoire has been extremely varied. We have guitarists performing with flute, violin, cello, percussion, piano, double bass, oboe, bassoon, and string quartets, as well as guitar duos, trios, and quartets. Duos have been formed that have survived far past the student's Yale years. Among them are the Threefifty Duo, Duo Noire, René Izquierdo and Elina Chekan, and the Z.o.o. guitar duo. The latter two are husband-and-wife duos and they are still married! What my students learn from their fellow instrumentalist has substantially shaped them musically. It is critical for guitarists to be playing as much chamber music as they can, especially in their early years. If it is difficult for a studio teacher to find other musicians to play with, I urge the teacher to play duets with his or her student. There is a plethora of great two-guitar music spanning the musical epochs.

*Beginner's Mind.* I have always loved the Zen expression "In the beginner's mind there are many possibilities. In the expert's mind there are few." In life as well as teaching music, maintaining a beginner's mind is critical. When I hear a student offer a completely different interpretation of a work or employ completely different fingerings in works I know well, I want to learn why. I have learned much from my students both when they were in my studio and certainly after they graduate. There is a reason for the expression "the student teaches the teacher."

*Become a Good Listener.* I am a talker. Anyone who knows me knows I talk too much. I am also fabulous at interrupting people. I should have a doctorate in that! Most of my blabbing in lessons is out of enthusiasm for my art and those that make it. I am happy to report, over the years, I have learned to be a better listener. It is quintessential for a music teacher to engage in deep listening.

*Being a Musical Detective.* Music teachers are musical and technical detectives. We need to notice that in a difficult passage it is usually one or two notes that are the troublemakers. It is our job to locate them, be certain the student hears them, and consequently improve the passage.

*Posture.* Observing what students do with their bodies when they play a difficult passage is one of our most important tasks. We need to teach them to play with minimum tension so as not to injure themselves. We see, for example, that they hold their breath as they play a given passage and how it is reflected in the sound they make. We notice how they have their heads buried in the neck of the instrument. We can see and even feel the excessive tension in both hands. We notice the tension in their necks and their unawareness of the perils of shortening the distance between themselves and the upper part of guitar. The list of the physical obstacles a teacher can notice can be extensive. It is documented that there are more injuries related to misuse of the body by guitarists than other instruments. Human contact is vital in communicating the complexities and subtleties of teaching an instrument.

*More Than One Answer.* Having one, two, or three ways to improve a given passage is something I tried to develop over the years. Many times I will take the extra time to try a couple of different solutions to a problem with the student on the spot. It is always been helpful to have a few different tools in the toolbox!

*Observing Their Practice Habits / Practicing with Them.* I like to evaluate students' practice techniques and habits. I find out what is not working for them and encourage them to change their practice methods/routines particularly when their habits get the better of them. I do not always succeed. I have found that even at an advanced level, occasionally practicing with a student can produce miraculous results. I am often horrified at how poorly and mindlessly students practice. This was certainly true in my early years. Seymour Bernstein's chapter on practicing in his book *With Your Own Two Hands* was seminal in improving my practicing habits. When first approaching a piece, students even at a high level have a reluctance to first sight-read through the piece several times, which allows them to get a sense of its architecture, its phrase structure, and the various emotions it conveys. If students "eavesdrop" on their own musical intuition during these readings and takes notes, they will begin to form what will be a personal and profound interpretation. I have asked many students to tape a card to their stands that reads "Where is my mind?" I love sharing with my students what I have learned through the years about practicing, including any recent discoveries. One's enthusiasm for one's work can inspire the students.

*Questioning Their Learning Methods.* I remember Rie Schmidt, David Leisner, and Seymour Bernstein playing a critical role in encouraging me to rethink how I learned music. Like many of my students, in my early years I neglected to look at the form, structure, and phrasing of a work before fingering it. Most of this was due to impatience and an overwhelming enthusiasm to dive into the notes and rhythms.

*To Memorize or To Learn.* Some students are quick to tell me with great pride that they memorized a piece. In their playing of the first phrase I notice the complete absence of the dynamic markings and the complete ignorance of the phrase structure. Yet, they have "memorized" it. This is not to say that they have not accomplished something. *Au contraire*, they have, but a greater attention to detail is needed from the start. Memorizing music, if one chooses to, should perhaps be the final act, not the initial.

*Become a Better Sight Reader.* Another reason I missed the architecture of a work in my early years was that I was (still am, ugh!) a terrible sight reader. Because so many of my students, like me, read poorly, I instituted a weekly sight-reading hour. We read all kinds of music, including certain string quartets, guitar quartets, trios, duos, violin music, flute music, Arban's *Cornet Method*, jazz charts, and even solos. Students have come to love it and they inevitably become better readers and better musicians.

*The Score is Your Trusted Friend.* I will often ask students at the outset to study a piece without the instrument in their hands, before playing a note, just to see what leaps out at them. The score must remain their trusted friend. It has been said by many a towering musician that the score is only part of what constitutes a great interpretation, but it is a critical part nonetheless.

*Highlight!* What a joy when I discovered the benefits of the highlighter pen! When one is confronted with a score like those of Toru Takemitsu, the detail on the manuscript can be intimidating. I found highlighting articulation, dynamic markings, expression markings, and more in different colors to be beneficial in executing detail more rapidly. The same can be said for a fugue. Highlighting the various subjects, countersubjects, cadences, and sequences can clarify much. I love highlighters so much I am almost to the point of distributing them to the students at the outset of the semester! As students move to iPads, highlighting might even be more exciting!

*Criticism, Encouragement, and Tact.* We must know when to say certain things and when not to. Given how sensitive certain students are and how emotionally charged the student-teacher relationship can be, it is critical. A few harsh words said with the wrong tone at the wrong time can wreak havoc. The opposite is also true. If I deliver a message with anger, the anger is what the student will remember more than the actual message. I can think of a few students I yelled at or said something with an edge or with a knee-jerk reaction. Afterwards I inevitably regret it. Upon reflection, I see that some of that anger was often based on ego. I thought, if a student phrases Bach like a machine and plays badly in public, it will reflect on me. My teaching career will be finished! Yale will fire me! Our criticism needs to be judicious and not judgmental. I have been taught that before I say something I should ask myself four questions: Is it true? Is it beneficial? Is it the right time to say it? Am I the right person to say it? Leo Brouwer changed my life with a few encouraging words when I first played for him in Arles, France, in 1974. I was a complete novice amongst some extraordinarily accomplished young guitarists. He did not go into detail about how inept my left or right hand technique was, but talked about my musical strengths to the entire class, simply, succinctly, and enthusiastically. I left the lesson literally jumping for joy. Leo sensed how much I admired him. He made me feel included in a world he knew I knew nothing about, but wanted desperately to be part of. Making someone believe they can do something when they are so vulnerable and uncertain is a tremendous gift.

*Building Confidence.* Leo's words and his later support was a confidence-builder. A student can never have enough confidence. If they do something well, congratulating them is essential. Being a professional musician can be a tough occupation. We teachers do not need to make it any tougher by not giving credit when and where it is due. Those well-deserved kind words can be the pillars that hold them up in a future difficult professional situation.

*Judging Your Teaching Abilities.* Although it is customary to congratulate the teacher when one of his or her students plays well or wins a competition, it has always felt awkward . . . almost embarrassing. I rarely feel like I had anything to do with these successes. That is not to say that they do not bring me joy; they do, but the joy is mostly for them. One could say that if you want to judge yourself as a teacher, then observe the progress of your least naturally gifted students. At the end of each year I try to assess my teaching. As I begin a new year I try to implement one or two new ideas or assignments. In-depth discussions with my colleagues about their teaching have been a welcome education. They have taught me much about my own teaching and teaching in general.

*A Student's Success.* How we measure success in this society is often tilted. Winning competitions, getting great reviews, having a million video hits on YouTube, getting a university position are all wonderful. Also impressive is changing people's lives through your teaching in a local music store or high school, or raising funds to teach guitar to children who would never be able to afford lessons or the instrument, as Matt Rohde, Adam Levin, and Scott Borg have done with their program the Kithara Project. I am overjoyed to meet up with many of my former students and discover they are leading healthy and happy lives. They are in their own way making the world a better place with their music, in whatever form it has taken shape.

*Students as Friends.* We all want to be liked, even loved, by our students. Who doesn't? It occurred to me after a few years that my job was to be as good a teacher as I could be to them, not necessarily be their good friends. They may later (as so many have) become my friends—in fact great friends—but that is not a key ingredient in the relationship. I am their teacher and they are my students. It certainly helps and I recommend having as friendly relationship as possible, but it is not essential. What is essential is to teach them to become better artists and guitarists.

*Caring for Your Students.* As much as what I said about the student-teacher relationship having necessary boundaries, there have been lessons with each of my students where deeply personal issues were brought up. Once in a post-Thanksgiving-break lesson, I asked: "So, how was your Thanksgiving holiday?" Student: "Oh, ok." Me: "Really? You don't sound very enthusiastic." Student: "Actually, it was horrible. My parents told me they are getting a divorce." He then burst into tears. Such occurrences are not atypical. One responds with empathy, of course, and guides the student the best one can at that point. I tell all of my students that in the course of their time at Yale, life will take many twists and turns. Things happen during their tenure that are often beyond their control. I ask them to keep me informed of any problems as best they can and as they see fit. I am not a mind reader, and the more I know, the better I can teach them. In the past twenty years in particular I have "loved and lost," to quote a line from one of the greatest music rockumentaries in history. I guide the students in times of distress and console to the best of my abilities. I am quick to point out that I am not a therapist. I always recommend some sort of professional help, which thankfully Yale provides. The same is true with any kind of pain or injury related to their playing. I am quick to send them to my own brilliant physical therapist Michele Semler. Knowing one's limitations in any area is helpful.

*Coffee Lessons.* With graduation in sight, inevitably comes the Coffee Lesson. That is the one lesson where clearly you need to leave the confines of the studio, go out, and treat them to a coffee, over which the topic is "Life after Yale." The Coffee Lesson is where I assess their work and the direction upon which I believe they should embark. Many questions are asked and hopefully answered to the degree to which we can see into the future accurately.

*Humor.* As mentioned earlier, humor is essential. One use of humor I use frequently is that of exaggerated exaggeration and gentle sarcasm. For example, if a pupil plays/noodles/repeats a phrase constantly while I am trying to discuss a point I may ask them, "Please play louder so we both don't have to hear what it is that I am saying" or "I can't tell you how I adore you cracking your knuckles loudly while someone is playing." When a student's posture is so twisted to the left, I will gently guide their head so close to the neck of the guitar that their nose is actually touching the neck. I then ask, "This is the correct posture, don't you think?" Needless to say, they get it instantly. Of course, I further elaborate about *not* shortening the distance between them and the guitar. The point is made and all have a good time.

*Playing in Your Lessons.* There are legendary pedagogues that never played a note in their teaching studio. We know that a gifted student can learn much from anyone whether they are a player or not. Right before my recording of BWV 1003, I played the fugue for my dear friend, harpsichordist and organist Mary Jane Newman. At the conclusion of the fugue, she said "It's interesting how you phrase the fugue subject. I don't phrase it that way at all." She then demonstrated how she phrased the subject on the harpsichord and all was revealed in seconds. It was magical and I shall never forget it. Such is the power of playing for the student. In my early years I played far too much in lessons. I'm ashamed to admit that I thought some of the lesson as an opportunity to keep my fingers moving if I had a concert approaching. Now I play less but I definitely play. I demonstrate this or that passage and certainly demonstrate different fingerings. If nothing else, the student is able to hear the sound you produce up close and personal. They can observe your physical relationship to the guitar. Occasionally, I will actually play through an entire piece. It is my hope that they will be inspired by the impromptu studio performance. I realize that for many teachers bringing your best instrument to lessons can be a danger, but experience has taught me that the student is inspired by hearing you on your concert guitar.

*Play Along with Christian Tetzlaff or Amandine Beyer*. There are those lessons when I have failed miserably to properly explain the importance of, say, letting a phrase breathe, or when my own playing of the phrase was not convincing enough to get the message across. This has led me to suggest—for example, in teaching Bach—that the student go online and play along with Christian Teztlaff or Amandine Beyer, who are two completely different violinists that I admire greatly. Of course, this is done with a student who deftly knows the work. In playing with them, along with me commenting here and there, they seem to really understand the music in an entirely new manner. This slightly odd approach has produced remarkably positive results.

*The Three-Point Rule*. Often my wife and I will finish our day discussing the lessons we taught that day. Were they successful? Did any of us learn anything? Rie, who is a dedicated and devoted Suzuki teacher, taught me the value of the One-Point Rule. Suzuki teachers stress that you need to get one point across to the student in each lesson. I have augmented it to three. Generally, between the student and myself we decide the week prior what we will be addressing and playing in the following week's lesson. There are those lessons, I am happy to say, in which I genuinely feel the student learned something valuable. And then there are those where I did not feel much was accomplished. The Three-Point Rule has helped those less-than-inspiring lessons. Even if I feel the lesson was a bit drab, I am sure to present at least three coherent points in the lesson that will benefit them. It has been very beneficial in masterclasses as well.

*Keeping a Student Folder*. I make a folder in my computer for each student, containing his or her résumé, entire repertoire both solo and chamber music dating as far back as they can, including simple etudes. Also in the folder is a type of journal which contains dates, comments, and assignments of various lessons. I will admit I get way too lax and forget to write in it often, but having it there has been beneficial.

*Play It My Way*. "Play it this way." "You have to use this fingering." These are phrases I did not hear while studying with Phillip de Fremery and Frederic Hand. It was not in their character, and they were wise enough to know that I had to find my own way of playing, whatever the repertoire was. That is not to say they did not show me the value of their particular fingering or phrasing, but it was never forced. It was generally followed by them saying, "Anyway, that's the way I do it." I have found that when I have been adamant about how something should be interpreted, it has backfired. I am a happy to agree to disagree with a student. I do not believe great art is concerned with "*a* way" or "*a* path."

*I Don't Know*. One of the most liberating phrases I learned late in my teaching days was the phrase "I don't know." It took me years to be able to admit to a student that I did not have the answer to a particular question. I am not a scholar and do not have all the answers. The good news is that I generally know the direction to point them; I try as much as I can to know and guide them to the proper source material or person who can better help them.

*The Internet and Cell Phones as Teaching Aids*. The internet and the cell phone have been welcome companions in the studio. As important as it is to articulate to the student what one is hearing, a picture and a recording can be worth a thousand words. It has been a timesaver to record or, better yet, to video the student when trying to make a point. In a video they can observe their posture while in the act of vigorously playing. By recording a passage and later following along with the score, we can locate precisely where the breaking up of a musical line occurs and numerous other problems. Even though one can argue that the sound quality of a cell phone is not recording-studio quality, a lot can be gained by recording the student on the spot. What a time saver and a neutralizer the cell phone has proven to be! I wish back in my early years of teaching that I had always carried a cassette recorder to lessons! Once, my student was playing an incorrect rhythm in Tansman's *Variation on a Theme of Scriabin*, which I pointed out to her. Her retort was, "Yes, but everyone plays it that way." I replied, "I bet so-and-so does not. Let's check on YouTube." Immediately we were online and, to my horror, so-and-so played the rhythm incorrectly, as did several others we listened to. Following that experience, she took great pride in playing it as written! YouTube has its merits in the teaching studio for sure.

*Your Teaching Studio, However Humble It May Be.* I am blessed to have a marvelous teaching studio at Yale. I have made it a bit like a guitar home. There is some memorabilia, a great plant, and tons of music and CDs. I did not always have a room. For at least ten years I was the wandering Yale School of Music guitar teacher. Often each lesson was in a different room. Even then, I tried to arrange the chairs and music stand to make it comfortable and acoustically better. You do not have to have to have a degree in *feng shui* to do this. I think my first studio was originally a closet on the second floor of Stoeckel Hall. I will never forget how wonderful the staff was when they first showed it to me. I loved that room even though it was tiny.

*Teaching Across from the Student, Not at Their Side.* I prefer teaching across from the student. I find I get a better perspective of their sound and posture. If the student is emoting in a given piece, they need more space. I ask the student to supply me with my own copy of whatever piece they are playing should I not have it.

*You Set the Example.* Like it or not, we are examples to our students both in and out of the studio. What you do and say sticks with them. Often former students approach me and recount something I said that resonated with them that I had no idea I said. Similarly, they will remember performances that touched them that I could barely remember playing. They will cite recordings that have been inspirational that were released when they were babies. Certain students look up to you in ways that would make your hair stand on end if you thought too much about it. It comes with the job. If you are a parent you know the feeling well.

*I May Not Be the Right Teacher for You.* I love to think that I have been or can be the best teacher for anyone and everyone. This is folly. In the audition process I have spotted people that I think: wow, I can help this person. I have also heard someone where I realize that I am not really the correct person for them at that point in their development. Consequently I reject them even if their playing is excellent. My teachers were primarily Phillip de Fremery, Frederic Hand, Anthony Newman, and Seymour Bernstein. Leo Brouwer, as I have stated, had a profound influence on me in the masterclasses I took with him. Later in life, I view John Williams and Paco Peña as my "graduate school" professors. The few recordings and performances I did with them, as well as the hours of conversation, provided a kind of teaching that is ineffable. The same can be said about Phil, Fred, Tony, and Seymour. They were all a perfect fit for me at the various stages in my life. We learn different truths from different teachers. It is healthy to remember that we cannot be the perfect teacher for everyone, but we can try. Though the years I have tried to have empathy for my students. I remind myself of where they are in their lives and what their dreams are.

## On Teaching Masterclasses

In my student years, masterclasses were a rarity. One traveled far to partake in them. The experience was treasured. As time progressed so did the classical guitar scene. More and more guitarists began to concertize and teach classes in remote parts of the country. Today, most classical guitar students have participated in several masterclasses. Festivals and weeklong classes in various exotic locations, including my own on Maui, are abundant.

All of my colleagues enjoy teaching masterclasses. The classes offer us a unique occasion to meet and hear young players that we may never meet again. In that short session, we aim to improve their music-making in whatever way we can. Masterclasses can be enriching experiences for both parties.

Over the years I have learned a few things that have had a positive impact on my masterclass teaching. Here are some.

Masterclasses by nature are classes and not lessons. I try to address the entire class, not only the student before me. I have observed a few classes in which the student and teacher are so engrossed in their lesson that the rest of the class feels entirely left out. I try to avoid that at all costs.

It is extremely helpful to know what the repertoire for the class will be in advance. This way, if possible, I can bring my own scores. They allow me to remember fingerings and several insights into the piece that may make for a far better lesson. Similarly, I urge the students and teachers to bring copies of the scores of all the music that will be played and to take copious notes. Not doing so is a wasted opportunity. It is easy to send PDF files of the pieces out to the various students or to have the music projected on an overhead screen. It makes all the difference.

When I am hosting a class, I make sure to give a formal introduction of my guest teacher. I list briefly some of their résumé so that the students and the audience are aware of their stature and accomplishments. I thank them for sharing their knowledge at the outset and of course at the end of the class. This is generally how I have had the good fortune of being introduced throughout my career. I am sad to say that there have been occasions when this has not happened. When that occurs, I introduce myself, say a bit about my career, and state how delighted I am to be teaching them. I often state that I do not consider myself a master but that I have been doing this for a number of years and will—I hope—have something beneficial to offer them. I am fond of saying "Whatever I say today, is just my opinion. While you're next to me, I would appreciate it if you say something like, 'Oh my God, you're a real genius for thinking of that. I owe you my life!'" I double-stress that whatever advice I give, it is just my opinion and they can forget it the minute the class is over! In addition, if it is a small class, I might ask each student in the room to identify himself or herself and say what year they are in school.

It is critical to set a positive and inclusive atmosphere from the outset. Seymour Bernstein introduced me to the idea of having the masterclass performers play a mini-concert at the beginning of the class. Prior to this mini-concert, for which the program order I arrange on the spot, I make a small speech stating that the concert is an opportunity for each to perform. I stress that all performers who are not regularly concertizing need to create their own performance opportunities. I continue briefly stating that retirement centers, prisons, and hospitals are desperate for live music. They can be wonderful places for a young performer to improve and share their gifts at the same time. The mini-concert allows me to observe how the student performs. I can assess their stage presence, observe their posture while playing, see if they are communicating their deepest emotions in the piece, hear if they have an imaginative interpretation of the given piece, and observe how they relate to an audience, however familiar it may be. In addition, I can map out the masterclass in terms of which student gets what lesson. In this way, I can address variety of topics. For example, one lesson will be focused on posture, another lesson on phrasing and interpretation, another on sound production, memory, and so on. I stress that much of what is taught in an individual lesson is directed to all of them and not just the person in the performer's seat. The mini-concert does take time. It is advisable to discuss the new format with your host. Because of the concert, your individual lessons might be shorter. Another benefit of the mini-concert is that it gives the student two opportunities to play.

At a class in Florida, a very gifted student performed the famous E major Prelude from BWV 1006. He was disgusted with his performance and let us all know. When it came time for his lesson, I complimented him and he grunted something to the effect that "It was awful," to which I replied, "Play it again." He did and played it gorgeously. He was pleased and we proceeded to have a great lesson. In the class, as a bare minimum, I try to maintain my aforementioned Three-Point Rule. If I can make one to three clear/helpful comments, I feel I have given something of value. No matter how glaring a technical nonproficiency may be, I try always to address a musical point somewhere in the lesson. Summarizing the three points at the conclusion of the lesson is a wonderful way of concluding. Often the lesson will cover three areas like form, some sort of technical issue, and interpretation.

Before I begin a lesson, I like to ask some basic questions. They tend to be the following: How long have you been working on this piece? Have you performed it before? Is this your first masterclass? What year are you in your conservatory training? or similarly, How long have you been studying the guitar? Knowing the answers to these will affect the tone and the direction of the lesson.

Before we begin working on the given piece, I ask for a show of hands as to how many in the audience know the piece. I like to know who in the audience does not know the work. I will also ask how many in the audience have played the piece.

Most lessons begin with a sincere compliment. I can always find something positive to say about any performance. The student may sound like nails on a blackboard and be scrunched up like a paper towel but play with great feeling and rhythmic drive. Complementing a solid sense of rhythm and emotion in their playing provides an entrance into the lesson. Once that is stated, I can more gently move into the criticism of their sound and posture. We have all seen students torn apart in classes. It is often not pretty. I was once attending a class and the teacher lit into the student and you could cut the negative vibe in the room with your index finger nail!!! All I could do was look for the exit sign. Ugh!!! The anger that a student can feel from a teacher may stem from the teacher's ego, insecurity, frustration, lack of sleep, or any number of other issues. It often is the passion they/we have for music that leads a teacher to criticize ruthlessly. We all care so deeply about the guitar and our art that it can get totally in the way of our teaching at a given moment. There should be a book of masterclass sayings or musings by various teachers. One teacher once asked a student, "How can you be so handsome and make such an ugly sound?" And your point is???????!!!! Yikes! Wisdom and compassion is required in one's criticisms as the situation is so emotionally charged. That having been said, the teacher should not be a threshold. There are students whose disrespect for the music and perhaps even the teacher needs to be addressed. That is where tact, wisdom, and compassion are handy. People's lives can be altered in a class. Usually the most difficult students are the most insecure. They respond quite well to great praise. If they know you are on their side and that you respect their talent, some excellent teaching and learning can occur.

I must have my instrument right by my side. I tune it and have it ready to go before we begin. In addition, I arrange the chairs to my liking and generally always teach on the left side of the student. I try to play at least a couple of phrases of whatever the piece may be. Even if I read wrong notes but play them with the correct dynamics and intent, the student benefits, as does the class. Demonstrating one or two passages on *their* instrument can delight a student, as they get to hear their guitar played, if briefly. Doing this can help to explain certain aspects of their playing.

Working in detail on fingerings in a masterclass can sometimes make for a boring class. When I see the students' fingerings are not working for them, I address one or two and then stress that they need to change several for a more a more successful performance. I do not dwell on them for fear of losing the energy in the room. I like to be sensitive to the flow of a lesson and the class in general. I want the audience to be engaged as much as possible. This is why I will often turn to the audience and ask them questions. If we are considering two different dynamics for a phrase, I will ask the audience which one they like and why.

There are several things the teacher can do to make the experience enriching for everyone present. Given the limited amount of time, one addresses the area or areas of the student's playing that requires the most urgent attention. You cannot fix all of a student's problems in one masterclass. Nor perhaps should you address them all. In my early classes, I was guilty of overwhelming the student with too many ideas. In time I learned less was more; hence, the Three-Point Rule.

What I most enjoy is transforming the student's playing right there on the spot. It is electrifying when the audience and the performer can immediately notice a positive difference in the playing of a certain phrase. If they leave the lesson playing more beautifully, we all are happy!

Beginning masterclass teachers ask me if they should teach the piece as they interpret it or work on the interpretation the student has presented. It is an excellent question. We teachers can have such passionate views of how we interpret particularly masterpieces like Bach's Chaconne or Benjamin Britten's *Nocturnal* that the second we hear something we absolutely would not do or do not do, we flinch in horror. "How dare you play it that way, you scoundrel you! You are ruining MY piece." These thoughts have occasionally gone through my head in certain classes! More frequently, I now try to improve/comment on the student's interpretation as it is presented. If it is convincing, then I am happy to forgo an extended explanation of how and why I play the given work the way I do. I am often enchanted to hear a completely different take on a work I adore and feel I own.

I always add a few comments about how I play the work or how I finger a passage. The students are, after all, coming to study with me at that class, so stating my views, however strong they are, is entirely appropriate. I particularly love hearing students play my own music in new and inventive ways I never thought of. They will finger passages in ways I wished I discovered!

From a game at an amusement fair, one of my children won a large plastic hammer. I decided this would be a perfect masterclass prop for loosening students up and providing a wee bit of humor. It was once employed in a class at the distinguished Peabody Conservatory. Sensing tension in his shoulder area, I started to whack the student on that spot with my large plastic hammer. Of course, at one point I gently hit him on the head as a type of exclamation point to whatever it was I was stressing. Both got a great laugh from all and the point was well taken. After the class my host asked, "Ben, have you been teaching a lot of classes lately?" I replied, "You can't imagine. I've done something like six in the last couple of months." To which my host replied, "Do yourself a favor, take a break!" It was quite a few years before I was asked back to teach at Peabody! Humor can be a magnificent asset in a class. That having been said, props like plastic hammers are not needed to get your points across. (Hmm, whatever happened to that hammer? I must get a new one!)

## The Maui Masterclasses

I will conclude my thoughts on teaching by saying that my favorite masterclass has been the one my wife and I started on the island of Maui in 1998. Maui and the other Hawaiian Islands are a kind of spiritual home.

I had the great honor of teaching for ten years at Paco and Karin Peña's legendary International Guitar Festival in Córdoba, Spain. Those years had a profound impact on both my wife and me. They provided a type of blueprint for our Maui class. When that chapter of our lives turned, for a few years I jointly taught a class with my first beloved teacher Phil de Fremery at Mount Holyoke College in Massachusetts. Phil was nice enough to let me join him and co-teach at his annual summer class. Those few years were also seminal in helping me become a better masterclass teacher as well as providing some insight for Rie and me into starting our own class. One of the highlights, besides teaching with Phil, were my late brother's insanely wonderful dinners that he would cook for us at the conclusion of each class. What terrific end-of-the-class parties we had! All that were there will remember!

After a time I thought, what if I held a class in my favorite place on earth? Why not on Maui? Eighteen classes and it is still thriving. In the past five years I have been able to bring a guest teacher due to an incredibly generous benefactor. (A crazy huge *mahalo* to them!) The main inspiration was the idea that if people could study the guitar in such a magnificent setting, it would transform their playing in a most positive manner. The class has always had a focus on performance. We have continually held four (now five) free concerts at different stunning locations on the island. We wanted to give the gift of music-making to the island. There are great musicians throughout the Hawaiian Islands, and being part of that music-making tradition in our humble way has been an honor.

Much has been written about the class, and there is a possible future documentary in the works, so I will not go into greater detail. Suffice to say it has been one of the most rewarding teaching experiences in my life. I thank my wife Rie, John Olson (who later took over Rie's work), Ian O'Sullivan, our incredible benefactors (they know who they are!), the community organizers, the faithful audiences, and all of the students who traveled far and wide to make it happen. *Mahalo* to all!

## ON RECORDING

On a cold November day in 1968, my dear childhood mate Jack Braider and I walked a few miles to Danbury, Connecticut to purchase the new Beatles record known as the "White Album." The anticipation of a new Beatles album was indescribable. We did whatever it took—including freezing ourselves to the bone, walking miles to Danbury, and paying with our last pennies—to own such a coveted album (or in that case, a double album). Purchasing a record like this was no casual affair. It was to be your life's new soundtrack for weeks, maybe months, to come, before the next "must-have" album presented itself to you. But it was more. The album provided a place of refuge. When life was too complicated and confused, you turned to "Sexy Sadie" and dreamed. When anger overtook you, it was "Yer Blues." When things were joyful, the needle was placed as skillfully as you could so as not to scratch the record on "Birthday." And so it went. We were committed to listening to it. There was the A side and the B side. If the recording was an opera or a symphony, the movements could not all be contained on side one. The act of flipping the album over and continuing the sonic journey was all part of the experience and excitement. The cover art and any and all liner notes were scrutinized, practically memorized, until the information was part of your being.

This type of intense record worship has been written about eloquently. Filmmakers have made movies and documentaries about record-store owners, their patrons, the artists they adored, the engineers, the producers, and the hallowed ground of the sacred studios. All of us who lived through this understand fully how life-altering and life-affirming a new recording by your favorite artist could be.

Records cost money. It was an investment. My copies of Bach's *Messe in H-Moll* on Das Alte Werk, Leo Brouwer's *Musique Contemporaine Pour Guitare* on Deutsche Grammophon, and the British release of Procul Harum's *A Salty Dog* cost more because they were imports. They were particularly coveted.

"Take 1: *Variations and Grand Contrapunctus*," said the voice through the monitor of a wooden paneled studio in the middle of some woodlands outside of Boston, Massachusetts. Filled with enough adrenaline to light up the wooded area at night time, I begin the opening measures of Anthony Newman's remarkable work for solo classical guitar. After years of filling my ears and heart with the glorious sounds of so many musical heroes and drooling over their record covers with excitement and awe, I was now doing what they all did. I was recording in a real studio! I could not believe that I was to be a guest artist on my musical hero's double album of his own compositions. I would be featured on an entire side of the four-sided release on Cambridge Records, a distinguished classical label. It was too indescribably exciting! To be chosen for such an opportunity was a gift. Making a recording in a studio—in any studio—in 1978 was not a simple task. It was a kind of rite of passage for a young musician. Today we make recordings and videos on our iPhones and computers with ease. Such was not the case in my beginning professional years.

"Take 2 . . . Take 3 . . . Insert 1 . . . Insert 2 . . ." said the producer. Tony instructed me to do three complete takes and then do what we call inserts, which are measures and phrases that the producer and I felt should be re-recorded. At the end of the session, one complete take was chosen as the foundation/blueprint for the final edit. It was the performance that we both agreed I played with the most musicality, vigor, emotion, and accuracy. Inserts of certain unclean runs and notes were edited/spliced-in to what would be the final recording.

Recordings are documents of your interpretations of pieces in a given period of your life. They are your opportunity to create a type of musical painting. The nature of the situation allows one to play the work several times and refine different musical phrases until they are to your liking. You are both performing and creating a performance. It is an art form unto itself. There is nothing like it.

Through the years I have recorded in acoustically gorgeous recital halls, churches, recording studios of every shape and size, and more.

"What are we going to do about these birds?" I asked the engineer with some irritation. Rie and I were recording our first CD, *Reverie: French Music for Flute and Guitar* in a church in Westchester County, New York. Each time Rie would play, the birds would gather outside the church window and want to jam with her! Each phrase Rie played would elicit many vocalizations. The clock is ticking and the dollars are flying by, and we are waiting for the birds to go to sleep? As we entered into the early evening we decided to begin the session, birds and all.

*J. S. Bach: Transcriptions for Guitar* was recorded in a church on the east side of Manhattan. If you listen really carefully in one movement you can hear a New York City bus drive by. On *Branches* and *Start Now* there are no buses or birds, although in one of the sessions we did have to break because of a lawn mower and thunderstorms.

It is possible that the Latitude records I made with Craig Peyton, my dear friend from our Wooster School years, had the biggest audience of my recording career. Randomly hearing your music on the car radio as I did a couple of times with Latitude is a thrill for any musician. Little did Latitude fans know that my classical guitar parts were recorded with me sitting in front of an AKG C414 microphone on the edge of the bathtub in Craig's tiny overheated bathroom in his studio apartment on East 80th Street!!!

The video *Improvisation Goyesque* was shot with me playing live to camera. It was a joy to make. I did a few improvisations based on my piece *Now and Ever* in different locations at the Roman arena in Arles, France. The video footage was brilliantly compiled and edited by Eben Bull. Ironically, this was very arena on whose steps a group photo was taken of our 1975 Leo Brouwer masterclass.

Not once, not twice, but three times did I record Manuel De Falla's masterpiece *Homenaje*. The first two recordings of the piece were done in my dear friend John Kiehl's Soundtrack Studio in lower Manhattan. I was unhappy with both of those interpretations and needed to do a third. The final *Homenaje* was most beautifully recorded and engineered by Darin Leong in his daughter's tiny bedroom at his house in Honolulu!

I received an email from Jim Benoit who had hired me years ago to play on a guitar series where he lived. At the time, Jim was a top employee for a computer music notational software company and asked if I would agree to do a recording session. They wanted to record me playing every note on my guitar to be used as the sample guitar sound for Notion software. They offered to fly me to London and do the session at Abbey Road Studios. It was surreal. There I was in the studio where The Beatles recorded the very first record I ever owned. It was the same studio years later where the "White Album" and so many others were recorded. During a break I was able to bang out a few notes on the piano Paul McCartney played on "Lady Madonna."

Renowned studios, like renowned concert halls, can contain a magical vibration. Great music can be recorded in a variety of studios and spaces, even on rooftops.

I am the guy that never quite believes he is "covered." "To be covered" means that at the session, all note mistakes, musical mistakes, guitar buzzes, and unclear notes were well-played, either in your complete takes or your inserts. "To be covered" is not to be confused with the "just one more take" syndrome. After one or two takes of our arrangement of the gorgeous Irish ballad "Peggy Gordon," Bill Coulter and I fell into the black hole of "just one more take." After each take we would say to each other "we can go deeper." Finally, after what felt like the 176th take, the vibe was so heavy and intense that after we played the final chord, we froze, milking the sacred sound of that final chord for all it was worth. It seemed like we held the chord for fifteen minutes, longer than the tune itself! In deep-freeze high-intensity mode, we hear in our headphones the engineer, Justin Mayer, say, "At ease, gentlemen." I still laugh when I think of it.

Not all recording is about putting down on tape a piece that you have polished and re-polished. It can be about letting the tape roll while you explore a musical idea and allowing spontaneity guide your musical intuition. If you are fortunate, you might find you created something enduring and magical. In any recording session you are bringing all of your experience and expertise to the microphone.

I am reminded of the genius jazz composer/pianist Thelonius Monk who said, "After two takes you are imitating yourself." After two takes of "Fingertips on Earth" from the recording *First You Build a Cloud*, our trusted engineer Dennis Smith remarked, "That was easy. In two takes we have a new tune;" to which Andy Summer replied, "Two takes and a lifetime of work."

As the record industry has dwindled to the point of many thinking it is pointless to even make a CD, the making of videos has flourished. Now performing soloists need to have videos posted on YouTube perhaps more than CDs. When a young guitar student wants to hear a piece of music, YouTube is their first and sometimes only source they turn to. On a whim, in 2012 I recorded Albeniz's *Córdoba*, de Falla's *Homenaje*, and Barrios's *Julia Florida*. I had no plans to put them on any kind of CD at that time. Upon reflection, I thought of making little "art guitar" videos. I wanted to be filmed playing these pieces in a beautiful location that complimented the music. My daughter Mitsuko had just graduated from Carnegie Mellon University with a degree in photography. I offered her a free trip to Honolulu to visit her cousins if she would make videos of these three works. She agreed and a new journey began. To our utter delight, the generous people at historic Shangri La, Doris Duke's estate in Honolulu, agreed to let us shoot on the days the museum was closed. It was an ideal location for these pieces given that we could not go to Córdoba or Cádiz, Spain. Mitsuko shot the video with the excellent video camera of my dear friend and world-renowned art photographer Christopher Burke. I played along with my pre-recorded track blasting in a speaker hidden from view. She edited the three videos with some executive producing help from her older brother and Rhode Island School of Design graduate John. Upon viewing the three videos, my then Yale student Solomon Silber asked, "What are you going to do with these?" I replied, "I don't know. Put them up on YouTube," to which Sol replied "Oh no no no, we are going to launch these with a plan." And so with Sol's help, we had a great time using all social media platforms for the release of the videos. From those three videos entitled *The Shangri La Series* began a new artistic journey.

This new journey leads me to Elm City Records. ECR is a New Haven-based production company founded by Sol and me. It was formed to record, film, and curate music and videos by musicians who we believe are making the world a better place through their art. My first release on ECR was *The Ben Verdery Guitar Project: On Vineyard Sound*. This CD is my third recording of American guitar music, the first two being *Ride the Wind Horse* and *Soepa*. It is comprised of guitar pieces written by the current composition faculty at Yale.

My son John Verdery had begun to do the graphics for all of my CDs. The cover art for *The Ben Verdery Guitar Project: On Vineyard Sound* tops his previous ones for its imagination and beauty. It was fitting as it represented a change of direction in my recording career.

Sergiu Celibidache, the legendary Romanian conductor, composer, and educator, was artistically opposed to making recordings. He felt the microphone could not possibly capture the divine acoustic subtleties of instruments. As much as I admire this towering musician and respect his artistic judgment, I for one wish he had recorded more.

We all can list the many recordings that have enriched our lives. Recordings of songs, symphonies, birds, and even the sea have helped us through the most troubling of times. Making recordings and videos is the one way we can get our music out into the world other than performing. My recording *J. S. Bach: Transcriptions for Guitar* was a cornerstone in my young career as was *Some Towns and Cities*. They were critically acclaimed and helped me get concert dates. A woman wrote to me several years ago, "Your Bach recording helped me get through a very difficult pregnancy. I listened to it constantly." I was speechless.

One of my latest recordings is Seymour Bernstein's *Searching for a Chorale*. It was recorded at ECR studios and produced by Sol Silber. Sean Hower and Scott Johnson of Polyphonic Industries LTD on Maui filmed the video. Mitsuko edited the video as she almost always does. Shortly after its release, I received an email from Seymour's 92-year-old friend and student, Jeanne Krausman. She took the time to write the most moving email an artist can receive. She concluded, "And now you have been added to my evening music to touch my soul." It affirmed my belief that if you create art with commitment and sincerity, it will enrich your life. If you put it out into the world, it can possibly enrich others.

## ON GUITARS AND STRINGS

We guitarists desire and seek guitars that do it all. They must have great color, be facile to play, responsive to our touch, have a gorgeous first string, they must sustain, be open and not tight, have great separation, have volume and projection and—simply put—they must be musical. That is the short list! Even when all the boxes are checked, we can still feel that a particular guitar lacks that inexplicable something. Why we play the guitar we do is extremely personal. Guitars essentially become part of our beings. We practice, perform, teach, and record with them. Without them, where would we be? It is one of the most intimate relationships we will have with any object. Maybe *the* most. Older guitars carry not just the soul of the maker but the soul of those who have played them. The much-loved and played guitar has stories to tell us. If we listen they will allow us to better tell ours.

I have essentially played five classical guitars thus far in my career. They were built by Thomas Humphrey, John Gilbert, Greg Smallman, Garrett Lee, and Otto Vowinkel. In addition, Chris Carrington was seminal in teaching me about the subtleties and advantages of owning a classical guitar with installed electronics. In the late 1990s and early 2000s, I played all of my digital-delay and amplified repertoire on Chris's guitars. There was a brief period when I greatly enjoyed playing on a Douglas Ching guitar. I met Doug and his wife in Honolulu and learned much from him during that time.

For twenty-five years I concertized and recorded on the extraordinary guitars of Greg Smallman. Greg's instruments were introduced to me by John Williams. John's work with Greg is well documented and another example of his vast contribution to the world of the classical guitar. I will always love my 1995 Smallman. Greg and his wife Robbie were so kind when I visited them in their home in Australia. It was a visit I shall always cherish.

I currently play and record a Garrett Lee guitar. Over the years Gary has become a dear friend. More than any other maker, Gary has educated me and continues to do so about the wonders and intricacies of our instrument. He is most beloved by all that are fortunate enough to know him, and for good reason.

In the last fifty years the development of the instrument has been unparalleled. Most classical guitarists at one point in their lives can afford to own a great instrument. How lucky are we? Very!!!!

In the very rare circumstance that I listen to my recordings, I am very aware of what guitar I was playing. I can hear what that particular guitar brought out in my playing. Ultimately I want whatever guitar I play to inspire me. The guitars I have played on over the years have done just that.

Ah, the sound and feeling of a new set of strings! The guitar smiles as do I when I begin playing on a fresh set of strings. As the classical guitar has developed, so has the classical guitar string. D'Addario strings remain the vanguard of the classical guitar string industry. Jim D'Addario is one of the more brilliant and generous people I know. He is an innovator. All of us who play on

D'Addario strings benefit from the relentless quest to make a better string. What he and the D'Addario Foundation have given us is unparalleled. What did Mauro Giuliani do when his strings wore out? Did he have sets of perfectly in-tune, beautifully sounding strings in his guitar case as he traveled? Did Llobet? I try to remind myself of just how lucky I am to not only know my guitar maker but my string maker as well. I remain close to my makers!

# Appendix A

# Compositions

The pieces are arranged alphabetically in each of the following categories:

Solo Classical Guitar
Solo Non-Classical Guitar
Two Guitars
Ensemble
Transcriptions/Arrangements, with sub-categories

R = recording
S = score

## SOLO CLASSICAL GUITAR

Actions
  S: *Easy Classical Guitar Recital* (Alfred)

Be Kind All the Time
  Electric classical guitar, digital delay and loop device, chopsticks,
    paper clips, and slide
  R: *Start Now*

Capitola, California
  R: *Some Towns and Cities*
  R: *Common Ground: New American Music for Guitar* (2012) by Kim Perlak
  S: *Some Towns and Cities* (Alfred)

Chicago, Illinois
  R: *Some Towns and Cities*
  S: *Some Towns and Cities* (Alfred)

Eleven Etudes
  Let Go; Now You See It, Now You Don't, Now You Do; Worry Knot;
    Cause and Effect; Passing; Monkey Mind; Start Now; Greed;
    Things Aren't Always What They Seem; Returning; Home is Here
  R: *Start Now*
  S: *Eleven Etudes* (Les Éditions Doberman-Yppan)

En Ti Los Ríos Cantan
  guitar and the voice of Pablo Neruda
  R: *On Vineyard Sound*

For Those Who Came Before Us

From Aristotle
  guitar and vocal percussion ("beatbox")
  co-written with Mark Martin

In Memory
  1. Arrival      2: Family      3. Gratitude
  R: *Ride the Wind Horse*

Keanae, Hawai'i
  R: *Some Towns and Cities*
  R: *Common Ground: New American Music for Guitar* (2012) by Kim Perlak
  S: *Some Towns and Cities* (Alfred)
  (see also Two Guitars)

Mahalo
    R: *Kahealani* (2003) by Jeff Peterson, Hula Records

Midnight Mango
    R: *Start Now*
    (see also Ensemble Music)

Milwaukee, Wisconsin
    R: *Some Towns and Cities*
    R: *Common Ground: New American Music for Guitar* (2012) by Kim Perlak
    S: *Some Towns and Cities* (Alfred)

New York, New York
    R: *Some Towns and Cities*
    S: *Some Towns and Cities* (Alfred)

Now and Ever
    R: *For David* (2009) by David Russell, Telarc

Philippe's Center
    Electric classical guitar, digital delay, spider capo

Prelude and Wedding Dance
    R: *Ufonia* (2002) and *Start Now*
    S: *Prelude and Wedding Dance* (Les Éditions Doberman-Yppan)

the rain falls equally on all things
    S: *the rain falls equally on all things* (Les Éditions Doberman-Yppan)

Satyagraha
    R: *Soepa* and *Start Now*
    R: *Departure* (2010) by Simon Powis
    S: *Satyagraha* (Les Éditions Doberman-Yppan)

Tears for Peace
    1. For Those Who Are Present
    2. For Those From the Past
    3. For the Children of the Future
    R: *Start Now*

Tread Lightly for You Tread on My Dreams
    R: *happy here*
    R: *Common Ground: New American Music for Guitar* (2012) by Kim Perlak

Waves/Olas

## SOLO NON-CLASSICAL GUITAR

The Bay
    for twelve-string guitar
    R: *Start Now*

The Estuary
    for twelve-string electric guitar, classical guitar, and loop device
    R: *Start Now*

Fix the Funk
    for solo baja guitar
    R: *Start Now*

A Ghost in Córdoba
    for cavaquinho and ebow
    R: *Start Now*

The Healing
    for electric guitar

San Francisco, California
    for solo harp guitar
    R: *Start Now*

Sarabane for Tony Williams
    for steel-string guitar

Ua Apuakea
    for double-neck baritone-tenor ukulele
    R: *Ufonia* (2002)

## TWO GUITARS

Camden, Maine
    R: *Some Towns and Cities*

Happy Here
    R: *happy here*

Keanae, Hawaiʻi

Miami, Florida
    R: *Some Towns and Cities* and *Ufonia* (1994)

Milwaukee, Wisconsin
   R: *threefifty duo* (2006) at http://www.threefiftymusic.com/albums

Mobile, Alabama
   R: *Some Towns and Cities*

Newport, Rhode Island
   R: *Some Towns and Cities*

Peace, Love and Guitars
   R: *Places Between: John Williams and John Etheridge Live in Dublin* (2006)

Sylacauga, Alabama
   R: *Some Towns and Cities*

What He Said
   S: *What He Said* (Les Éditions Doberman-Yppan)

ENSEMBLE

Chant for Peace
   R: *Ufonia* (2002)
   (see also Appendix C, Video and Audio Files)

Dennis, Massachusetts
   flute and guitar
   R: *Some Towns and Cities*

Firefly
   R: *Ufonia* (2002)

Give
   eight guitars
   R: *Recinto de la Piedra* (2016) by Ensamble de Guitarras de Chile,
      Javier Farías, director; released and financed by the
      Chilean Council of Culture and the Arts

Groundhog Day
   R: *Ufonia* (2002)

In the Garden: The Girl and the Butterfly
   R: *Ufonia* (2002)

Los Angeles, California
  R: *Some Towns and Cities*

Midnight Mango
  R: *Ufonia* (2002)

Penzacola Belongs To All

Scenes from Ellis Island
  R: *Ufonia* (2002) and *Ufonia* (1994)
  R: *Air and Ground* (2000) by the Los Angeles Guitar Quartet

Seattle, Washington
  R: *Some Towns and Cities, Ufonia* (2002), and *Ufonia* (1994)

Song Before Spring
  R: *Ufonia* (2002) and *A Winter Solstice Reunion*

Soul Force
  guitar, cello, flute, African hand drum

Tucson, Arizona
  R: *Some Towns and Cities*

Voices in the Pajaro Valley
  R: *Ufonia* (2002)

## TRANSCRIPTIONS/ARRANGEMENTS

### Solo Guitar

Abel (The National)

Adagio, K. 540 (W. A. Mozart)
  R: *Branches*
  S: *Adagio, K. 540* (Doberman-Yppan)

Amazing Grace
  R: *Branches*

Cello Suite No. 4, BWV 1010 (J. S. Bach)
  R: *Branches*

Cello Suite No. 6, BWV 1012 (J. S. Bach)
  R: *J. S. Bach: Transcriptions for Guitar*

Ciaconna from Partita No. 2 in D minor, BWV 1004 (J. S. Bach)
R: *Branches*

Don't Be Cruel (Otis Blackwell, as sung by Elvis Presley)
R: *A Guitar for Elvis* (2010) by various artists
S: *A Guitar for Elvis* (Hal Leonard)

Ezy Ryder (Jimi Hendrix)
R: *Branches*

For the Tears in Your Eyes (Prince)
R: *Soepa*

Gottes Zeit ist die allerbeste Zeit, BWV 106 (J. S. Bach)

Happy Xmas (John Lennon/Yoko Ono)
R: *Song for Our Ancestors*
R: Stephen Robinson, *A Christmas Feeling* (2000)

Kiss (Prince)
R: *Soepa*

Let's Go Crazy (Prince)
R: *Soepa*

little eye (David Lang) with pedal steel accompaniment
R: *The Ben Verdery Guitar Project: On Vineyard Sound*

Little Wing (Jimi Hendrix)
R: *Branches*

On the Beautiful Blue Danube (Johann Strauss II)
R: *Branches*
S: *On the Beautiful Blue Danube* (Les Éditions Doberman-Yppan)

Purple Haze (Jimi Hendrix)
R: *Branches*

Purple Rain (Prince)
R: *Soepa*

Violin Sonata No. 2 in A minor, BWV 1003 (J. S. Bach)
R: *J. S. Bach: Transcriptions for Guitar*

Two Guitars

Pua Lililehua (music by Kahauanu Lake, lyrics by Mary Kawena Puku'i)
by Benjamin Verdery and Jeff Peterson, after Keola Beamer

Two Guitars
arranged by William Coulter and Benjamin Verdery
for steel string guitar and classical guitar

An Daingean (William Coulter)
R: *Song for Our Ancestors*

Costa de Galicia (Traditional Galician)
R: *happy here*

Drop of Brandy (Traditional Irish)
R: *Song for Our Ancestors*

Flow Gently Sweet Afton (Traditional Scottish)
R: *Song for Our Ancestors*

Frieze Britches (Traditional Irish)
R: *Song for Our Ancestors*

Herzlich tut mich verlangen
(Melody: Hans Leo Hassler; harmonization: J. S. Bach)
R: *Song for Our Ancestors*

How Great is the Pleasure (Traditional Shaker)
R: *Song for Our Ancestors*

Loch Laven Castle / Le Funque Trunk
(Traditional Scottish / David Surette and Steve Baughman)
R: *Song for Our Ancestors*

Muiñeira de Chantada / Maestoso from Symphony No. 3
(Traditional Galician / Camille Saint-Saëns)
R: *Song for Our Ancestors*

Music for a Found Harmonium (Simon Jeffes, Penguin Café Orchestra)
R: *happy here*

Peggy Gordon (Traditional Irish)
R: *happy here*

Rise (Eddie Vedder)
R: *happy here*

Sheep May Safely Graze (J. S. Bach)
R: *happy here*

Song Four Our Ancestors (Traditional African)
R: *Song for Our Ancestors*

Tibetan Prayer Song (Traditional Tibetan)
R: *Song for Our Ancestors*

White Room (Cream)
R: *happy here*

Women of Ireland (Mná na hÉireann) (Seán Ó Riada)
R: *happy here*

## Flute and Guitar

Forlane en Rondeau (François Couperin)
R: *Reverie*

Kinderszenen, Op.15 (Robert Schumann)

Loro (Egberto Gismonti)

Miami, Florida (Benjamin Verdery)
R: *Ufonia* (1994)

La Musette en Rondeau (Jean-Philippe Rameau)
R: *Reverie*

Rigaudons: Premier, Deuxième, Double (Jean-Philippe Rameau)
R: *Reverie*

Le Rossignol-en-Amour (François Couperin)
R: *Reverie*

Seattle, Washington (Benjamin Verdery)

## Flute, Percussion, and Steel String Guitar

Refuge of the Road (Joni Mitchell); flute parts arranged by Keith Underwood
R: *Ufonia* (1994)

*Appendix A*

## Guitar and Baritone

A Case of You (Joni Mitchell)

Die schöne Müllerin (Franz Schubert)

## Guitar and String Quartet

Clarinet Sonata (Leonard Bernstein)

## Concerti

Concerto in A Minor, Wq. 170, H 432 (C. P. E. Bach)

Concerto in D Minor, BWV 1052 (J. S. Bach)

# Appendix B

# Discography

The recordings are listed in reverse chronological order
in each of the following categories:

Solo Recordings
Collaborative Recordings

SOLO RECORDINGS

*The Ben Verdery Guitar Project: On Vineyard Sound*
Elm City Records 2016 (digital album)
https://elmcityrecords.bandcamp.com/
   1–3. Joaquin is Dreaming (Martin Bresnick)
      Joaquin Imagines a Part of His History
      Joaquin Foresees a Future
      Joaquin is Sleeping, Joaquin is Dreaming
   4–7. On Vineyard Sound (Ezra Laderman)
      With Rhythmic Drive and Compulsion
      Andantino
      Brusque, Strident
      With Rhythmic Drive and Compulsion – Coda
   8. Lullaby (Aaron Jay Kernis); with Rie Schmidt, flute
   9–11. For Ben (Hannah Lash)
      Movement Number One
      Play These Notes
      This Dances Slowly
   12. January Echoes (Christopher Theofanidis)
   13. The Mentioning of Love (Ingram Marshall); with Rie Schmidt, flute
   14. En Ti Los Ríos Cantan (Benjamin Verdery)
   15. little eye (David Lang); with Jack Vees, pedal steel guitar
   16. National Anthem (Jack Vees)
Produced by Benjamin Verdery, Jack Vees, Greg Diacosta, Adam Abeshouse,
   Elizabeth Brown, and Eugene Kimbal
1, 2, 3: Recorded and engineered by Adam Abeshouse
4, 5, 6, 7, 8, 12, 13: Recorded in Sprague Hall, Yale School of Music,
   engineered and mastered by Eugene Kimbal
9, 10, 11, 14, 15: Recorded and mixed at Fire House 12 Studios by Greg Diacosta
16: Recorded and mixed by Jack Vees at CSMT, Yale School of Music
Final mastering: Fire House 12 Studios by Greg Diacosta
Guitars:
   1, 2, 3, 4, 5, 6, 7: Greg Smallman, 1995
   8, 12, 13, 14, 16: Garrett Lee, 2013
   9, 11: Gibson, Super 400, 1956
   10: Collings 290DC electric
   15: Otto Vowinkel baritone classical guitar, 2013; Emmons pedal steel guitar
   16: Jeff Traugott, R.001-181.080; Stratocaster. 1974; Gibson Firebird, 1963;
      Veillette baritone 12 string; Harmony H1 lap steel
D'Addario strings

*Branches*
Mushkatweek Records 300, 2006
1. Ciaccona from Partita No. 2 in D minor, BWV 1004 (J. S. Bach)
2. Adagio, K. 540 (W. A. Mozart)
3–8. Cello Suite No. 4 in E-flat major, BWV 1010 (J. S. Bach)
   Prelude
   Allemande
   Courante
   Sarabande
   Bourrée
   Gigue
9. The Blue Danube (Johann Strauss)
10. Amazing Grace (Traditional)
11. Ezy Ryder (Jimi Hendrix)
12. Little Wing (Jimi Hendrix)
13. Purple Haze (Jimi Hendrix)
All arrangements by Benjamin Verdery
Produced by Adam Abeshouse and Benjamin Verdery
Engineered, edited, and mastered by Adam Abeshouse
Recorded July and September 2005
The Mozart and the Strauss arrangements are published by Les Éditions
   Doberman-Yppan: https://www.productionsdoz.com
Guitar: Greg Smallman, 1998
D'Addario strings
Online: Search for "All Tracks - Benjamin Verdery - Youtube" or
   https://www.youtube.com/playlist?list=
   PLe-nyU0D9BgvLymSv8kgF2LbdiJICgiN_

*Start Now*
Mushkatweek Records 4782, 2005
    All compositions by Benjamin Verdery
      1–2. Prelude and Wedding Dance
      3–14. Eleven Etudes
        Let Go
        Now You See It, Now You Don't, Now You Do
        Worry Knot
        Cause and Effect
        Passing (two tracks)
        Monkey Mind
        Start Now
        Greed
        Things Aren't Always What They Seem
        Returning
        Home is Here
      15–17. Tears for Peace
        I: For Those Who Are Present
        II: For Those from the Past
        III: For the Children of the Future
      18. Be Kind All the Time
      19. Satyagraha
      20. A Ghost in Córdoba
      21. Fix the Funk
      22. Capitola
      23. Midnight Mango
      24. Milwaukee
      25. The Bay
      26. The Estuary
Produced by Adam Abeshouse and Benjamin Verdery
Engineered, edited, and mastered by Adam Abeshouse
Guitars by Greg Smallman and Chris Carrington ("Blackie" electric guitar)
Baja guitar by Antonio Aparicio
Twelve-string guitar by Aria
D'Addario strings
Online: Search for "All Tracks - Benjamin Verdery - Youtube" or
    https://www.youtube.com/playlist?list=
      PLe-nyU0D9BgvLymSv8kgF2LbdiJlCgiN_

*Soepa*
Mushkatweek Records MR200, 2001
1. 4 the tears in your eyes (Prince, arranged by Benjamin Verdery)
2. Strummage (Jack Vees)
3. On Wet Roads on Autumn Nights (Van Stiefel)
4–6. Your Cry Will Be a Whisper (Daniel Asia)
7. Sonatina (John Anthony Lennon)
8. Purple Rain (Prince, arranged by Benjamin Verdery)
9. Kiss (Prince)
10. Let's Go Crazy (Prince, arranged by Benjamin Verdery)
11. Satyagraha (Benjamin Verdery)
12–14. Soepa (Ingram Marshall)
All premiere recordings
Produced by Benjamin Verdery and Dominic Barbera
Engineers: Dominic Barbera, John Kiehl, and Bill Kovatch
Edited, mixed, and mastered by Dominic Barbera
Guitar: Greg Smallman, 1995
In *Strummage,* the Soloette guitar was used for the volume pedal passages and
  a Chris Carrington guitar was used for the harmonics
Online: Search for "All Tracks - Benjamin Verdery - Youtube" or
  https://www.youtube.com/playlist?list=
    PLe-nyU0D9BgvLymSv8kgF2LbdiJICgiN_

*Ride the Wind Horse: American Guitar Music*
Newport Classic NPD 85509, 1991
  1. Serenade (Lou Harrison)
  2. Toccata y Lamento (Robert Sierra)
  3–6. Four Pieces (David Leisner)
     Prelude
     Episode
     Ritual
     Dance
  7-11. Serenade for Guitar (Lou Harrison)
     Round
     Air
     Infinite Canon
     Usul
     Sonata
  12–13. Ride the Wind Horse (Anthony Newman)
     Larghetto
     Presto
  14–16. In Memory (Benjamin Verdery)
     Arrival
     Family
     Gratitude
  17. Little Wing (Jimi Hendrix)
  18. Purple Haze (Jimi Hendrix)
Produced by Lawrence J. Kraman and Christopher Lewis
Engineer: Lawrence J. Kraman
Digital Editor: Allan Tucker
Guitar: Millenium Guitar by Thomas Humphrey
D'Addario strings

*Guitar Player Magazine Presents Legends of Guitar: Classical*
Rhino R70563. 1987
  Ben plays on one track: *Gigue* by Anthony Newman


*J. S. Bach: Transcriptions for Guitar*
Sine Qua Non, 1983 (cassette) / GRI Music GRI 002, 1994
  1–6. Cello Suite No. 6 in D major, BWV 1012
     Prelude
     Allemande
     Courante
     Sarabande
     Gavottes I and II
     Gigue
  7–10. Violin Sonata No. 2 in A minor, BWV 1003
     Grave
     Fuga
     Andante
     Allegro
Producer/Recording Engineer: David Hancock
Remastered in 1994 at DOREMI Digital Audio Laboratories by Jacob Harnoy
Guitar: Thomas Humphrey
D'Addario strings


*Music by Anthony Newman*
Cambridge Records CRS B 2833, 1978
Re-released as *Anthony Newman: The Jesus Cantata*
  Ben plays on two tracks: *Variations and Grand Contrapunctus* and
*Ride the Wind Horse*

COLLABORATIVE RECORDINGS

*happy here*
William Coulter and Benjamin Verdery, guitars
Mushkatweek Records 400, 2011
   1. Rise (Eddie Vedder)
   2. Music for a Found Harmonium (Simon Jeffes)
   3. Sheep May Safely Graze (J. S. Bach)
   4. White Room (Cream)
   5. Costa de Galicia (Traditional Galician)
   6. Mysterious Barricades (François Couperin)
   7. Women of Ireland (Seán Ó Riada)
   8. One Night in Bethlehem (Traditional Irish)
   9. Happy Here (Benjamin Verdery)
   10. Tread Lightly (Benjamin Verdery)
   11. Redwood Waltz (William Coulter)
   12. Peggy Gordon (Traditional Irish)
Nos. 1, 2, 4, 5, 7, and 12 arranged by William Coulter and Benjamin Verdery
No. 3 arranged by Quine, Coulter, and Verdery
No. 6 arranged by Alirio Díaz
No. 8 arranged by William Coulter
Engineered by Justin Mayer, Steve Coulter, and Chris Chase
Mixed by William Coulter
Mastered by Rainer Gembalczyk
William Coulter plays an SCGC Brazilian OM with D'Addario strings
Benjamin Verdery plays 1998 and 2003 Greg Smallman guitars with
   D'Addario strings

*First You Build a Cloud*
Andy Summers and Benjamin Verdery, guitars
R.A.R.E. RAR 1001, 2007
    All selections by Andy Summers and Benjamin Verdery except where noted
    1. First You Build a Cloud
    2. Skywalking Woman
    3. Fez
    4. Bring on the Night (Sting)
    5. World Piece
    6. Love in the Time of
    7. Now I'm Free (A. Summers)
    8. Stone Town
    9. Fingertips on Earth
    10. The Girl from Reykjavik
    11. Flow
    12. Sarabande (J. S. Bach)
    13. Brotherhood of the Grape
Produced by Andy Summers, Ben Verdery, and Dennis Smith
Recorded and mixed by Dennis Smith
Online: Search for "All Tracks - Benjamin Verdery - Youtube" or
    https://www.youtube.com/playlist?list=
        PLe-nyU0D9BgvLymSv8kgF2LbdiJICgiN_


*Bassoon Brasileiro*
Frank Morelli, bassoon, with Orpheus Chamber Orchestra and
    Benjamin Verdery
MSR Classics MS1110, 2004
    Ben plays on one track: "Aria" from *Bachianas Brasileiras no. 5* by Heitor
    Villa-Lobos, arranged for bassoon and guitar

*Ufonia*
Vicki Bodner, oboe; John Marshall, percussion; Harvie Swartz, bass; Keith
  Underwood, flutes; Benjamin Verdery, guitar; Sanghamitra Chatterjee,
  vocals on *Chant for Peace*
Mushkatweek Records 100, 2002
  All compositions by Benjamin Verdery
  1. Seattle
  2. Song before Spring (for Jim and Janet)
  3. Voices in the Pajaro Valley
  4. Prelude and Wedding Dance
  5. In the Garden: The Girl and the Butterfly (for Mitsuko)
  6. Midnight Mango
  7. Ellis Island
  8. Ua Apuakea
  9. Firefly (for John)
  10. Groundhog Day
  11. Chant for Peace
Chief Engineer: Dominic Barbera
Assistant Engineers: Evan Benjamin, Scott Cannizzaro, Vince Reynolds, and
  Matthew Thrasher
Mixed by Dominic Barbera, Vicki Bodner, Keith Underwood, and
  Benjamin Verdery

*Song for Our Ancestors*
William Coulter and Benjamin Verdery, guitars
Solid Air Records SACD 2024, 2001
1. Drops of Brandy (Traditional Irish)
2. How Great is the Pleasure (Traditional Shaker)
3. Muiñera de Chantaga / Saint-Saëns
   (Traditional Galician / C. Saint-Saëns)
4. An Daingean (William Coulter)
5. Song for our Ancestors (Traditional African)
6. Herzlich tut much verlangen (Hans Leo Hassler / J. S. Bach)
7. Frieze Britches (Traditional Irish)
8. Flow Gently Sweet Afton (Traditional Scottish)
9. Loch Lavan Castle / Le Funque Trunk
   (Traditional Scottish / David Surette and Steve Baughman)
10. Happy Xmas, War is Over (John Lennon)
11. Tibetan Prayer Song (Traditional Tibetan)
12. Keanae, Hawaii (Benjamin Verdery)
All arrangements by William Coulter and Benjamin Verdery
Produced by William Coulter and Benjamin Verdery
Executive Producer: James Jensen
Recorded, edited, mixed, and mastered by Justin Mayer and William Coulter
Ben plays a Greg Smallman guitar with D'Addario strings
Bill plays a Jeff Traugott guitar with D'Addario strings

*The Enchanted Dawn*
Rie Schmidt, flute; Benjamin Verdery, guitar
GRI Music, GRI005, 1998/2007
    1. Haru No Umi ("The Sea in Springtime") (Michio Miyagi)
    2–5. L'Histoire du Tango (Astor Piazzolla)
        Bordei 1900
        Café 1930
        Nightclub 1960
        Concert d'aujourd'hui
    6. Psalm 100 (Frederic Hand)
    7–9. Selections from "On an Overgrown Path" (Leoš Janáček)
        (Arranged for solo guitar by Martin Bresnick)
        In Tears
        A Faded Leaf
        The Virgin Mary of Frydek
    10. Armenian Song (Gilbert Biberian)
    11. Armenian Dance (Gilbert Biberian)
    12. L'Aube Énchantée ("The Enchanted Dawn") (Ravi Shankar)
        sur la Raga Todi; with Samir Chatterjee, tablas
Recorded by Steve Epstein
Produced by Vicki Bodner and Tom Clippert
Ben plays a Greg Smallman guitar with D'Addario strings


*A Celtic Christmas: Peace on Earth*
Windham Hill WH 11461, 1999
    One track: "Flow Gently Sweet Afton" featuring William Coulter and
Benjamin Verdery, guitars

*The Mask*
The New York Concert Singers; St. Luke's Chamber Ensemble;
Judith Clurman, conductor
New World Records 80547-2, 1998
   1–4. Hymns from the Old South (Virgil Thomson)
     My Shepherd Will Supply My Need; The Morning Star;
     Green Fields; Death, 'tis a Melancholy Day
   5–10. The Mask (William Bolcom)
     We Wear the Mask; Heritage; Shadow; Worn Faces;
     Interlude for Natalie; Portrait
       Margaret Kampmeier, piano
   11–14. Four Songs to Poems of Thomas Campion (Virgil Thomson)
     Follow Your Saint; There is a Garden in Her Face;
     Rose Cheek'd Laura, Come; Follow Thy Fair Sun
       William Blount, clarinet; Sara Cutler, harp; Louise Shulman, viola
   15–21. Romancero Gitano (Mario Castelnuovo-Tedesco)
     Baladilla de los Tres Rios; La Guitarra; El Puñal;
     Procesión (Procesión, Paso, Saeta); Memento; Baile; Crótalo
       Benjamin Verdery, guitar
Producer: Elizabeth Ostrow
Engineer: Tom Lazarus


*The Crooked Road*
William Coulter & Friends
Gourd Music GM129, 1999
Ben plays a duet with Bill on two tracks:
   Mná na hÉireann ("The Women of Ireland") (Seán Ó Riada)
   Eleanor Plunkett (Turlogh O'Carolan)
Executive producer: Neal Hellman
Produced and arranged by William Coulter with assistance of Justin Mayer
Recorded and mixed by William Coulter and Justin Mayer; Steve Coulter; and
   Jay Ryan and Scott Good
Mastered by Rainer Gembalczyk


*A Winter Solstice Reunion*
Windham Hill 01934-11369-2, 1998
   Ufonia plays on one track: "Song Before Spring"

*The Romantic Handel: Love Duets and Cantatas*
Helicon Classics HE 1007, 1997
   No se emenderá jamás, HWV 140 (George Frideric Handel)
   Edward Brewer, harpsichord; Benjamin Verdery, guitar;
   Faye Robinson, soprano

*Celtic Crossing: Airs, Reels, and Jigs from Ireland and Beyond*
William Coulter & Friends
Gourd Music GM121, 1995
Ben plays a duet on one track with Bill: O'Carolan's Farewell to Music
Produced and arranged by William Coulter with assistance from Justin Mayer
   and Barry Phillips
Executive producer: Neal Hellman
Recorded and mixed by Justin Mayer and William Coulter

*Ufonia*
Benjamin Verdery: classical and steel string guitars; John Marshall: dumbek,
   bodhran, rig, udu, gaval, darbukka, ocean drum, zanz, Venezuelan maraca;
   Keith Underwood: c flute, alto flute, bass flute, African wooden flute, bass
   recorder, tenor recorder, Irish whistle, panpipes; Vicki Bodner: oboe, English horn; Harvie Swartz: acoustic bass, vertical bass.
Mushkatweek Records, 1994
   All compositions by Benjamin Verdery except where noted
   1. Seattle, Washington
   2. Ellis Island
   3. Margaret & Dan
   4. Miami, Florida
   5. Refuge of the Road (Joni Mitchell)
Engineers: Larry Alexander, Mark Conese
Audio consultant: Michael P. Hese
Mixed by Larry Alexander, Vicki Bodner, John Marshall, Benjamin Verdery
Recorded February 1993, Ambient Recording Company, Stamford, Connecticut

*Some Towns and Cities*
Newport Classic 85519, 1991
All compositions by Benjamin Verdery
1. Capitola, California
   Benjamin Verdery, guitar
2. Miami, Florida
   Paco Peña and Benjamin Verdery, guitars
3. Seattle, Washington
   Keith Underwood, flute; Vicki Bodner, oboe; Harvie Swartz, double
        bass; Glen Velez, riq; Benjamin Verdery, guitar; Rhythm Exchange
        (John Marshall, Dean Lindenmuth, Nick Mainella, Mike Lategano),
        percussion
4. Sylacuaga, Alabama
   John Williams and Benjamin Verdery, guitars
5. Chicago, Illinois
   Benjamin Verdery, guitar
6. Camden, Maine
   John Williams and Benjamin Verdery, guitars
7. Tucson, Arizona
   Paco Peña and Benjamin Verdery, guitars; Craig Peyton, marimba;
        Rhythm Exchange
8. Dennis, Massachusetts
   Rie Schmidt, flute and alto flute; Benjamin Verdery, guitar
9. Newport, Rhode Island
   Frederic Hand and Benjamin Verdery, guitars
10. San Francisco, California
    Benjamin Verdery, solo harp guitar
11. Los Angeles, California
    Keith Underwood and Rie Schmidt, flutes; Vicki Bodner, oboe;
        Christopher Lewis, piano; Harvie Swartz, double bass; Glen Velez,
        frame drum and shaker; Benjamin Verdery, 12-string guitar;
        Rhythm Exchange
12. Keanae, Hawaii
    Benjamin Verdery, guitar
13. New York, New York
    Benjamin Verdery, guitar
14. Milwaukee, Wisconsin
    Benjamin Verdery, guitar
15. Mobile, Alabama
    Leo Kottke and Benjamin Verdery, guitars

*John Williams Plays Vivaldi Concertos*
Franz Liszt Chamber Orchestra, János Rolla, conductor
Sony Classics SK 46556, 1991
    John Williams and Benjamin Verdery play on one track: Concerto in
G Major for Two Mandolins, RV 532, transcribed for guitars


*Emotional Velocity*
Craig Peyton: keyboards, mallet instruments, computers; Benjamin Verdery,
guitars, bagpipes
Sona Gaia ND-62759, 1989
All compositions by Craig Peyton and Benjamin Verdery
    1. Emotional Velocity
    2. Lonesome Dove
    3. Love One's Lost (with Rie Schmidt, bass and alto flutes, and
       Vicki Bodner, oboe and oboe d'amour)
    4. Our Land
    5. Baby (with Bendik, saxophone)
    6. Play Ball
    7. Sharing a Smile
    8. Sacred Landing
    9. In This Moment (with Vicki Bodner, oboe and oboe d'amour)
    10. Hearts Connecting to Hearts
    11. Tears of Joy (with Carl Stormer, electronic percussion)
Recorded Spring 1989 at The Mighty P-Factor, New York
Engineered, mixed, and produced by Craig Peyton
Executive Producer: Michael Sullivan
Guitars by John Gilbert and Greg Smallman
D'Addario strings

*Latitude: 40 Degrees North*
Craig Peyton, Fairlight III, vibes, percussion; Benjamin Verdery, classical and
   electric guitars
CD: Lifestyle LSCD 3110, 1987
   Earthflight EFCD 7372, 1987/1992
LP: Lifestyle LSR 6010, 1987
   1. Trust
   2. Al Campo de Paco
   3. She Slowly
   4. There's a Hole in the Ozone
   5. 40 Degrees North
   6. The Champ
   7. Pilot
   8. Partial Recall
   9. Mombasa (Yogi Lee, vocals)
   10. Wishing for Wings (Julie Eigenberg, vocals) (1992 recording only)
Recorded and mixed at The Mighty P-Factor, New York, by Craig Peyton
Nos. 4 and 5 mixed by Gary Rindfuss
Digital mastering at New York Digital Recording by Paul Zinman


*Latitude*
Craig Peyton, Fairlight III, vibes; Benjamin Verdery, guitars
CD: Lifestyle LSCD 3104, 1986
   Earthflight EFCD 7371, 1992
LP: Lifestyle LSR 6004, 1986
   1. At a Heart's Glance
   2. Wing and a Prayer
   3. A Boy's Fortune
   4. Spring Training
   5. Open Water
   6. Private Island
   7. Rock Pool Dreams
   8. Cloud Dancing
   9. Making the Most (1992 recording only)
Recorded and mixed at The Mighty P-Factor, New York, by Craig Peyton
Executive Producer: John Golden

*Reverie: French Music for Flute and Guitar*
Rie Schmidt, flute; Benjamin Verdery, guitar
Newport Classic NC60010, 1986
1. Forlane en Rondeau (François Couperin)
2. Les Barricades Mystérieuses (François Couperin), solo guitar
3. Le Rossignol-en-Amour (François Couperin)
4. La Musette en Rondeau (Jean-Philippe Rameau)
5. Rigaudons: Premier, Deuxième, Double (Jean-Philippe Rameau)
6. Le Montagnard, Op. 34: Introduction-Andantino (Napoléon Coste)
7. Consolazione, Romance, Op 25: Andante Cantabile (Napoléon Coste)
8. Rondeau Montagnard: Allegretto (Napoléon Coste)
9. Allegretto (Benjamin Godard)
10. Rêverie (Claude Debussy)
11. Mouvements Perpétuels: Assez modéré (Francis Poulenc)
12. Mouvements Perpétuels: Tres modéré (Francis Poulenc)
13. Mouvements Perpétuels: Alerte (Francis Poulenc)
14. Pavane pour une infante défunte (Maurice Ravel), solo guitar
15. Pièce en forme de Habañera (Maurice Ravel)
16. Entracte (Jacques Ibert)
Nos. 1, 3, 4, 5, and 10 transcribed by Benjamin Verdery
No. 2 transcribed by Alirio Díaz
No. 9 transcribed by Eliot Fisk
No. 11, 12, and 13 transcribed by Arthur Levering
No. 14 transcribed by Frederic Hand
No. 15 transcribed by Phillip de Fremery
John Gilbert guitar with D'Addario strings


*Bach: Two Generations. Concerti for Guitar and Chamber Orchestra*
Benjamin Verdery, guitar; Dennis Masuzzo, bass; Laurentian String Quartet;
Brandenburg Collegium; Anthony Newman, harpsichord and conductor
LP: Musical Heritage Society MHS 7397A, 1986.
Concerto in D minor, BWV 1052 (J. S. Bach)
    I: Allegro;  II: Adagio;  III: Allegro
Concerto in A major, Wq. 172 (C. P. E. Bach)
    I: Allegro;  II: Largo con sordini, mesto;  III: Allegro assai

# Appendix C

# Online Video and Audio Files

The citations in each of the following categories are in reverse chronological order by the date the video or audio was uploaded (in parenthesis):

Solo Performer
Performing with Other Musicians
Ensemble Conductor
Compositions Performed by Other Musicians
Masterclass
Interviewee
Interviewer

151

SOLO PERFORMER

*Purple Haze* (Jimi Hendrix)
https://www.youtube.com/watch?v=eUWSPCmThpQ
(23 November 2017)

*Searching for a Chorale* (Seymour Bernstein)
https://www.youtube.com/watch?v=7KTf_zNACag
(4 August 2017)

*January Echoes* (Christopher Theofanidis)
https://www.youtube.com/watch?v=PpXHQ4T7c40 (audio only)
(3 August 2017)

*On Vineyard Sound: I. With Rhythmic Drive and Compulsion* (Ezra Laderman)
https://www.youtube.com/watch?v=sfjLMdh7vnY (audio only)
(3 August 2017)

*On Vineyard Sound: II. Andantino* (Ezra Laderman)
https://www.youtube.com/watch?v=cR9YYUu6MTs (audio only)
(24 July 2017)

*On Vineyard Sound: III. Brusque, Strident* (Ezra Laderman)
https://www.youtube.com/watch?v=zTAiKpNEbjU (audio only)
(24 July 2017)

*On Vineyard Sound: IV. With Rhythmic Drive and Propulsion - Coda* (Ezra Laderman)
https://www.youtube.com/watch?v=m8Lhdeowd-k (audio only)
(24 July 2017)

*En Ti Los Ríos Cantan* (Benjamin Verdery)
https://www.youtube.com/watch?v=p81cuC7-o_M (audio only)
(24 July 2017)

*For Ben: I. Movement Number One* (Hannah Lash)
https://www.youtube.com/watch?v=7tQ3WKP9n4A (audio only)
(24 July 2017)

*For Ben: II. Play These Notes* (Hannah Lash)
https://www.youtube.com/watch?v=BylM7AHFRas (audio only)
(24 July 2017)

*For Ben: III. This Dances Slowly* (Hannah Lash)
https://www.youtube.com/watch?v=yfontOAByjM (audio only)
(24 July 2017)

*Joaquin is Dreaming: I. Joaquin Imagines a Part of His History* (Martin Bresnick)
https://www.youtube.com/watch?v=-VXWOOYMbUI (audio only)
(24 July 2017)

*Joaquin is Dreaming: II. Joaquin Foresees a Future* (Martin Bresnick)
https://www.youtube.com/watch?v=EbcB5bZGjT0 (audio only)
(24 July 2017)

*Joaquin is Dreaming: III. Joaquin is Sleeping, Joaquin is Dreaming* (Martin Bresnick)
https://www.youtube.com/watch?v=A1Cs86nHQuc (audio only)
(24 July 2017)

*little eye* (David Lang)
https://www.youtube.com/watch?v=4wdmS56-f3Q (audio only)
(24 July 2017)

*J. S. Bach: Chaconne*
https://www.youtube.com/watch?v=quf_ukqCXN0 (audio only)
(9 December 2016)

*On Vineyard Sound: With Rhythmic Drive and Compulsion* (Ezra Laderman)
https://www.youtube.com/watch?v=WlNyJ2XPyvs (audio only)
(23 June 2016)

*Ben Verdery – Joaquin is Sleeping, Joaquin is Dreaming* (Martin Bresnick)
https://www.youtube.com/watch?v=0UyqhoDa_hw (audio only)
(10 May 2016)

*Mozart: Adagio*
https://www.youtube.com/watch?v=xpoFAO-AbO0 (audio only)
(8 January 2016)

*Adagio, K. 540* (W. A. Mozart)
https://www.youtube.com/watch?v=NYn2J5GZ4Hc (audio only)
(23 May 2015)

*Allemande* (J. S. Bach, from Cello Suite No. 4)
https://www.youtube.com/watch?v=N0GKH8P-Fjk (audio only)
(23 May 2015)

*Amazing Grace*
https://www.youtube.com/watch?v=N_UBk5zh48M (audio only)
(23 May 2015)

*Blue Danube Waltz* (J. Strauss II)
https://www.youtube.com/watch?v=ac_p4BGmY8Y (audio only)
(23 May 2015)

*Ciaconna* (J. S. Bach)
https://www.youtube.com/watch?v=ydPJ0arhIus (audio only)
(23 May 2015)

*4 the Tears in Your Eyes* (Prince)
https://www.youtube.com/watch?v=LKSZLGUwUXo (audio only)
(23 May 2015)

*Gigue* (J. S. Bach, from Cello Suite No. 4)
https://www.youtube.com/watch?v=BJ0JLBv0-vw (audio only)
(23 May 2015)

*Kiss* (Prince)
https://www.youtube.com/watch?v=jVluW8XQmVU (audio only)
(23 May 2015)

*Let's Go Crazy* (Prince)
https://www.youtube.com/watch?v=_gazqn6bVxg (audio only)
(23 May 2015)

*Little Wing* (J. Hendrix)
https://www.youtube.com/watch?v=wqahF3O4VTs (audio only)
(23 May 2015)

*Purple Haze* (J. Hendrix)
https://www.youtube.com/watch?v=9nC15zFnwNU (audio only)
(23 May 2015)

*Purple Rain* (Prince)
https://www.youtube.com/watch?v=TE2uICJzsmY (audio only)
(23 May 2015)

*Satyagraha* (B. Verdery)
https://www.youtube.com/watch?v=zmi9zTeoe9Y (audio only)
(23 May 2015)

*Your Cry Will Be a Whisper* (Daniel Asia)
Mvmnt. 1: https://www.youtube.com/watch?v=v1XWrkgekbY (audio only)
Mvmnt. 2: https://www.youtube.com/watch?v=O14u6Bb7ZHY (audio only)
Mvmnt. 3: https://www.youtube.com/watch?v=vXVg6hSewpc (audio only)
(23 May 2015)

*Improvisation Goyesque*
(Free adaptation of the 2nd movement of *Now and Ever* by Benjamin Verdery)
https://www.youtube.com/watch?v=FmbdJVSA5HM&index=3&list
   =RDzjfIMh613Fo
(25 January 2015)

*Benjamin Verdery – Julia Florida* (Agustin Barrios Mangore)
Shangri La, Honolulu, Hawai'i, August 2014
https://www.youtube.com/watch?v=3vyMDmhMIxA
(7 December 2014)

*Benjamin Verdery – Homenaje* (Manuel de Falla)
Shangri La, Honolulu, Hawai'i, August 2014
https://www.youtube.com/watch?v=P9zUe_iG-d0
(9 November 2014)

*Benjamin Verdery – Córdoba* (Isaac Albéniz)
Shangri La, Honolulu, Hawai'i, August 2014
https://www.youtube.com/watch?v=-NEZ8BMaSnQ
(26 October 2014)

*Prelude and Wedding Dance* (B. Verdery)
https://www.youtube.com/watch?v=poNRUPsvTM8 (audio only)
(30 September 2014)

*Benjamin Verdery: Studio Concert playing Bach and Newman* [1980s]
J. S. Bach: Prelude, Sarabande, Gavottes and Gigue from Cello Suite No. 6
Anthony Newman: Courante, Sarabande, and Gigue
https://www.youtube.com/watch?v=9AZrCZ2Gnco
(2 November 2013)

*Benjamin Verdery – JS Bach – Sarabande*
KBS-TV, Seoul, Korea, March 2010
https://www.youtube.com/watch?v=p7yHVCkYEao
(20 June 2013)

*Benjamin Verdery Plays J.S. Bach's Prelude to the Fourth Cello Suite*
https://www.youtube.com/watch?v=bcw5Q9cUBLs
(23 May 2013)

*Benjamin Verdery Plays Randy Newman's "In Germany before the War"*
https://www.youtube.com/watch?v=f5AIuxnstUM
(20 May 2013)

*Be Kind All the Time* (B. Verdery)
The Monkey, New York, N.Y., 17 May 2007
Part I: https://www.youtube.com/watch?v=HMSOLQWvytc&index=10&list
=RDP9zUe_iG-d0
Part II: https://www.youtube.com/watch?v=m6BYiyIbb3g&list=RDP9zUe
_iG-d0&index=19
(5 July 2012)

*Benjamin Verdery plays Bach, Cello Suite No. 6 in D major, BWV 1012*
(Prelude, Sarabande, Gavottes)
92 Street Y, New York, N.Y., 30 January 2010
https://www.youtube.com/watch?v=3IIOpUd0uDg
(22 February 2012)

*Benjamin Verdery – Milwaukee*
KBS-TV, Seoul, Korea, March 2010
https://www.youtube.com/watch?v=m0_3qaHSUh4&index=28&list=
   RDP9zUe_iG-d0
(29 January 2012)

*Waves[/Olas]* (B. Verdery)
Festival Guitares au Palais 2010, Perpignan, France, 29 August 2010
https://www.youtube.com/watch?v=-_cHO6lEIDg
(19 December 2011)

*Bach: Prelude from Cello Suite No. 6*
Festival Guitares au Palais 2010, Perpignan, France, 29 August 2010
https://www.youtube.com/watch?v=F7SJlrulJt4
(15 December 2011)

*Gigue* (Anthony Newman)
https://www.youtube.com/watch?v=TVM9SfVulYc
(16 July 2010)

*Couperin: Mysterious Barricades*
KBS-TV, Seoul, Korea, March 2010
https://www.youtube.com/watch?v=TdvJKT50794
(20 June 2010)

*Ben Verdery plays Jimi Hendrix*
(An arrangement of "Ezy Ryder")
The Monkey, New York, N.Y., 17 May 2007
https://www.youtube.com/watch?v=Tj5P_90y3Jw
(22 July 2009)

*Philippe's Center* (B. Verdery)
Wooster School, Danbury, Connecticut
https://www.youtube.com/watch?v=-IybPiXk8Xg
(31 May 2009)

*Prelude and Wedding Dance* (B. Verdery)
New York Guitar Festival, 16 March 1999
https://www.youtube.com/watch?v=URG_1ArVc1U
(26 December 2006)

## PERFORMING WITH OTHER MUSICIANS

*Chant for Peace* (B. Verdery)
Billy Dean Thomas, vocals; Nano Stern, vocals; and Benjamin Verdery, guitar
https://www.youtube.com/watch?v=pKGHCPGt_6I
(16 September 2017)

*Lullaby* (Aaron Jay Kernis)
Rie Schmidt, flute, and Benjamin Verdery, guitar
https://www.youtube.com/watch?v=ci_y14zrfCI (audio only)
(24 July 2017)

*The Mentioning of Love* (Ingram Marshall)
Rie Schmidt, flute, and Benjamin Verdery, guitar
https://www.youtube.com/watch?v=c2YgsFevjRM (audio only)
(24 July 2017)

*National Anthem* (Jack Vees)
Jack Vees, pedal steel guitar, and Benjamin Verdery, guitar
https://www.youtube.com/watch?v=OpsY3-FHFpg (audio only)
(24 July 2017)

*Hoochie Coochie Man* (Willie Dixon)
Billy Dean Thomas, vocals, and Benjamin Verdery, guitar
https://www.youtube.com/watch?v=Yjil1v3Hyhs
(26 December 2015)

*Ellis Island* (B, Verdery)
Ufonia
https://www.youtube.com/watch?v=LBv5KB8-Oes (audio only)
(14 October 2015)

*Voices in the Pajaro Valley* (B. Verdery)
Ufonia
https://www.youtube.com/watch?v=SrUXQv9HxV8 (audio only)
(14 October 2015)

*Start Now* (B.Verdery)
Billy Dean Thomas, vocals, and Benjamin Verdery. guitar
https://www.youtube.com/watch?v=zjfIMh613Fo
(9 April 2015)

*Black Bach*
Billy Dean Thomas, vocals, and Benjamin Verdery, guitar
J. S. Bach: Allegro, BWV 998, with lyrics by Billy Dean Thomas
https://www.youtube.com/watch?v=gt6_-dRlrNI
(9 April 2015)

*Fez* (Andy Summers and Benjamin Verdery)
Andy Summers and Benjamin Verdery
https://www.youtube.com/watch?v=l9LXnB_rZW0 (audio only)
(21 February 2015)

*Fingertips on Earth* (Andy Summers and Benjamin Verdery)
Andy Summers and Benjamin Verdery
https://www.youtube.com/watch?v=iQajz8LwPd4 (audio only)
(21 February 2015)

*First You Build a Cloud* (Andy Summers and Benjamin Verdery)
Andy Summers and Benjamin Verdery
https://www.youtube.com/watch?v=TLQHph0XcaA (audio only)
(21 February 2015)

*Flow* (Andy Summers and Benjamin Verdery)
Andy Summers and Benjamin Verdery
https://www.youtube.com/watch?v=vZcfuT6RdZU (audio only)
(21 February 2015)

*Love in the Time of* (Andy Summers and Benjamin Verdery)
Andy Summers and Benjamin Verdery
https://www.youtube.com/watch?v=4UGd9kWQgII (audio only)
(21 February 2015)

*Skywalking Woman* (Andy Summers and Benjamin Verdery)
Andy Summers and Benjamin Verdery
https://www.youtube.com/watch?v=XavTNWp2tJE (audio only)
(21 February 2015)

*Stone Town* (Andy Summers and Benjamin Verdery)
Andy Summers and Benjamin Verdery
https://www.youtube.com/watch?v=sugzImzeYpw (audio only)
(21 February 2015)

*Chant for Peace* (B.Verdery)
Ufonia
https://www.youtube.com/watch?v=UO1dKbJC8-c (audio only)
(30 September 2014)

*Ellis Island* (B.Verdery)
Ufonia
https://www.youtube.com/watch?v=O8kXewIImqQ (audio only)
(30 September 2014)

*Midnight Mango* (B.Verdery)
Ufonia
https://www.youtube.com/watch?v=wS-6UIq48eU (audio only)
(30 September 2014)

*Song Before Spring* (B.Verdery)
Ufonia
https://www.youtube.com/watch?v=8OlFixByUGo (audio only)
(30 September 2014)

*Concerto in G major, RV 532* (Antonio Vivaldi)
John Williams and Benjamin Verdery
Franz Liszt Chamber Orchestra, János Rolla, conductor
Part I: https://www.youtube.com/watch?v=_V3HEFgTgdo (audio only)
Part II: https://www.youtube.com/watch?v=iCxSlT9iYjY (audio only)
Part III: https://www.youtube.com/watch?v=1QiRghRFuMc (audio only)
(8 September 2014)

*Amsterdam Electric Guitar Heaven 2012, Andy Summers & Ben Verdery*
De Melkweg, Rabozaal, Amsterdam, The Netherlands, 7 December 2012
https://www.youtube.com/watch?v=XalGRngY1YQ
(8 December 2012)

*Peggy Gordon* (Traditional)
William Coulter and Benjamin Verdery, July 2011
https://www.youtube.com/watch?v=tXnb_zHegv8&index=33&list
   =RDP9zUe_iG-d0
(26 June 2012)

*White Room* (Jack Bruce and Pete Brown)
William Coulter and Benjamin Verdery, July 2011
https://www.youtube.com/watch?v=tXnb_zHegv8&index=33&list
   =RDP9zUe_iG-d0
(23 May 2012)

*World Piece* (Andy Summers and Benjamin Verdery)
Andy Summers and Benjamin Verdery
https://www.youtube.com/watch?v=m9eUKNB4NoM (audio only)
(10 April 2011)

ENSEMBLE CONDUCTOR

*Scenes from Ellis Island*
Maui Masterclass Orchestra conducted by Benjamin Verdery
Keawala'i Congregational Church, Makena, Maui, 2000
https://www.youtube.com/watch?v=L3i7N52FCHs
(14 June 2015)

*Scenes from Ellis Island*
Festival of Sound, Parry Sound, Ontario, 24 July 2007
conducted by Benjamin Verdery
Pre-performance talk: https://www.youtube.com/watch?v=rMBb8MtdkwE
Part I: https://www.youtube.com/watch?v=MwA2BnD7L6w
Part II: https://www.youtube.com/watch?v=vvEVD-XWwmU
(14 August 2007)

*Scenes from Ellis Island: Rehearsal and Performance*
Guitar Ensemble, University of California, Santa Barbara
http://www.uctv.tv/shows/Scenes-from-Ellis-Island-Rehearsal-and
   -Performance-A-Master-Class-with-Benjamin-Verdery-5949
http://podcast.uctv.tv/vod/5949.mp4
(27 August 2001)

## COMPOSITIONS PERFORMED BY OTHER MUSICIANS

*Now and Ever*
Chris Garwood, Yale School of Music
https://www.youtube.com/watch?v=X6_b4jZgFUc
(23 June 2017)

*Satyagraha*
Hernán Léon Martínez, Yale School of Music, 30 April 2016
https://www.youtube.com/watch?v=LTdgi7nciKY
(14 June 2016)

*Seattle*
Hernán Martínez, guitar; Andrew Robson, flute; Sam Suggs, double bass;
   Georgi Videnov, percussion; Yale School of Music, 6 May 2016
https://www.youtube.com/watch?v=zfNiKSqjY7I
(14 June 2016)

*Start Now*
Kithara Project, Mid-Maryland Guitar Festival, 2016
https://www.youtube.com/watch?v=bNpvFRLY6mw
(13 May 2016)

*Dennis, Massachusetts*
Duo Paradiso (Melanie Sabel, flute, and Štěpán Matějka, guitar)
https://www.youtube.com/watch?v=-XMANC_12wY (audio only)
(5 May 2016)

*Miami, Florida*
Duo Paradiso (Melanie Sabel, flute, and Štěpán Matějka, guitar)
https://www.youtube.com/watch?v=F9wMwALB54g (audio only)
(5 May 2016)

*Seattle, Washington*
Duo Paradiso (Melanie Sabel, flute, and Štěpán Matějka, guitar)
https://www.youtube.com/watch?v=mYx5Oxjq6mo (audio only)
(5 May 2016)

*Dennis, Massachusetts*
Duo Paradiso (Melanie Sabel, flute, and Štěpán Matějka, guitar)
https://www.youtube.com/watch?v=J9G1rN_onXg
(4 November 2015)

*Tread Lightly*
Kim Perlak
Boston Guitarfest 2015, Fenway Center, Northeastern University, 18 June 2015
https://www.youtube.com/watch?v=7gFqSp3HqWo
(25 August 2015)

*Scenes from Ellis Island*
Maui Honu Guitar Orchestra, Maui Masterclass, July 2015
https://www.youtube.com/watch?v=N3D7xamanhA
http://www.benverderymauiclass.com/past-classes/
(17 July 2015)

*Milwaukee, Wisconsin*
Chris Mallet and Ian O'Sullivan
St. John's Episcopal Church, Kula, Maui, July 2015
https://www.youtube.com/watch?v=yqXY6dOL9tY
(13 July 2015)

*Scenes from Ellis Island*
The McCallum Classical Guitar Chamber Orchestra
https://www.youtube.com/watch?v=Ev-f9oUEQ9A
(10 June 2015)

*Keanae, Hawai'i*
Kim Perlak
https://www.youtube.com/watch?v=wTm9ITN3-pg
(23 May 2015)

*Scenes from Ellis Island*
Northwest Guitar Orchestra conducted by Mark Wilson
Cornish College of the Arts, Seattle, Washington, 19 April 2015
https://www.youtube.com/watch?v=Lw1oOPYkht4
(20 April 2015)

*Let Go*
Appassionata Guitar Trio
https://www.youtube.com/watch?v=MmRb0bakKsk (audio only)
(4 March 2015)

*Now You See It, Now You Don't, Now You Do*
Appassionata Guitar Trio
https://www.youtube.com/watch?v=R7iO4I-i-cs (audio only)
(4 March 2015)

*Start Now*
Appassionata Guitar Trio
https://www.youtube.com/watch?v=sDgwDt8aNEs (audio only)
(4 March 2015)

*Scenes from Ellis Island*
Los Angeles Guitar Quartet
https://www.youtube.com/watch?v=3MgnoTSQyyU (audio only)
(5 November 2014)

*Capitola, California*
John Williams and Timothy Kain
https://www.youtube.com/watch?v=r6HqO639vzo (audio only)
(8 September 2014)

*Peace, Love, and Guitars*
John Etheridge and John Williams
Part I: https://www.youtube.com/watch?v=cQ-0whelg28 (audio only)
Part II: https://www.youtube.com/watch?v=UPGqtukzCeE (audio only)
Part III: https://www.youtube.com/watch?v=ZsxdKy-ETeY (audio only)
(7 September 2014)

*Greed, Things Aren't Always What They Seem*, and *Passing* from *Eleven Etudes*
Koh Kazama, Yale School of Music
https://www.youtube.com/watch?v=R9EwLtHahFE
(27 August 2014)

*Passing* and *Monkey Mind* from *Eleven Etudes*
Koh Kazama, Yale School of Music, 13 April 2013
https://www.youtube.com/watch?v=QyI9ZT3dLlU
(26 August 2014)

*Keanae, Hawai'i*
Zane Forshee
https://www.youtube.com/watch?v=ggcHvKfuCa4
(25 August 2014)

*Tears for Peace: III. For the Children of the Future*
Ray Zhou
https://www.youtube.com/watch?v=kIrPw2tq6ZQ
(14 May 2014)

*Scenes from Ellis Island*
Santa Cruz Guitar Orchestra, Kuumbwa Jazz Center, 27 April 2013
https://www.youtube.com/watch?v=CrdRp12WQ9U
(29 April 2013)

*Let Go*
Pia Gazarek-Offermann
https://www.youtube.com/watch?v=K4ykqBGIoPM
(27 April 2013)

*Satyagraha*
Pia Gazarek-Offermann
https://www.youtube.com/watch?v=WBOIJ_UrATE
(26 April 2013)

*Scenes from Ellis Island*
Tokyo guitar ensemble conducted by Harumi Nakajima
Part I: https://www.youtube.com/watch?v=H-naaCjc030
Part II: https://www.youtube.com/watch?v=9PD6JKRlMyU
(31 January 2011)

*Scenes from Ellis Island*
MacPhail Guitar Quartet
Hoyt Sherman Place, Des Moines, Iowa, November 2008
https://www.youtube.com/watch?v=8v9zooxRe-A
(14 January 2009)

*Give*
Hochschule für Musik und Theater, Rostock, Germany, 29 October 2009
Part I: https://www.youtube.com/watch?v=2s-Mxa_IDVc
Part II: https://www.youtube.com/watch?v=YdzPN8bibvE
(30 October 2009)

*Home is Here* from *Eleven Etudes*
Christopher Mallett, Windsor Arts Center, Windsor, Connecticut
https://www.youtube.com/watch?v=E4X9l17RuAw
(24 December 2008)

*Scenes from Ellis Island*
B A Applied Music and RSAMD Guitar Ensembles
Part I: https://www.youtube.com/watch?v=Fq66CzxXCs8
Part II: https://www.youtube.com/watch?v=yJaIbDk3Rho
(26 March 2008)

MASTERCLASS

*Soundscape: A Master Class with Benjamin Verdery*
University of California, Santa Barbara
https://www.youtube.com/watch?v=q8ihXPVLFCU
(31 January 2008)

INTERVIEWEE

*Ben Verdery - Jimi Hendrix Matters - Notes with Ray White*
https://www.youtube.com/watch?v=im7TYSEESNs
(23 November 2017)

*ArTravel (Ep.2) A Musical Journey in Korea – Classic Guitarist
     Benjamin Verdery*
https://www.youtube.com/watch?v=2SJgvK-V06U
(9 October 2016)

*Classical Guitarist Ben Verdery Plays at Heckscher Museum of Art*
https://www.youtube.com/watch?v=D5VrF7nlZAU
(2 November 2014)

*Composer Benjamin Verdery on "What He Said" for Two Guitars*
18 November 2010
https://www.youtube.com/watch?v=vpG4qBdkCHM
(12 March 2012)

*Benjamin Verdery Interview at Yale University*
13 January 2012
https://www.youtube.com/watch?v=BXW4WTZQSx8
(10 February 2012)

*Benjamin Verdery KBS-TV, Seoul, Korea*
March 2010
Part I: https://www.youtube.com/watch?v=YOnIsylaUvo
Part II: https://www.youtube.com/watch?v=2lN8ETl57vY
(8 June 2010)

*Ben Verdery on Good Playing Posture*
https://www.youtube.com/watch?v=Fkz2jnMJVlE
(9 February 2009)

*Ben Verdery on Classic Technique*
(An arrangement of *Kiss* by Prince)
https://www.youtube.com/watch?v=6mne7wo3s48
(9 February 2009)

*An Interview with Benjamin Verdery*
Soundscape, University of California, Santa Barbara
Interviewed by Brian Head
https://www.youtube.com/watch?v=_JuoHbk1icA
(31 January 2008)

INTERVIEWER

*Guitarist Ben Verdery Interviews Composer David Lang*
https://www.youtube.com/watch?v=CdPCzZKLNh8
(19 October 2017)

Alternate website for the following videos:
http://92yondemand.org/category/guitar-talks

*Los Angeles Guitar Quartet*
https://www.youtube.com/watch?v=QQkO3_KnR1s
(3 August 2017)

*Pablo Sáinz Villegas*
25 March 2017
https://www.youtube.com/watch?v=m6zHBBjYG1A
(7 July 2017)

*Ana Vidović*
https://www.youtube.com/watch?v=g0MLFX8ei_M
(26 June 2017)

*Paul O'Dette*
3 November 2011
Part I: https://www.youtube.com/watch?v=clxoDOwK-qI
Part II: https://www.youtube.com/watch?v=tQ5vltWA0IY
(6 and 9 April 2016)

*Sérgio Assad*
9 May 2015
https://www.youtube.com/watch?v=p2XEtVTi6Ds
(20 August 2015)

*American Guitarist-Composers: Andrew York, Gyan Riley, Frederic Hand, David Leisner*
28 March 2015
https://www.youtube.com/watch?v=7j6OFhq5V4Y
(20 August 2015)

*Pepe Romero*
22 November 2014
https://www.youtube.com/watch?v=7AWbGH-gjzw
(20 August 2015)

*Eliot Fisk and Paco Peña*
24 April 2014
https://www.youtube.com/watch?v=GitzNDAuRPo
(20 August 2015)

*David Russell*
22 March 2014
https://www.youtube.com/watch?v=AuqZqdVLpO4
(20 August 2015)

*Christopher Parkening on Andrés Segovia*
26 October 2013
https://www.youtube.com/watch?v=pvqitrUbVNk
(20 August 2015)

*Raphaella Smits*
23 March 2013
https://www.youtube.com/watch?v=iCDBlg2qZwo
(20 August 2015)

*Los Angeles Guitar Quartet: Scott Tennant, Matthew Greif, John Dearman,*
    *William Kanengiser*
9 February 2013
https://www.youtube.com/watch?v=i4St2zpfNIk
(20 August 2015)

*On Leo Brouwer: Ricardo Cobo, Louis Trépanier, Philip Candelaria,*
    *Christopher Stell, Raphaella Smits, Mark Eden, René Izquierdo*
23 April 2011
https://www.youtube.com/watch?v=FrFHPZydtrs
(20 August 2015)

*On Julian Bream: Frederic Hand, William Kanengiser, David Leisner, David*
    *Tanenbaum, Scott Tennant*
1 March 2008
https://www.youtube.com/watch?v=Y93Ho_G9Ktg
(20 August 2015)

# Appendix D

# Programs

Pieces marked with an asterisk were written for Benjamin Verdery

A person's year of death in brackets indicates the person was alive the year the concert was given, but is now deceased. The year of death is given for the sake of completeness.

*Appendix D*

25th Long Island Guitar Festival
Hillwood Recital Hall, Tilles Center for the Performing Arts
LIU Post, Brookville, New York, 9 April 2017

Benjamin Verdery                Prelude and Wedding Dance
(b. 1955)

*Three Works Inspired by J. S. Bach*

Heitor Villa-Lobos              Aria from Bachianas Brasileiras No. 5, W389
(1887–1959)                     arr. Roland Dyens

Seymour Bernstein               Searching for a Chorale (2016)*
(b. 1927)

Ingram Marshall                 Soepa (1999)*
(b. 1945)                       in three movements; for electric classical guitar,
                                digital delay, and loops

INTERMISSION

René Eespere                    In Doubt
(b. 1953)                       (world premiere)

Benjamin Verdery                From Aristotle
                                1. The Poet Being an Imitator
                                2. A Noun
                                3. A Verb
                                4. A Wineless Cup
                                with Mark Martin, mixed vocals

Benjamin Verdery                Now You See It
                                Music: Six Etudes by B. Verdery
                                Choreography: Michiyaya Dance Company
                                1. Let Go
                                2. Now You See It, Now You Don't, Now You Do
                                3. Worry Knot
                                4. Start Now
                                5. Greed
                                6. Home is Here
                    Michiyaya Dance Company: Hannah Seiden, Aliza Russell,
                    Alexandra Wood, Núria Martin Fandos, Belinda Adam

Benjamin Verdery, guitar
Morse Recital Hall, Yale University, New Haven, Connecticut
19 January 2016

Benjamin Verdery
(b. 1955)

Prelude and Wedding Dance
Tread Lightly
Satyagraha
Now and Ever

Benjamin Verdery
and Mark Martin

For Aristotle
1. The Poet Being an Imitator
2. A Noun
3. A Verb
4. The Wineless Cup
with Mark Martin, mixed vocals

INTERMISSION

Benjamin Verdery

What He Said
with Simon Powis, guitar

En Ti Los Ríos Cantan (In You the Rivers Sing)
for classical guitar and the voice of Pablo Neruda

Capitola, California

Mobile, Alabama
with Jack Vees, lap steel guitar

Start Now
with Billy Dean Thomas and Mark Martin, vocals

Chant for Peace
Billy Dean Thomas, Mark Martin, and
    Kelly Hill, vocals
Simon Powis, An Tran, Gulli Bjornsson.
    Solomon Silver, Jiycon Kim, Chris Garwood,
    and Max Lyman, guitars

New Sounds Live
121 Guitars and More
Students from Third Street Music School
New York, New York, 14 October 2015

David Lang
(b. 1957)

questionnaire
    Performed by Third Street guitarists
    Sheer Pluck Orchestra
    William Anderson, conductor
    Commissioned by the Roger Shapiro Fund for
        New Music for Third Street's 120th
        anniversary; world premiere

David Lang

little eye
wavy
before gravity
after gravity
    Performed by Third Street students

Benjamin Verdery
(b. 1955)

Ellis Island
    William Anderson, Pat Bianculli, Steve Bloom,
    Marco Capelli, Oren Fader, Kevin Gallagher,
    Paul Hemmings, Koh Kazama, Nadav Lev,
    Dan Lippel, Jeff Litman, David Moreno,
    Marc Wolf, Max Zuckerman, guitars;
    Bomita Lubinsky, flute;
    Mark Martin, beatboxer;
    Ina Litera, violin;
    Benjamin Verdery, conductor

Benjamin Verdery, guitar    Rie Schmidt, flute
Morse Recital Hall, Yale University, New Haven, Connecticut
11 February 2015

Christopher Theofanidis    January Echo*
(b. 1967)

Ezra Laderman                On Vineyard Sound*
(b.1924–[2015])             1. With rhythmic drive and propulsion
                                     2. Andantino
                                     3. Brusque, strident
                                     4. With rhythmic drive and propulsion – Coda

Benjamin Verdery           En Ti Los Ríos Cantan (In You the Rivers Sing)
(b. 1955)                        for classical guitar and the voice of Pablo Neruda

Aaron Jay Kernis           Lullaby
(b. 1960)                        with Rie Schmidt, flute

INTERMISSION

Hannah Lash                  For Ben*
(b. 1981)                        1. Movement Number One
                                     2. Play These Notes
                                     3. This Dances, Slowly
                                     (world premiere)

Jack Vees                       National Anthem*
(b. 1955)                        for electric guitar and fixed media

Martin Bresnick             Joaquin is Dreaming*
(b. 1946)                        1. Joaquin Imagines a Part of History
                                     2. Joaquin Foresees a Future
                                     3. Joaquin is Sleeping, Joaquin is Dreaming

Benjamin Verdery, guitar    Rie Schmidt, flute
Morse Recital Hall, Yale University, New Haven, Connecticut
25 January 2014

| | |
|---|---|
| Benjamin Verdery (b. 1955) | Now and Ever |
| J. S. Bach (1685–1750) | Cello Suite in E-flat Major, BWV 1010 arr. B. Verdery Prelude; Allemande; Courante; Sarabande; Bourrée I; Bourrée II; Gigue (performed on an Otto Vowinkel baritone classical guitar) |

INTERMISSION

| | |
|---|---|
| Ingram Marshall (b. 1945) | The Mentioning of Love* with Rie Schmidt, flute |
| Hannah Lash (b. 1980) | Play These Notes* for electric guitar (world premiere) |
| Robert Schumann (1810–1856) | Mai Lieber Mai from Album für die Jugend arr. Andrés Segovia |
| Felix Mendelssohn (1809–1847) | Song Without Words, Op. 19, No. 4 arr. Andrés Segovia |
| Manuel de Falla (1876–1946) | Homenaje (Le Tombeau par Claude Debussy) |

*Three American Songs arranged by Benjamin Verdery*

| | |
|---|---|
| Prince (1958–[2016]) | Kiss |
| Randy Newman (b. 1943) | In Germany Before the War |
| Otis Blackwell (1932–2002) | Don't Be Cruel |

Benjamin Verdery, guitar
Yumi Kurosawa. koto
Elizabeth Brown, shakuhachi, theremin
Sprague Memorial Hall, Yale University, New Haven, Connecticut
18 February 2013

| | |
|---|---|
| Isaac Albéniz (1860–1909) | Córdoba, Op. 232, No. 4 arr. John Williams |

| | |
|---|---|
| Martin Bresnick (b. 1946) | Joaquin is Dreaming* 1. Joaquin Imagines a Part of History 2. Joaquin Foresees a Future 3. Joaquin is Sleeping, Joaquin is Dreaming |

Benjamin Verdery, guitar

| | |
|---|---|
| Traditional Yumi Kurosawa (b. 1975) | Takeda Lullaby Inner Space |

Yumi Kurosawa, koto

| | |
|---|---|
| Yatsuhashi Kengyo (1614–1685) | Midare ("Disorder") |

Elizabeth Brown, shakuhachi; Yumi Kurosawa, koto

INTERMISSION

| | |
|---|---|
| W. A. Mozart (1756–1791) | Adagio in B minor, K. 540 arr. B. Verdery |

Benjamin Verdery, guitar

| | |
|---|---|
| Elizabeth Brown (b. 1953) | Shakuhachi Solos from Isle Royale 1. Loons   2. Black-throated Blue Warbler |

Elizabeth Brown, shakuhachi

| | |
|---|---|
| Benjamin Verdery (b. 1955) | Standing in Your Own Light |

Yumi Kurosawa, koto; Benjamin Verdery, guitar

| | |
|---|---|
| Elizabeth Brown | Atlantis* |

Elizabeth Brown, theremin; Benjamin Verdery, guitar

A Tribute to Leo Brouwer
92 Street Y
Benjamin Verdery, Artistic Director
New York, New York, 23 April 2011


All compositions by Leo Brouwer

| | |
|---|---|
| Paisaje cubano con lluvia | The Canadian Guitar Quartet |
| Canticum<br>    Eclosión; Ditirambo<br>Elogio de la danza<br>    Lento; Ostinato | René Izquierdo |
| Estudio sencillo no. 6<br>La espiral eterna | Benjamin Verdery |
| Un dia de noviembre<br>El decamerón negro<br>Ojos brujos | Christopher Stell |
| Per suonare à due | Eden Stell Guitar Duo |

INTERMISSION

| | |
|---|---|
| "Cambío el rimo de la noche"<br>    from Canciones remotas | The Canadian Guitar Quartet |
| Estudio sencillo no. 7<br>Hika "In memoriam Toru Takemitsu" | Raphaella Smits |
| Sonata del Caminante<br>    Visión de la Amazonia<br>    El gran sertão<br>    Danza festiva<br>    Toccata nordestina | Odair Assad |

Benjamin Verdery, guitar      Rie Schmidt, flute
92 Street Y
New York, New York, 6 December 2008

| | |
|---|---|
| Martin Bresnick<br>(b. 1946) | Joaquin is Dreaming*<br>1. Joaquin Imagines a Part of History<br>2. Joaquin Foresees a Future<br>3. Joaquin is Sleeping, Joaquin is Dreaming<br>(New York premiere) |
| Benjamin Verdery<br>(b. 1955) | Satyagraha |
| Johann Sebastian Bach<br>(1685–1750) | Chaconne, BWV 1004<br>arr. B. Verdery |
| Ingram Marshall<br>(b. 1945) | The Mentioning of Love*<br>(alto flute and guitar) |

INTERMISSION

| | |
|---|---|
| Benjamin Verdery | Tears for Peace<br>1. For Those Who Are Present<br>2. For Those from the Past<br>3. For the Children of the Future |
| Leoš Janáček<br>(1854–1928) | from On An Overgrown Path<br>arr. Martin Bresnick<br>1. A Faded Leaf<br>2. The Virgin Mary of Frydek |
| Johann Strauss II<br>(1825–1899) | Blue Danube Waltz<br>arr. B. Verdery |

## Guitar Gala
### Charles W. Stockey Centre for the Performing Arts
### Parry Sound, Ontario, Canada, 24 July 2007

| Canadian Guitar Quartet | Benjamin Verdery, guitar |
| Andrew Scott, guitar | Russell Braun, baritone |
| Suzanne Shulman, flute | Guitar Orchestra |

Benjamin Verdery
(b. 1955)

A Tribute to Jimi Hendrix
1. Ezy Ryder
2. Little Wing
3. Purple Haze

Benjamin Verdery

Be Kind All the Time

Patrick Roux
(b. 1962)

Soledad

Franz Schubert
(1797–1828)

Die schöne Müllerin
1. Morgengruß
2. Wohin
3. Ner neurieige

Patrick Roux

Concerto Épisodique
1. Éveil
2. Envol

INTERMISSION

Louis Trépanier
(b. 1971)

Cuerda pa' rato

Leo Brouwer
(b. 1939)

Acerca del cielo, el aire y la sonrisa

Benjamin Verdery

Ellis Island

Benjamin Verdery Tribute Concert
Morse Recital Hall, Sprague Hall, Yale University,
New Haven, Connecticut, 25 March 2006

All compositions by Benjamin Verdery
performed by Yale School of Music alumni

Start Now    Now You See It . . .    Let Go
Appassionata Guitar Trio:
Amanda Cook, Rebecca Baulch, Hayley Savage

Let Go    Worry Knot    Passing    Monkey Mind
Scott Morris

Capitola    Milwaukee
René Izquierdo and Elina Chekan

Keanae
Kim Perlak

Miami    Mobile
Threefifty Duo:
Geremy Schulick and Brett Parnell

Satyagraha
Marc Teicholz

Sap Dream    Prelude and Wedding Dance
Bryce Dessner and David Nadal

Be Kind All the Time
Mesut Ozgen

Ellis Island
Alumni and current students

William Coulter and Benjamin Verdery, guitars
Shadyside Presbyterian Church
Pittsburgh, Pennsylvania, 19 March 2006

Traditional Shaker — How Great is the Pleasure
Traditional Galician — Muiñeira de Chantada
(arr. C. Saint-Saëns)
William Coulter — An Daingean
(b. 1959)

William Coulter, guitar

Johann Sebastian Bach — Cello Suite No. 4, BWV 1010
(1685–1750) — arr. B. Verdery
1. Prelude
2. Sarabande
3. Gigue

Benjamin Verdery, guitar

Traditional Irish — Frieze Britches
Traditional African — Song for Our Ancestors

William Coulter and Benjamin Verdery, guitars

INTERMISSION

Traditional Galician — Costa de Galicia
Traditional Irish — Bill Malley's Barndance
Traditional — Amazing Grace

William Coulter, guitar

Benjamin Verdery — from Eleven Etudes
(b. 1955) — Let Go
Now You See It, Now You Don't, Now You Do
Start Now
Home is Here

Benjamin Verdery, guitar

Traditional Tibetan — Tibetan Prayer Song
Traditional Irish — Drops of Brandy
Anonymous — Olde English Ballad

William Coulter and Benjamin Verdery, guitars

American Composers Orchestra
Robert Beaser, Artistic Director
Dennis Russell Davies, Conductor Laureate
Carnegie Hall, New York, New York, 23 February 2005

Manly Romero          Blanco, Azul, Rojo
(b. 1966)             1. Bolero
                      2. El Gardin del Eden
                      3. Balajú

American Composers Orchestra
Steven Sloane, Music Director and Conductor
(ACO/Whitaker Commission and world premiere)

Ingram Marshall       Dark Florescence: Variations for
(b. 1945)             Two Guitars and Orchestra

Andy Summers, electric guitar     Benjamin Verdery, classical guitar
(Yale University Irving S. Gilmore Music Library Commission and world premiere)

INTERMISSION

Danny Elfman          Serenada Schizophrana
(b. 1953)             1. Pianos
                      2. Blue Strings
                      3. A Brass Thing
                      4. Quadruped Patrol
                      5. "I Forget"
                      6. Bells and Whistles

ACO Singers
Judith Clurman, Director
(ACO Commission and world premiere)

Guitar Extravaganza 4
Yale School of Music, 15 November 2003

9:00–5:00 Exhibits     Guitar Makers, Music Publishers

9:00–5:00 Exhibit     "Guitar, Lute, and Related Instruments: Treasures from the Irving S. Gilmore Music Library"

10:00 Concert     Curtis High School Guitar Ensemble
Lou Mannarino, Director
Suzuki Guitar Ensemble, Hartt School of Music
Dave Madsen, Director

11:00 Lecture     Meeting with Roland Dyens

12:00 Masterclass     The Canadian Guitar Quartet

12:30 Lecture     "Influences and Inspirations in Classical Guitar Making"
Thomas Humphrey

2:00 Concert     New Music for Guitar
Mesut Ozgen
Matthew Rohde
Yale Guitar Ensemble
Yale Collegium Musicum, Richard Lalli, Director

3:15 Masterclass     "Tárrega Loves Tablas!"
Samir Chatterjee

4:00 Lecture     "Flamenco Techniques for the Classical Guitarist"
Dennis Koster

4:30 Lecture     "Mauro Giuliani: A Guitarist's Life in Old Vienna"
Thomas F. Heck

5:30 Concert     The Canadian Guitar Quartet

8:00 Concert     Roland Dyens

Bach: Guitar Works
St. Bartholomew's Church
New York, New York, 2 April 2003


Johann Sebastian Bach    "Jesu, Joy of Man's Desiring"
(1685–1750)              from Cantata No. 147
                         arr. Hector Quine

Bryce Dessner and Benjamin Verdery, guitars


J. S. Bach                Prelude from Prelude, Fugue, and Allegro, BWV 998

J. S. Bach                Cello Suite No. 4, BWV 1010
                          arr. B. Verdery
                          1. Prelude
                          2. Allemande
                          3. Courante
                          4. Sarabande
                          5. Bourée I & II
                          6. Gigue

J. S. Bach                Chaconne from Violin Partita No. 2, BWV 1004
                          arr. B. Verdery

Benjamin Verdery, guitar


J. S. Bach                Vivace from Organ Sonata No. 6
                          arr. B. Verdery

Bryce Dessner and Benjamin Verdery, guitars
Simone Uranovsky, cello

Guitar Extravaganza 3
Yale School of Music, 6 November 1999

10:00 Concert  Curtis High School Guitar Ensemble
Lou Mannarino, Director
Suzuki Guitar Ensemble, Hartt School of Music
Dave Masdsen, Director

11:00 Lecture  "Toward the Guitar: A Brief Discussion of Some of the
Instruments that Led to the Development of the
Modern Classical Guitar"
Richard Savino

12:00 Concert  New Music for Guitar
Audubon Ensemble: Janet Axelrod, Bryce and Jessica
Dessner, Lars Frandsen, Andrew Leonard,
Scott Sanchez

1:30–3:30  Yale Collection of Musical Instruments

2:00 Lecture  "John Dowland's Songs"
Dave Nadal

2:30 Sight-Reading  Lou Mannarino

2:30 Lecture  "The Cause and Prevention of Musician's Muscle
Injuries"
James Z. M. Wang, PT, PC

3:30 Masterclass  Seymour Bernstein

5:15 Concert  Stephen Aron and Richard Savino

8:00 Concert  Andrew York and Hubert Kappel

Benjamin Verdery, guitar
Concertgebouw
Amsterdam, Netherlands, 12 December 1998

| | |
|---|---|
| Prince<br>(1958–[2016]) | A Little Prince Sweet<br>arr. B. Verdery<br>1. Kiss<br>2. Purple Rain<br>3. Let's Go Crazy |
| Johann Sebastian Bach<br>(1685–1750) | Cello Suite No. 4, BWV 1010<br>arr. B. Verdery<br>1. Allemande<br>2. Courante<br>3. Sarabande<br>4. Bourée I & II<br>5. Gigue |
| Leoš Janáček<br>(1854–1928) | from On An Overgrown Path<br>arr. Martin Bresnick<br>The Virgin Mary of Frydek |

INTERMISSION

| | |
|---|---|
| John Anthony Lennon<br>(b. 1950) | Sonatina<br>(dedicated to Benjamin Verdery) |
| Benjamin Verdery<br>(b. 1955) | Satyagraha |
| Jack Vees<br>(b. 1955) | Strummage |
| Benjamin Verdery | Prelude and Wedding Dance |
| Stephen Funk Pearson | Pongue |

*Appendix D*

The Schmidt/Verdery Duo
Rie Schmidt, flute      Benjamin Verdery, guitar
Guitar Foundation of America Festival
Akron, Ohio, 9 October 1998

| | |
|---|---|
| Béla Bartók<br>(1881–1945) | Six Romanian Folk Dances<br>1. Stick Dance<br>2. Sash Dance<br>3. In One Spot<br>4. Dance from Bucsum<br>5. Romanian Polka<br>6. Fast Dance |
| Stephen Dodgson<br>(1924–[2013]) | In Search of Folly (1986) |
| Anthony Newman<br>(b. 1941) | Ride the Wind Horse |
| Manuel de Falla<br>(1876–1946) | Four Songs<br>1. Nana<br>2. El Pano Moruno<br>3. Cancion<br>4. Asturiana |

INTERMISSION

| | |
|---|---|
| Roberto Sierra<br>(b. 1953) | The First Chronicle of Discovery (1988)<br>(world premiere)<br>written for the Schmidt/Verdery Duo |
| Benjamin Verdery<br>(b. 1955) | In Memory (1988) |
| Robert Beaser<br>(b. 1954) | Mountain Songs<br>1. The Cuckoo<br>2. Fair and Tender Ladies<br>3. The House Carpenter<br>4. Cindy |

Benjamin Verdery, guitar
Festival Internacional de Guitarra
Teatro Ocampo, Morelia, Michoacán, Mexico, 3 March 1998

| | |
|---|---|
| Prince<br>(1958–[2016]) | A Little Prince Sweet<br>arr. B. Verdery<br>1. Kiss<br>2. Purple Rain<br>3. Let's Go Crazy |
| Johann Sebastian Bach<br>(1685–1750) | Cello Suite No. 4, BWV 1010<br>arr. B. Verdery<br>1. Allemande<br>2. Courante<br>3. Sarabande<br>4. Bourée I & II<br>5. Gigue |
| Leoš Janáček<br>(1854–1928) | from On An Overgrown Path<br>arr. Martin Bresnick<br>1. In Tears<br>2. The Virgin Mary of Frydek |

INTERMISSION

| | |
|---|---|
| John Anthony Lennon<br>(b. 1950) | Sonatina<br>(dedicated to Benjamin Verdery) |
| Isaac Albéniz<br>(1860–1909) | Torre Bermeja |
| Benjamin Verdery<br>(b. 1955) | Satyagraha<br>Sarabande for Tony Williams |
| Stephen Funk Pearson | Pongue |

Liederabend
Residenzschloß
Bad Urach, Germany, 29 September 1997

Hermann Prey, baritone            Benjamin Verdery, guitar

Franz Schubert (1797–1828)

Die schöne Müllerin, D. 795
(The Lovely Maiden)

Based on poems by Wilhelm Müller (1794–1827)

| | |
|---|---|
| Das Mandern | Wandering |
| Wohin? | Where to? |
| Halt! | Stop! |
| Danksagung an den Bach | Thanksgiving to the Brook |
| Am Feierabend | Evening's Rest |
| Der Neugierige | Curiosity |
| Ungeduld | Impatience |
| Morgengruß | Morning Greeting |
| Des Müllers Blumen | The Miller's Flowers |
| Tränenregen | Rain of Tears |
| Mein! | Mine! |
| Pause | Interlude |
| Mit dem grünen Lautenbande | With the Green Lute-Ribbon |
| Der Jäger | The Hunter |
| Eifersucht und Stolz | Jealousy and Pride |
| Die liebe Farbe | The Beloved Color |
| Die böse Farbe | The Hateful Color |
| Trock'ne Blumen | Withered Flowers |
| Der Müller und der Bach | The Miller and the Brook |
| Des Baches Wiegenlied | The Brook's Lullaby |

Orchestral Fireworks
South Arkansas Symphony
Kermit Poling, Music Director and Conductor
Harton Theatre, Southern Arkansas University
Magnolia, Arkansas, 29 October 1995

Michael Torke                    Bright Blue Music
(b. 1961)

Joaquín Rodrigo                  Concierto de Aranjuez
(1901–99)                          1. Allegro con spirito
                                   2. Adagio
                                   3. Allegro gentile

Benjamin Verdery, guitar

INTERMISSION

Igor Stravinsky                  Firebird Suite (1919)
(1882–1971)                        1. Introduction
                                   2. Dance of the Firebird
                                   3. Dance of the Princess
                                   4. Danse Infernale
                                   5. Lullaby
                                   6. Finale

Benjamin Verdery, guitar
International Guitar Week
Denver, Colorado, 10 July 1994

Lou Harrison                     from Serenade for Guitar (1987)
(b. 1917–[2003])                 1. Round
                                 2. Air
                                 3. Sonata

Johann Sebastian Bach            Prelude from BWV 1006a
(1685–1750)                      Sarabande from BWV 995
                                 Prelude from BWV 1007
                                 Sarabande from BWV 1012
                                 Prelude from BWV 1012

Benjamin Verdery                 For Those Who Were Here Before Us
(b. 1955)

INTERMISSION

Roberto Sierra                   Toccata y Lamento (1987)
(b. 1953)

Anthony Newman                   Gigue
(b. 1941)

John Majors                      Sea Changes
(b. 1954)                        1. The Practise of Waters
                                 2. Tidal Pools
                                 3. Kelp Dreams
                                 4. Ocean Flashes

Leoš Janáček                     from On An Overgrown Path
(1854–1928)                      arr. Martin Bresnick
                                 1. Our Evenings
                                 2. A Faded Leaf
                                 3. The Virgin Mary of Frydek
                                 4. In Tears

Ufonia
Kane Hall, University of Washington
Seattle, Washington, 26 February 1994


Benjamin Verdery          Tucson
(b. 1955)                 Miami
                          Margaret & Dan

Benjamin Verdery &        For Those Who Were Here Before Us
John Marshall

Benjamin Verdery          Los Angeles
                          Seattle

                     INTERMISSION

Benjamin Verdery          Capitola
                          (solo guitar0

Jimi Hendrix              Little Wing
(1942–1970)               (solo guitar)

Joni Mitchell             Refuge of the Roads
(b. 1943)

Benjamin Verdery          Miriam
                          untitled
                          Ellis Island

Benjamin Verdery, guitar
Classical Guitar Festival of Great Britain
22 August 1993

Benjamin Verdery                from Some Towns and Cities
(b. 1955)                           Capitola CA
                                    Chicago IL
                                    Keanae HI
                                    New York NY
                                    Milwaukee WI

Daniel Asia                     Your Cry Will Be a Whisper
(b. 1953)

Roberto Sierra                  Toccata y Lamento (1987)
(b. 1953)

David Leisner                   Freedom Fantasy No. 3
(b. 1953)


                          INTERMISSION

Benjamin Verdery               The Healing
(b. 1955)

Lou Harrison                   from Serenade for Guitar (1987)
(b. 1917–[2003])                    1. Round
                                    2. Air
                                    3. Sonata

John Majors                    ˙ Sea Changes
(b. 1954)                           1. The Practise of Waters
                                    2. Tidal Pools
                                    3. Kelp Dreams
                                    4. Ocean Flashes

Jimi Hendrix                   Little Wing
(1942–1970)                    Purple Haze

Ufonia
Merkin Concert Hall, Abraham Goodman House
New York, New York, 28 March 1992

Benjamin Verdery, guitar          Harvie Swartz, double bass
Keith Underwood, flute            Vicki Bodner, oboe
John Marshall, percussion         Dominic Frasca, guitar
          Christopher Lewis, piano


Some Towns and Cities
All selections composed by Benjamin Verdery

Capitola CA
Chicago IL
Keanae HI
New York NY
Milwaukee WI
(solo guitar)

Dennis MA
(flute and guitar)

Miami FL
(guitar, bass, flute, oboe, percussion)

Los Angeles CA
(guitar, bass, flute, oboe, percussion, piano)

A Scene from Ellis Island (premiere)
(guitar, bass, flute, oboe, percussion)

INTERMISSION

Mobile AL
Newport RI
(guitar duo)

Tucson AZ
(two guitars, bass, flute, oboe, persussion)

Miriam (premiere)
Seattle WA
(guitar, bass, flute, oboe, percussion)

The Schmidt/Verdery Duo
Rie Schmidt, flute    Benjamin Verdery, guitar
New York, New York, 15 April 1989


Stephen Dodgson       In Search of Folly
(1924–[2013])        (New York premiere)

Roberto Sierra        The First Chronicle of Discovery
(b. 1953)           1. Leyenda Taina
                  2. Danza
                  (New York premiere)

Anthony Newman     Ride the Wind Horse
(b. 1941)          (New York premiere)

Astor Piazzolla       Histoire du Tango
(1921–[1992])        1. Bordel 1900
                  2. Café 1930
                  3. Night Club 1960
                  4. Concert d'Aujourd'hui

INTERMISSION

Toru Takemitsu       Toward the Sea (1981)
(1930–[1996])        1. The Night
                  2. Moby Dick
                  3. Cape Cod

Benjamin Verdery    In Memory
(b. 1955)          in three movements

Robert Beaser        from Mountain Songs
(b. 1954)          1. Barbara Allen
                  2. Fair and Tender Ladies
                  3. The House Carpenter
                  4. Cindy

Benjamin Verdery, guitar
Covarrubias Hall, National Theatre of Cuba,
Havana, Cuba, 23 May 1988

| | |
|---|---|
| Lou Harrison (1917–2003) | Serenade |
| Roberto Sierra (b. 1953) | Toccata y Lamento |
| David Leisner (b. 1953) | Four Pieces<br>Prelude<br>Episode<br>Ritual<br>Dance |
| Leo Brouwer (b. 1939) | La Espiral Eterna |
| Ludovico Roncalli (1654–1713) | Passacaglia |
| Johann Sebastian Bach (1685–1750) | Chaconne |

INTERMISSION

| | |
|---|---|
| John Dowland (1563–1626) | Fantasia |
| Anthony Newman (b. 1941) | Ride the Wind Horse<br>Larghetto<br>Presto |
| Isaac Albéniz (1860–1909) | Córdoba |
| Benjamin Verdery (b. 1955) | In Memory |
| Jimi Hendrix (1942–70) | Little Wing<br>Purple Haze |

*Appendix D*

Rie Schmidt, flute      Benjamin Verdery, guitar
Festival Internacional de la Guitarra, Córdoba, Spain, 16 July 1985

Francis Poulenc                Mouvements perpétuels
(1899–1963)                    1. Assez modéré
                               2. Tres modéré
                               3. Alerte
                               (flute and guitar)

Toru Takemitsu                 Hacia el mar (Toward the Sea)
(1930–[1996])                  1. The Night
                               2. Moby Dick
                               3. Cape Cod
                               (alto flute and guitar)

Frederic Hand                  Trilogy
(b. 1947)                      1. Moderato
                               2. Gently
                               3. Allegro
                               (guitar)

Johann Sebastian Bach          Sonata in C major, BWV 1033
(1685–1750)                    1. Andante – Presto
                               2. Allegro
                               3. Adagio
                               4. Menuets I and II
                               (flute and guitar)

INTERMISSION

David Leisner                  Dances in the Madhouse
(b. 1953)                      1. Tango Solitaire
                               2. Waltz for the Old Folks
                               3. Ballad for the Lonely
                               4. Samba!
                               (flute and guitar)

Isaac Albéniz                  Torre Bermeja
(1860–1909)                    (guitar)

Claude Debussy                 Syrinx
(1862–1918)                    (flute)

Béla Bartók                    Six Romanian Dances
(1881–1945)                    (flute and guitar)

Benjamin Verdery, guitar
Wigmore Hall, London, England, 24 March 1985

| | |
|---|---|
| François Couperin<br>(1668–1773) | Les Moissonneurs<br>Les Barricades Mystérieuses<br>Le Moucheron |
| Anthony Newman<br>(b. 1941) | Chaconne |
| Johann Sebastian Bach<br>(1685–1750) | Chaconne |
| | INTERMISSION |
| Frederic Hand<br>(b. 1947) | Trilogy<br>1. Moderato<br>2. Gently<br>3. Allegro |
| Leo Brouwer<br>(b. 1939) | La Espiral Eterna |
| Isaac Albéniz<br>(1860–1909) | Torre Bermeja<br>Córdoba |

Benjamin Verdery, guitar
Dallas Classic Guitar Society
Majestic Theater, 21 November 1983

Fernando Sor                         Introduction and Thême Varié, Op 20
(1778–1839)

Anthony Newman                       Courante*
(b. 1941)                            Sarabande*
                                     Gigue*

Johann Sebastian Bach                Cello Suite No. 6 in D Major, BWV 1012
(1685–1750)                          arr. B. Verdery
                                     1. Prelude
                                     2. Allemande
                                     3. Courante
                                     4. Sarabande
                                     5. Gavottes I & II
                                     6. Gigue

INTERMISSION

Heitor Villa-Lobos                   Etudes 1–7
(1887–1959)

Leo Brouwer                          La Espiral Eterna
(b. 1939)

Manuel de Falla                      Danse du Corregidor
(1876–1946)                          Fisherman's Song
                                     The Miller's Dance

Benjamin Verdery, guitar
Festival Internacional de la Gitarra
Córdoba, Spain, 27 July 1983

| | |
|---|---|
| Fernando Sor<br>(1778–1839) | Introduction and Thême Varié, Op 20 |
| Anthony Newman<br>(b. 1941) | Courante*<br>Sarabande*<br>Gigue* |
| Johann Sebastian Bach<br>(1685–1750) | Cello Suite No. 6 in D Major, BWV 1012<br>arr. B. Verdery<br>1. Prelude<br>2. Allemande<br>3. Courante<br>4. Sarabande<br>5. Gavottes I & II<br>6. Gigue |

INTERMISSION

| | |
|---|---|
| Robert Beaser<br>(b. 1954) | Notes on a Southern Sky |
| Maurice Ravel<br>(1875–1937) | Pavane pour une infant défunte |
| Giulio Regondi<br>(1822–1872) | Introducción y Capricho, Op. 23 |

198

*Appendix D*

Rie Schmidt, flute    Benjamin Verdery, guitar
Merkin Concert Hall, Abraham Goodman House
New York, New York, 8 December 1980

| Johann Sebastian Bach<br>(1685–1750) | Sonata in C major, BWV 1033<br>1. Andante – Presto<br>2. Allegro<br>3. Adagio<br>4. Menuets I and II |
|---|---|
| Johann Sebastian Bach | Cello Suite No. 6 in D Major, BWV 1012<br>arr. B. Verdery<br>1. Prelude<br>2. Allemande<br>3. Courante<br>4. Sarabande<br>5. Gavottes I & II<br>6. Gigue |
| Wolfgang Amadeus Mozart<br>(1756–91) | from Serenade in C major, K. 439b<br>1. Allegro<br>2. Larghetto<br>3. Rondo |

INTERMISSION

| Leo Brouwer<br>(b. 1939) | La Espiral Eterna (1971) |
|---|---|
| Alvin Brehm<br>(1925–[2014]) | Ayu Variations (1980) |
| Jacques Ibert<br>(1890–1962) | Pièce pour flute seule |
| Maurice Ravel<br>(1875–1937) | Pièce en forme de Habañera |
| Ferdinando Carulli<br>(1770–1871) | Nocturne in D major, Op. 115<br>1. Allegro<br>2. Theme and Variations |

# Appendix E

# Publications

♮ = music scores

Cooper, Colin, ed. *Guitar Interviews: The Best from Classical Guitar Magazine Volume 1*, ed. Colin Cooper. Fenton, Missouri: Mel Bay Publications, 2016. Interview with Ben on pp. 99–104.

Mallet, Christopher. "Benjamin Verdery: Playing and Composing Outside the Box" *Classical Guitar*, September 2016. http://classicalguitarmagazine.com /benjamin-verdery-playing-and-composing-outside-the-box/

♮ Mozart, Wolfgang Amadeus. *Adagio, K. 540*. Arranged by Benjamin Verdery. Les Éditions Doberman-Yppan, DO-595.

Perlak, Kimberley. *"Finding a Voice" in the American Classical Guitar Vernacular: The Work of Andrew York, Benjamin Verdery, Bryan Johanson, and David Leisner*. DMA dissertation, University of Texas at Austin, 2008. https://www.lib.utexas.edu/etd/d/2008/perlakd24849/perlakd24849.pdf

♮ Strauss, Johann II. *On the Beautiful Blue Danube*. Arranged by Benjamin Verdery. Les Éditions Doberman-Yppan, DO-601.

♮ Verdery, Benjamin. *Benjamin Verdery's Some Towns and Cities: The Solos*. Edited by Nathaniel Gunod. Van Nuys, California: Workshop Arts, Alfred Publishing, 1994. Scores with commentary and CD.

199

♩ Verdery, Benjamin. *Easy Classical Guitar Recital.* Van Nuys, California: Workshop Arts, Alfred Publishing, 1998. Scores with commentary and CD.

♩ Verdery, Benjamin. *Eleven Etudes.* Lévis, Québec: Les Éditions Doberman-Yppan, DO-539.

Verdery, Benjamin. "My Time with Anthony Newman." In *Anthony Newman: Music, Energy, Spirit, Healing.* Edited by Thomas Donahue. Lanham, Md.: Scarecrow Press, 2001, pp. 51–55.

♩ Verdery, Benjamin. *Prelude and Wedding Dance.* Lévis, Québec: Les Éditions Doberman-Yppan, DO-613.

♩ Verdery, Benjamin. *the rain falls equally on all things.* Lévis, Québec: Les Éditions Doberman-Yppan, DO-1095.

♩ Verdery, Benjamin. *Satyagraha.* Lévis, Québec: Les Éditions Doberman-Yppan, DO-611.

♩ Verdery, Benjamin. *The Verdery Guitar Series.* Two volumes. Oakville, Ontario: Frederic Harris Music, 1996. Scores of new music by other composers.

♩ Verdery, Benjamin. *What He Said.* Lévis, Québec: Les Éditions Doberman-Yppan, DO-1028.

Verdery, Benjamin, and Gunod, Nathaniel. *Benjamin Verdery: The Essentials of Classical Guitar.* VHS video. Van Nuys, California: Workshop Arts, Alfred Publishing, 1989/2000.

# Appendix F

# Websites

Benjamin Verdery
http://www.benjaminverdery.com

Yale University
http://music.yale.edu/faculty/verdery/

92nd Street Y: Art of the Guitar
http://www.92y.org/uptown/concerts/classical/art-of-the-guitar.aspx
http://92yondemand.org/category/guitar-talks

Management Agency: GAMI/Simonds
http://www.gamisimonds.com/verdery/

Music Publisher: Alfred Music
https://www.alfred.com

Music Publisher: Les Productions d'Oz / Doberman-Yppan
https://www.productionsdoz.com

Elm City Records
http://www.elmcityrecords.com/

*Appendix F*

cd baby
https://store.cdbaby.com/cd/verdery/

Maui Masterclass
http://www.benverderymauiclass.com

Facebook
https://www.facebook.com/benjamin.verdery/

YouTube
https://www.youtube.com/user/benverdery

Instagram
https://www.instagram.com/benverdery/

Twitter
https://twitter.com/benverdery

# Index

♪ = musical composition
❷ = recording

203

# About the Contributors

SÉRGIO ASSAD. Guitarist, composer, arranger, and teacher. By the age of fourteen, he was writing and arranging original compositions for two guitars, performing with his brother Odair. At seventeen, he began his studies with Monina Tavora, a former pupil of Andrés Segovia. Later, he studied conducting and composition at the Escola Nacional de Música in Rio de Janiero, and also studied composition with Esther Scliar. For the past two decades, he has been most active creating a repertoire for guitar duo, performing extensively with his brother Odair. As a composer, he has written over fifty pieces for guitar, and has recorded thirty albums. In addition to teaching masterclasses, he taught at the Conservatoire Royal de Musique in Brussels from 1994 to 1996, and at the Chicago College of Performing Arts and Roosevelt University from 2003 to 2006. Currently, he teaches at the San Francisco Conservatory of Music.
http://assadbrothers.com

SEYMOUR BERNSTEIN. Pianist, composer, writer, and lecturer. He began teaching piano at the age of fifteen when his teacher at the time, Clara Husserl, arranged for him to supervise the practicing of some of her gifted younger pupils. He soon had a class of pupils of his own, some of whom are still studying with him. At age seventeen he won the Griffith Artist Award. During the Korean War, he gave concerts on the front lines and for top military leaders. His teachers have included Alexander Brailowsky, Sir Clifford Curzon, Jan Gorbaty, Nadia Boulanger, and Georges Enesco. He made his debut in 1969 with the Chicago Symphony Orchestra, playing the world premiere of Concerto No. 2 by Heitor Villa–Lobos. His concert career has taken him to Asia, Europe, and throughout the Americas. His awards include the First Prize and Prix Jacques Durand at Fontainebleau, the National Federation of Music Clubs Award for Furthering American Music Abroad, a Beebe Foundation grant, two Martha

Baird Rockefeller grants, and four State Department grants. His compositions range from teaching material for students of all levels to the most sophisticated concert pieces. He is the author of *With Your Own Two Hands: Self-Discovery through Music, 20 Lessons in Keyboard Choreography* (both published in multiple languages), *Monsters and Angels: Surviving a Career in Music*, and *Chopin: Interpreting His Notational Symbols*. He is the subject of the documentary *Seymour: An Introduction* (theatrical release 2015), directed by Ethan Hawke. He maintains a private studio in New York City, and is an Adjunct Associate Professor of Music and Music Education at New York University.
http://seymourbernstein.com

JACKSON BRAIDER. Writer and independent radio producer. Between 1990 and 2010, he wrote notes for more than three hundred compact discs for Sony Classical and Newport Classic labels. His audio work has been broadcast both locally and nationally on public radio. He is a proud member of both the Association of Independents in Radio and PRX, the Public Radio Exchange. His book, *The Mystic Chords of Memory*, is due out in 2018.

LEO BROUWER. Guitarist, composer, and conductor. He was born in Havana, Cuba and began playing the guitar at age 13. His teacher was Isaac Nicola, who was a student of Emilio Pujol, who in turn was a student of Francisco Tárrega. He studied at the Hartt College of Music and the Juilliard School of Music; his teachers included Vincent Persichetti and Stefan Wolfe. In 1960, he created the Cuban Institute of Art and Film Industry and helped to organize conservatories. He is also involved in the Concurso y Festival Internacional de Guitarra de la Habana. He has composed music for guitar, orchestra, and various chamber ensembles, as well as music for over one hundred movies, including *Like Water for Chocolate*.

WILLIAM COULTER. Guitarist and teacher. He was exposed early in his life to the classical techniques of choral music, being the son of a classical singer who founded the professional choral group Pro Arte Chorale. At age nine he began piano lessons, switching to electric guitar in his teens, then to the classical guitar at age eighteen. He earned a bachelor's degree from the University of California Santa Cruz, a master's degree in music from the San Francisco Conservatory, and a second master's degree in ethnomusicology from the University of California Santa Cruz. His particular interest is in American folk music and traditional Celtic music. He has released eleven recordings, including a track on the Grammy-winning album, *Henry Mancini: Pink Guitar*. When not performing, he works as a recording engineer and producer, and teaches guitar at the University of California Santa Cruz, as well as at summer music camps including the National Guitar Summer Workshop, Alasdair Fraser's Valley of the Moon Scottish Fiddling School, and the Puget Sound Guitar Workshop.
williamcoulterguitar.com

JAMES D'ADDARIO. Chairman and CEO of D'Addario & Company, Inc. The company designs, manufactures, and markets complete lines of strings for fretted and bowed musical instruments, drumheads, drum practice pads, and guitar and reeds and woodwind accessories under the proprietary brand names D'Addario, Evans, Planet Waves, Rico, and HQ Percussion. The company was founded in 1973 by his father John, his brother John Jr., and himself. The family's history of string making extends back to the seventeenth century in Salle, Italy. He and his wife JANET founded the James D'Addario Family Foundation that supports charities such as Providence House, St. Francis Hospital, pediatric kidney research at UCLA, and WFUV in New York City.

www.daddario.com

DON DAWSON. Musician and road dawg. He has been an employee of D'Addario & Company, Inc. since 1984. He began his career pushing a broom on the shipping/receiving docks and has had the pleasure of working in sales, R & D, artist relations, advertising, marketing, website management, and now social media. He has played in original and cover bands, combining his work life and personal life of music into one most enjoyable journey.

BRYCE DESSNER. Composer and guitarist. He earned bachelor's and master's degrees from Yale University. He is a member of the Grammy-nominated band The National, and also a member of Clogs, a mostly-instrumental improvising quartet. With Alec Hanley Bemis and Aaron Dessner, he founded Brassland Records, which has released five Clogs albums since 2001. He is the founder and curator of the annual MusicNOW Festival based in Cincinnati, Ohio. His long list of compositions may be found on his website. In October 2015, he collaborated with Ryuichi Sakamoto and Alva Noto to provide the score for the film *The Revenant* directed by Alejandro González Iñárritu. They received a nomination for Best Original Score at the 2016 Golden Globes and a nomination at the 2017 Grammys in the category of Best Score Soundtrack for Visual Media. He has produced several recordings: *Filament* by eight blackbird, which won Best Chamber Music/Small Ensemble Performance at the 2016 Grammys; Richard Reed Parry's album *Music for Heart and Breath* (2014); David Lang's album *death speaks* (2013); and Pedro Soler and Gaspar Claus's album *Barlande* (2011).

http://brycedessner.com

THOMAS DONAHUE. Editor. He received the D.D.S. degree from the State University of New York at Buffalo. His masterclass participations include studying harpsichord with Joyce Lindorff at Cornell University, and organ and harpsichord with Anthony Newman at SUNY Purchase. He has a strong interest in new music for the harpsichord, having participated as a composer in three Aliénor Harpsichord Composition Competitions, and serving as a preliminary judge for the 2015 Competition. His compositions have been published in

Aliénor Anthologies and have been included on the recordings *Shadow Journey: 21st Century Music for Harpsichord* (2014) and *Bela Cycles: New Music for Harpsichord* (2016). His piece *Five Shapes* was included in the program for the tenth anniversary concert of the British Harpsichord Society (2013). His articles have been published in *The American Organist*, *The Diapason*, *ISO Information*, *De Clavicordio IX*, *Early Keyboard Journal*, *Journal of the American Musical Instrument Society*, and *Galpin Society Journal*. He has writte n/edited eight books: *The Modern Classical Organ* (1991), *Gerhard Brunzema: His Work and His Influence* (1998, including his companion recording *Brunzema in Ontario*), *Anthony Newman: Music, Energy, Spirit, Healing* (2001), *A Guide to Musical Temperament* (2005), *Music and Its Questions: Essays in Honor of Peter Williams* (2007), *A Style and Usage Guide to Writing About Music* (2010), *Essays in Honor of Christopher Hogwood: The Maestro's Direction* (2011), and *The Harpsichord Stringing Handbook* (2015).

ELIOT FISK. Guitarist and teacher. He holds a B.A., summa cum laude, from Yale College, and an M.M. from Yale School of Music. He studied guitar with Oscar Ghiglia and Alirio Díaz, and was the last direct pupil of Andrés Segovia. He also studied with the harpsichordists Ralph Kirkpatrick and Albert Fuller. Upon graduating from Yale in 1977, he started the guitar department at Yale University School of Music. He has taught at the Cologne Hochschule für Musik, and in 1989 started teaching at the Salzburg Mozarteum and at the New England Conservatory since 1996. He is Founder and Artistic Director of the annual Boston GuitarFest (www.bostonguitarfest.org), co-sponsored by the New England Conservatory and Northeastern University. He has commissioned new pieces by Leonardo Balada, Luciano Berio, William Bolcom, Nicholas Maw, Xavier Montsalvatge, George Rochberg, and Kurt Schwertsik. With flutist Paula Robison, he recorded Robert Beaser's *Mountain Songs*, which was nominated for a Grammy in 1987.

http://www.eliotfisk.com

FREDERIC HAND. Guitarist and composer. He is a graduate of the Mannes College of Music. He studied with Julian Bream in England on a Fulbright scholarship. He has been the guitarist and lutenist for the Metropolitan Opera since 1986. As a composer, his music has been featured in films such as *This Boy's Life*, *Kramer vs. Kramer*, and *The Next Man*, as well as television programs *Sesame Street*, *As the World Turns*, and *The Guiding Light*, for which he won an Emmy award in 1996. He has also been nominated for a Grammy for his composition *Prayer*. His original compositions and arrangements have been published by G. Schirmer, Theodore Presser, Cherry Lane, and Mel Bay. His recordings are on the Sony, BMG and the Musical Heritage Society labels. Formerly head of the guitar departments at SUNY Purchase and Bennington College, he is on the faculty of Mannes College The New School for Music.

http://www.frederichand.com

HANNAH LASH. Composer. She received a bachelor's degree in composition from the Eastman School of Music, a performance degree from the Cleveland Institute of Music, a doctorate in composition from Harvard University, and an artist diploma from Yale University. Her teachers include Martin Bresnick, Bernard Rands, Julian Anderson, Steven Stucky, Augusta Read Thomas, and Robert Morris. She has received numerous awards, including the ASCAP Morton Gould Young Composer Award, a Charles Ives Scholarship from the American Academy of Arts and Letters, a Fromm Foundation Commission, a fellowship from Yaddo Artist Colony, the Naumburg Prize in Composition, the Barnard Rogers Prize in Composition, and the Bernard and Rose Sernoffsky Prize in Composition. She has held teaching positions at Harvard University (teaching fellow) and Alfred University (guest professor of composition). She is currently on the composition faculty at Yale University School of Music.
http://hannahlash.com

GARRETT LEE. Luthier. He started in the academic world and biotechnology industry, having earned a doctorate in biochemistry. He started building guitars in 1999 as a hobby; by 2007 he was making them full-time. His current output is ten instruments a year. His approach is to combine traditional techniques with contemporary elements such as double top soundboards, elevated fingerboards, and adjustable-action necks. He is on the board of advisors of the New Jersey Guitar and Music Society, and lectures on lutherie at guitar festivals and societies.
http://www.leeguitarworks.com

DAVID LEISNER. Guitarist, composer, and teacher. He graduated from Wesleyan University. He studied guitar with John Duarte, David Starobin, and Angelo Gilardino, and composition with Richard Winslow, Virgil Thomson, Charles Turner, and David Del Tredici. He has premiered works by David Del Tredici, Virgil Thomson, Ned Rorem, Philip Glass, Richard Rodney Bennett, Peter Sculthorpe, and Osvaldo Golijov, and revived interest in the nineteenth-century composers J. K. Mertz and Wenzeslaus Matiegka. He has recorded CDs for the Azica, Naxos, Telarc, Koch and Etcetera labels, and a solo concert DVD on the Mel Bay label. He taught at the New England Conservatory for 22 years, and is currently the co-chair of the guitar department at the Manhattan School of Music.
http://www.davidleisner.com

INGRAM MARSHALL. Composer. He studied at Lake Forest College, Columbia University, and California Institute of the Arts, where he received an M.F.A. in 1971. His teachers included Vladimir Ussachevsky and Morton Subotnick. He has received awards from the National Endowment for the Arts, the Rockefeller Foundation, the Fromm Foundation, the Guggenheim Foundation, and the American Academy of Arts and Letters, and was the recipient of a Fulbright Scholarship. Though the composer uses the term "expressivist" to describe his music, he is often associated with post-minimalism. His music often reflects an interest in world music, particularly Balinese gamelan tradition, as well as influence from the American minimalism trends of the 1960s. In the mid-seventies he developed a series of "live electronic" pieces such as *The Fragility Cycles*, *Gradual Requiem*, and *Alcatraz* in which he blended tape collages, extended vocal techniques, Indonesian flutes, and keyboards. In recent years he has concentrated on music combining tape and electronic processing with ensemble and soloists. He lived and worked in the San Francisco Bay Area from 1973 to 1985, and taught at The Evergreen State College in Washington State until 1989. He is now a professor at the Yale School of Music.

http://www.ingrammarshall.net/

MARTHA MASTERS. Guitarist. She received both the bachelor's and master's degrees from the Peabody Conservatory, where she studied with Manuel Barrueco, and completed the D.M.A. degree at the University of Southern California as a student of Scott Tennant. In 2000 she won first prize in the Guitar Foundation of America International Concert Artist Competition. That same year she also won the Andrés Segovia International Competition in Linares, Spain, and was named a finalist in the Alexandre Tansman International Competition of Musical Personalities in Lodz, Poland. She is currently president of the Guitar Foundation of America, has five recordings on the Naxos and GSP labels, and has published three books: *Alfred's Guitar 101* (Alfred Music, with Tom Dempsey), *The Total Classical Guitarist* (Alfred Music), and *Reaching the Next Level* (Mel Bay). She is on the guitar faculty of Loyola Marymount University and California State University Fullerton.

http://www.marthamasters.com/

ANTHONY NEWMAN. Keyboardist, conductor, and composer. At age ten he began his organ studies with Richard Key Biggs. At eighteen, he studied at l'École Normale de Musique in Paris with Pierre Cochereau (organ), Madeleine de Valmalete (piano), and Marguerite Roesgen-Champion (harpsichord). After returning to the United States, he studied at the Mannes School of Music with Edgar Hilliar (organ), Edith Oppens (piano), and William Sydemann (composition), receiving his B.S. in 1963. He received the Nice Prize for composition in 1964. As a master's student at Harvard University, he studied with Leon Kirchner (composition) and was a teaching fellow at Boston University. His doctoral studies were at Boston University, where he studied with George Faxon (organ), Gardner Read (composition), and Luciano Berio (composition), serving with the latter as a teaching assistant. His professional debut was at Carnegie Hall in 1967, at which he played Bach's organ music on the pedal harpsichord. His teaching positions have been at The Juilliard School, Indiana University, and the State University of New York at Purchase. He has made over 200 recordings for such labels as Columbia, Digitech, Excelsior, Helicon, Infinity Digital, Sony, Vox, Newport Classic, Sheffield, Sine Qua Non, Deutsche Grammophon, and 903 Records. He is the author of *How Music is Composed: A Systematic Approach to the Teaching of Composition* and *Bach and the Baroque*.

http://www.anthonynewmanmusician.org

JOHN OLSON. Scientist and guitarist. He received his Ph.D. from the Massachusetts Institute of Technology and has performed research for over twenty years in academic and industrial settings. As a guitarist, he is active primarily as an ensemble player, currently performing in several groups, including the Olson/De Cari Duo, the Contemporanea Guitar Duo, the Brooklyn Guitar Quartet, and the Nylon Wound Guitar Quartet. He also serves as a section leader and soloist with the New York City Guitar Orchestra. Committed to the generation of new music, John has commissioned over a dozen new works. He has studied guitar with David Leisner, Benjamin Verdery, Jon Harris, and Neil Anderson, and organ and baroque performance practice with organists Rick Erickson and Rodney Gehrke. In 2006, the recording *Quiet Songs* was released by the Olson/De Cari Duo, containing Baroque and twentieth-century music for solo guitar, and guitar and voice. Since 2007, John has served as President of the New York City Classical Guitar Society, which is recognized nationally and internationally for its important programming. Since 2014, John has been a member of the Board of Trustees of the Guitar Foundation of America.

http://www.johnolsonguitar.com          http://www.olsondecariduo.com

IAN O'SULLIVAN. Guitarist, composer, and teacher. He grew up on the north shore of Oʻahu. He is a graduate of The Kamehameha Schools, the University of Hawaiʻi at Mānoa, and Yale University, being the first guitarist from Hawaiʻi to be accepted at the Yale School of Music. At Yale, he earned the Eliot Fisk Prize in Guitar. His expertise includes not only the classical guitar but also Hawaiian slack-key guitar and the *ʻukulele*. His CD *Born and Raised* features new music for solo guitar by Hawaiian composers. He was a finalist for the 2014 Nā Hōkū Hanohano Award in three categories: Most Promising Artist of the Year, Instrumental Composition (*Mokule ʻia*), and Instrumental Album of the Year (*Born and Raised*). He is a lecturer in guitar at the University of Hawaiʻi at Mānoa.

http://ianosullivanguitar.com

PACO PEÑA. Guitarist and composer. Born in Córdoba, Spain, he started playing guitar at age six and gave his first professional performance at age twelve. In the late 1960s he moved to London to pursue a solo career. He is considered one of the world's foremost flamenco guitarists. He founded the world's first university course on flamenco guitar at the Rotterdam Conservatory of Music, created the Centro Flamenco Paco Peña in Córdoba, and founded the annual Córdoba Guitar Festival. He has thirty recordings to his credit. He contributed the chapter on flamenco guitar for the book *The Guitar: A Guide for Students and Teachers* (Oxford University Press, 1988/2000). His most famous compositions include *Misa Flamenca* and *Requiem for the Earth*. In 1997 he was named Oficial de la Cruz de la Orden del Mérito Civil, and in 2012 was awarded the Gold Medal in the Arts by the John F. Kennedy Center for the Performing Arts in Washington, D.C.

http://www.pacopena.com

DAVID RUSSELL. Guitarist. Born in Glasgow, his family moved to Minorca when he was five. At age 16 he went to London to attend the Royal Academy of Music, where his primary teacher was Hector Quine. He also studied French horn and violin. He twice won the Julian Bream Prize in guitar. He graduated in 1974 with a Ralph Vaughan Williams Trust Scholarship, and in 1975 he was awarded a grant by the Spanish Government to return to Spain and study with José Tomás in Santiago de Compostela. He was the winner of several major prizes: the Ramirez Competition of Santiago de Compostela (1975), the Andrés Segovia Prize of Palma de Mallorca (1977), the Alicante Prize, and the Francisco Tárrega Competition. In 1981 he made both his London and New York debuts. In 1997 he was named a Fellow of The London Royal Academy of Music, and in November 2003 he was given the Medal of Honour of the Conservatory of the Balearics. In 2004 he won a Grammy for his recording *Aire Latino* in the category of Best Classical Instrumental Solo. Since 1995 he has recorded exclusively with Telarc international, with sixteen CDs to date.
http://www.davidrussellguitar.com

RICHARD SAVINO. Guitarist and lutenist. He received his D.M.A. degree from SUNY at Stony Brook where he studied under Jerry Willard. He has also studied with Oscar Ghiglia, Eliot Fisk, and Albert Fuller. He was director of the California State University Summer Arts Guitar and Lute Institute from 1987 to 1998. He has been visiting artistic director of the Aston Magna Academy and Music Festival (1993, 1995, 2005, 2009, 2010), the Connecticut Early Music Festival (2002), Ensemble Rebel (2010) and was coordinator of performance practice at the Monadnock Music Festival in New Hampshire from 1994 to 1997. He is presently director of the ensemble El Mundo, a chamber group dedicated to the performance of Latin American, Spanish, and Italian chamber music from the sixteenth to the nineteenth centuries. He has been principal theorbist/lutenist for several opera companies: Santa Fe, Glimmerglass, San Diego, Dallas, Denver, Central City, Portland, San Francisco, and Houston Grand. He is a recipient of a Diapason d'Or (a French Grammy) and was nominated for a Grammy in 2012 for El Mundo's recording *The Kingdoms of Castille*; he also worked with Ars Lyrica of Houston on their 2010 Grammy-nominated recording. His discography includes over thirty recordings on the Harmonia Mundi, Naxos, Koch, Stradivarius, and Dorian labels. He is contributing author to the Cambridge University Press Studies in Performance Practice series, and has edited the complete works of Fernando Sor (Editions Chanterelle) as well as a collection of secular monodies by Francesca Caccini (Indiana University Press). He is presently a Collegiate Professor at the San Francisco Conservatory of Music, and Professor of Music at the California State University at Sacramento.
http://www.richardsavino.net

JOHN SCHAEFER. Radio host and writer. He has hosted and produced WNYC's radio series *New Sounds* since 1982 and the *New Sounds Live* concert series since 1986. He has also hosted the program *Soundcheck* since its inception in 2002. He is the author of *New Sounds: A Listener's Guide to New Music* (Harper & Row, 1987; Virgin Books, 1990) and *The Cambridge Companion to Singing: World Music* (Cambridge University Press, 2000). He also wrote the television program *Bravo Profile: Bobby McFerrin*, is a contributing editor for *Spin* and *Ear* magazines, and has written liner notes for over 100 recordings. He is a regular contributor to the World Science Festival and the White Light Festival at Lincoln Center. He has also written about horse racing (*Bloodlines: A Horse Racing Anthology*, Vintage, 2006) and was a regular panelist on the BBC's soccer-based program *Sports World*.

http://soundcheck.wnyc.org

ANDY SUMMERS. Guitarist, composer, photographer, writer, and producer. He began playing the guitar at age thirteen. Starting in the mid-1960s, he performed with several bands in London. In the late 1970s and early 1980s, he was the guitarist for The Police. After The Police, he has released fourteen solo albums and several collaborative albums with such musicians as Robert Fripp, John Etheridge, Victor Biglione, Benjamin Verdery, Fernanda Takai, and Rob Giles. He has composed scores for such films as *Down and Out in Beverly Hills*, *End of the Line*, *Weekend at Bernie's*, *Motorama*, and *And the Circus Leaves Town*. His memoir *One Train Later* was published in 2006, and the film *Can't Stop Losing You: Surviving The Police* based on that book was released in 2015. His work in photography has been shown in exhibitions around the world, including Los Angeles, Paris, Cologne, Shanghai, Beijing, Sao Paolo, and Rio de Janeiro, and his photographs have been published in several books: *Throb* (1983); *I'll Be Watching You: Inside the Police 1980–83* (2007); and *Desirer Walks the Streets* (2009). His awards include five Grammys, induction into the Rock and Roll Hall of Fame, inclusion in the *Guitar Player* magazine Hall of Fame, and recipient of the Chevalier De L'Ordre Des Arts et Des Lettres by the Ministry of Culture in France.

http://andysummers.com

THOMAS SYDORICK. Teacher, portfolio manager, and playwright. He received his bachelor's degree from the University of Pittsburgh and an M.B.A. from New York University. He taught in the English departments at Santa Fe Preparatory School, Santa Fe, New Mexico (being one of the founding members), The Harvey School in Katonah, New York, and the Rippowam Cisqua School in Bedford, New York. He also taught in the Department of Communications at the University of California at San Diego. In the business world, he worked at Drexel Burnham Lambert in New York City, was a vice president at Coast Federal Bank in Los Angeles, and was Chairman and CEO of Northview Corporation in San Diego, California. His writing experiences include Playwright-in-Residence at the College of Santa Fe and at Jerome Robbins's American Theater Lab. He was honored with an OBIE Award—the off-Broadway theater award—in recognition of distinguished directing for his play *20th Century Tar*, selected as one of the ten best off-Broadway plays (1970–71) by International Theater Institute and Scribners.

SCOTT TENNANT. Guitarist and teacher. He studied at the University of Southern California from 1980 to 1986 where he studied with Pepe Romero and James Smith. He won silver medals in the Toronto International Guitar Competition in 1984, and in the Paris Radio France Competition in 1988, and won the gold medal/first prize in the Tokyo International Competition in 1989. He has written several articles and books, most notably *Pumping Nylon*. He is a founding member of the Los Angeles Guitar Quartet (LAGQ). He has made several solo recordings on the GHA and Delos labels, and with the LAGQ he has recorded for GHA, Delos, Sony Classical, Windham Hill, Deutsche Grammophon and Telarc labels. Their Telarc recording *LAGQ Latin* was nominated for a Grammy, and their Telarc recording *LAGQ's Guitar Heroes* won the Grammy for Best Classical Crossover Album of 2005. He taught guitar at the San Francisco Conservatory of Music from 1989 to 1993, and has since been on the faculty of the Thornton School of Music at the University of Southern California.
http://www.scott-tennant.net/

JACK VEES. Guitarist and composer. He holds an undergraduate degree from Glassboro State College and an M.F.A. from California Institute of the Arts. Composition teachers include Louis Andriessen, Vinko Globokar, Stephen L. Mosko, Bernard Rands, and Morton Subotnick. Influences include Louis Andriessen, John Cage, George Crumb, Charles Ives, Erik Satie, Joel Thome, and Captain Beefheart (Don Van Vliet). He has written music for his own ensemble, Chez Vees, and for groups such as Ensemble Modern, California EAR Unit, and Zeitgeist. He has collaborated with performers Ashley Bathgate, Libby Van Cleve, Amy Knoles, Jeffrey Krieger, and Benjamin Verdery, as well as various choreographers and video artists. He is the operations director and instructor of the Center of Studies in Music Technology at the Yale School of Music.
http://jackvees.com

ANDREW YORK. Guitarist and composer. He received a bachelor's degree in classical guitar performance from James Madison University in 1980 and a master of music degree from the University of Southern California in 1986. He played lute with the USC Early Music Ensemble, and was a member of the Los Angeles Guitar Quartet for sixteen years. He has over fifty published works for guitar. As a solo guitarist, he has ten CDs for the Sony-U.S., Sony-Japan, Telarc, GSP and Delos labels; has appeared in three DVDs; and has published the three-volume *Jazz Guitar for Classical Cats*. His ten recordings with the Los Angeles Guitar Quartet includes *LAGQ's Guitar Heroes* (2005), which won a Grammy. He teaches undergraduate and graduate guitar at California State University, Fullerton, School of Music.
http://www.andrewyork.net